Bully Glares At Anti-Bully

The story of morality

When I was 14 or 15 my grandfather said something that has stayed with me for all the years since his death. He spent his life mining coal in Haydock, a Lancashire village on the eastern edge of St. Helens, where I was born in 1952. He said 'you can learn all there is to know about life without going any further than Billinge' another village, on the northern edge of St. Helens. Well I went off to University, became a Structural Engineer, and lived in the Midlands and then the South West for awhile, but after the 1970s were over came back to where I started. He was right, that tough old man, I could have figured it all out without moving away, see what you think…

Bully Glares At Anti-Bully

The story of morality

David Knowles

Arena Books

First published simultaneously in Great Britain & the USA in 2010 by Arena
Books

Arena Books
6 Southgate Green
Bury St. Edmunds
IP33 2BL

www.arenabooks.co.uk

Distributed in America by Ingram International, One Ingram Blvd., PO Box 3
LaVergne, TN 37086-1986, USA.

David Knowles, 1952-
   Bully Glares At Anti-Bully *The story of morality*
   1. Ethics, Modern – 21st Century
   I. Title
   170-dc22

ISBN 978-1-906791-56-8

BIC classifications: JFM, HPX, JFF, HRAM1.

Printed & bound by Lightningsource UK

Cover design
by Jason Anscomb

Typeset in Times New Roman

Author's Introductory Note

This Volume contains two of a total of three Books, the third is half written, but will be given its final shape by the observations, comments and criticisms received from you - dear reader. Happy reading…

Via Website: www.bullyantibully.org

Book 1 – Birth, Hidden Face and … Secret Core
"Well then," said I, "as heir to this argument, tell me, what is this saying of Simonides that you think tells us the truth about doing right?"
    Socrates asks Polemarchus a question in the Prelude of **The Republic**

Book 2 – What it is, What it is not and … Where it has been
"What is all this nonsense, Socrates? Why do you go on in this childish way being so polite about each other's opinions? If you really want to learn what justice is, stop asking questions and then playing to the gallery by refuting anyone who answers you. You know that it's easier to ask questions than to answer them. Give us an answer yourself, and tell us what you think justice is."
    Thrasymachus interrupts Socrates in Book One of **The Republic**

Book 3 – And Anti-bully Glares Back
"Then shall we not fairly plead in reply that our true lover of knowledge normally strives for reality, and will not rest content with each set of particulars which opinion takes for reality, but soars with undimmed and unwearied passion till he grasps the nature of each thing as it is…"

Socrates sets forth his argument for the ideal philosopher in Book Six of **The Republic**

Acknowledgements

Book 1 – Birth, Hidden Face and ... Secret Core

The quotations in Chapter 7 and elsewhere are from *The Republic*. Penguin Classics Edition. The quotation in Chapter 16 is *from The Descent of Man* by Charles Darwin, Princeton University Press. The quotations in Chapter 25 are from *The Bhagavad Gita*. Penguin Classics, translated into English by Juan Mascaro. Quoted with permission.

Book 2 – What it is, What it is not and ... Where it has been

Quotations in Section 1.5 are from the *Selected Essays* of Ralph Waldo Emerson, Penguin Books. Quotation in Section 2.5 is from *The Descent of Man* by Charles Darwin, Princeton University Press.

CONTENTS

Book 1 - Birth, Hidden Face and ... Secret Core

Book 2 - What it is, What it is not and ... Where it has been

Section 1 - What it is

Contents

Book 1

Birth, Hidden Face and ... Secret Core

"Well then," said I, "as heir to this argument, tell me, what is this saying of Simonides that you think tells us the truth about doing right?"

Socrates asks Polemarchus a question in the Prelude of

THE REPUBLIC

CHAPTER 1
Ruth Carrim

He watched her, for a moment saying nothing.
She stared back at him. Then he started off again.

"Which am I then Ruth? Good or Evil?"

"That remains to be seen. Meanwhile as I said, I won't be going back there, it's history, and I don't need it."

"I think you do", he said quietly.

She looked at Gregory, deciding what to say next, a little less friendly than she had been up to now.

"My answer is no, a definite unequivocal no."

"And that's final?"

"Of course it's final, otherwise I wouldn't say it."

"No, I suppose not."

"It's too late to go back Gregory. It's not possible, just not possible, for the last time my answer is no. I hear you, and I suppose I owe you a favour of sorts, and I will repay it, but not this way."

She took a breather. *Good and Evil, why had she said that? Despite his left wing politics such terms didn't come into Gregory's vocabulary, he was more of a "in my best interests" or "not in my best interests" kind of guy.*

Her eyes wandered away to the house behind him, inside it the party people were partying, she could hear them through the open windows, one of them was trying the handle of the glass door, she could see it move. It was locked, Gregory standing next to her had the key, they had the first floor patio to themselves. 'You old hypocrite', she had thought when he'd locked it after them and led her over to the table by the railings, all equal, but some more equal than others.

"I can't explain. I don't want to explain, and I certainly don't have to. I don't want to think about any of it, I just want to forget it and put it all behind me."

She turned her back on him, to lean forwards against the railing now in front of her. The greenness of the park stretched away for what seemed forever. Neither of them spoke.

Below them a car drifted along the road that bounded the park, separating the trees from the houses, he moved away from her slightly, to pour champagne from the bottle in the ice bucket into their glasses. There were three other tables, all empty, their parasols bright red, freshly washed, the metal of the tables painted white. It was a May Day party, May Day in Liverpool. *A May Day a little while after our comrades got themselves kicked out of the Kremlin, a time when only the last diehard intellectuals are still hanging onto their dreams, or pretending to.*

A pale imitation of a May Day, the last May Day ever, as far as Ruth was concerned. 'A party for old times sake, and for Old Timers, like me,' Gregory had said, and as for the kids who made up most of those present, why to them it was just any old party, any party in a storm, any party is better than no party.

Someone else tried the door handle, and knocked loudly, but the noise drifted out and was soon lost in the trees. He left the newly charged glasses where they were on the table as he turned back to her, his chubby pink face was older and fatter than she remembered, too much good living, too many long lunches, his flat sleek swept back silver hair looked thinner, too much smooth talking. He wore a dark three-piece suit covering his tall tubby figure, too much bloody money.

"Listen Gregory", she began again.

"No you listen Ruth. What the hell have you been doing these last three years? Writing nothing, seeing no one, lecturing when you feel like it, poncing about with some Art Historian. Art Historian!"

"My aren't you well informed."

"We were always good at that. Come on, this isn't Ruth Carrim, not the Ruth Carrim I know..."

"You knew another Ruth Carrim - she's retired."

"Retired? What's ... retired," he spat the word with scorn. "Forget retirement, no one retires at thirty seven, no one retires with your ... no one retires with so ... when they're still so angry."

She looked at him, spluttering away, and smiled for the first time since they'd met, he'd been doing his homework, and she liked that. Actually she liked him; she always had, in spite of herself, and in spite of his nonsensical rhetorical bullshit. In theory he wasn't her cup of tea at all, Ruth liked actions to match words, she liked logic, consistency and directness. Gregory wasn't any of these, he was a wheeler dealer come up to see her from London with one of his offers.

He was devious, given to long bouts of circumlocution, loquaciously expressing emotions he didn't really feel, about motives he didn't really have. He was a businessman, he was rich, Ruth liked her Socialists poor.

"Tell me about what it is you are doing these days, what's going on down there in the big city?"

"Do you miss that big city?"

"Maybe", she shrugged.

"I'm helping to tidy things up, that's all."

"Tidying things up ... or tidying people up?"

He turned away, picked up the glasses in one smooth movement, and wheeled back to her. She took one this time and raised it, watching him over the top of the glass.

"To May Day," he said. She nodded.

"To May Day," she repeated, but carried on watching him.

They touched glasses, he smiled, and then they drank.

"Mmmmm, not bad" he said, with a little raise of his eyebrows. He looked at Ruth, she looked good, damn good for such a casual dresser. Tight fitting jeans, a red shirt, tied at the midriff, the top button open to show the edge of a black bra, and a hint of cleavage that his eyes kept straying towards. Her hair hung in loose black curls, but fairly short, just brushing her shoulders, surrounding a pointy brown face, with an expression that closely resembled granite.

"The KGB are gone Ruth, and the new broom is sweeping clean. All they want is for you to find a man. Just go and find him, as a favour to me, as a favour to yourself, that's all. Simple as that."

Granite, it was here that the show was over, here that the boys stopped leering. It wasn't a pretty face, it wasn't a friendly face, it was not; 'I'm nice to know', or 'I like you, do you like me', it was the hardest face you've ever seen on a woman, and one of the hardest you've ever seen on anyone. It was, 'don't speak fool unless you've got something to say' it was 'God help you if you say something stupid,' it was 'don't ogle me, unless I owe you a favour'.

"You old queen," she grinned after another sip, "I don't understand why you think I would be remotely interested in seeing either of them again. So tell me. I am wanting to hear from you, in your own words, as they say."

Don't foul this up he repeated to himself for the umpteenth time, this is it, don't foul up. For some reason she's got a soft spot for you, she always has had, don't mouth off, just say what you have to say and then keep quiet. Like almost every man she'd ever met, beneath his urbane exterior Gregory Allen was permanently uneasy in the presence of Ruth Veronica Carrim.

"Because this battle between them is important to you."

He put the glass down, took one deep breath and was off, speaking fairly quickly, as if by rote, as if frightened she would stop him, would suddenly break in with a caustic comment, with a 'hang on a minute Gregory', preceding a damning indictment of whatever was being said.

"You are still in love with this Steven Morris, you fell in love with him three years ago even though you stuck with Peter, out of loyalty at first. Later, after the rumpus was over, you left Peter, came up here to Liverpool and took up with this boffin, this Arty Farty God knows what - - that you're with now. God knows why, something different, someone untainted, someone from a different world."

He faltered for a moment, and then gathered himself again.

"You thought you wanted out, you did want out, but now it doesn't feel right. Inside things just don't feel so good, you don't feel alive like you used to, every fibre doesn't spark the way it used to, you don't crackle with that energy you always carried with you.

"You told yourself it would be OK, that it was OK not to feel like that anymore, everyone gets older, that it was a price worth paying to be free of it all. But now you're not so sure, three years of peace is long enough, long enough for you to want in again. This academic you're with, he's OK, he's cultured, suave, amusing, a raconteur, good in bed, all the usual stuff. All the usual stuff Ruth Carrim, except it happens to cut no ice with us, it breaks no privileged skulls, changes no worlds, kills no greedy Fascists."

His voice increased now in intensity, his fat pink face becoming red. "It just happens Ruth Carrim that you and I, we don't give that," and he clicked his pudgy pink fingers with a flourish, "for all that suavity, that culture, that smoothy smoothy let's have fun. It just happens Ruth that all that is totally bloody meaningless to you and I, it just happens that all that, is" he sought for a final phrase, "is just … just fiddling while Rome burns".

He stopped and took a breath.

Then he swept his jacket back, stuck his hands in his pockets and stood there looking at her, daring her to disagree. She almost didn't.

"That's a nicely thought out summary." she said, tilting her head back appraisingly. Silence. He willing her to respond, she desperately trying not to, remembering now why they were once friends, for awhile. She looked pretty cool, but she wasn't, her mind was racing like a speeding film, back in time, a whole series of emotions, like some mad science fiction machine. If Gregory had had the impudence to put out his hand, to press against the shirt where it covered her breasts, he'd have felt a heart beating ready to burst. Beating for what Gregory had said, the way he'd summed things up, she felt like putting her head back and just screaming out loud.

She actually turned away from him, and opened her mouth to do it, and as she did, from nowhere a breeze sprung up, it gusted suddenly through the trees. Quick, and quite strong, it literally took her breath away, caught her with a lungful and blew into her open mouth, she coughed in surprise. It came, blowing into Liverpool from the west, from the northern seaboard of Wales, it would bring rain soon, but for now it disappeared as fast as it had come, rustling its way through the trees at the back of the house.

"You've got it wrong Gregory." How in hell could he have got it so right? How could this wealthy socialist, with half an eye on his money, and the other eye on his own self-aggrandisement, how could this old roué be tuned into her so well?

She finished her cough and looked at him properly.

"You've got it wrong", she said again, keeping her voice flat and eyeing him coldly.

"I don't think so," he said.

They looked at each other, back and forth eyeball to eyeball, but not as a confrontation, just looking, trying to outguess each other. Does he know, does she know, does he know that she knows? Does she know that he knows that she knows?

She broke the silence.

"You're talking about you, not me."

"I don't think so," he said again, in a slow calculating manner.

Another silence…

"You don't think so?"

"No."

"Who the hell are you? Who the hell do you think you are? To have the temerity to think you can guess what's in my mind?"

He shrugged. Looked a little confused and started fiddling with the drinks again. Her heart was slowing. Thank God she hadn't screamed, that would have been madness, he'd have known everything then, have known he'd gotten everything right.

"Did you ever meet him?"

"Who?"

"Who do you think? I know you've met Peter Barrow, right?"

"Right."

"So?"

"Did I ever meet Steven Morris?"

"Right," she said with heavy sarcasm.

"No."

"What do you think he was?" she asked.

"How do you mean?"

"Well was he in the construction business like Michael Barrow, or maybe some kind of fellow traveller, one of those, what did you used to call them, 'communists after their first pint of lager'? Was he an intellectual, like I'm supposed to be, or maybe a thug-for-hire like my own darling Peter? Maybe that's what you think? That they're two ex-Communist bully boys about to slug it out in a field somewhere at dawn?"

No reply, Gregory put down his glass. "If that were the situation why would I get in the middle of it? Why would I leave my Art Historian, who you despise so much for that?" Still no reply, "Come on don't be shy, you know what he did, but what was he?"

"I don't..."

"And you know what I did?"

"I know what people say, but I don't know..."

"Stop it, don't give me that. I had one lover Peter...? Come on, fill in, you know plenty, tell me. "

"Peter Barrow obviously."

"Obviously, but I was greedy and took a second Steven...?"

"Steven Morris."

"And the second one...?"

"Used you to get at the first."

"And?"

"He ... people say the second lover kidnapped Peter's niece."

"Some say eloped, some say kidnapped - and some say rescued. Whatever you say, he stole her from under our noses, and he never gave her back. So you know what people say he did - but what was he? Are you deaf - what was he?"

"I still don't understand you."

"Understand this, I was used Gregory and no one likes to be used. I was used by Steven bloody Morris and I didn't see it coming, and I see everything coming. Why would I want to go back? Do you remember me as the forgiving type? If you do you are sadly mistaken. I'm strictly Old Testament remember, an eye for an eye, and a tooth for an equal sized tooth? What was he, what was Steven Morris?" She insisted suddenly aggressive. "What was he?"

"I know some things, talk I've heard, Peter's mentioned the subject. I know what the file says."

"Oh we have a file, we have a file do we? Of course we do." Ruth trilled with sudden glee. "We have a file, we know what Peter Barrow has told us and we have a file. How edifying that must be."

Gregory looked uncomfortable, standing there now taking Ruth's offered empty glass in his hand, and setting it down. This was exactly how he hadn't wanted things to go. How had this gone wrong, how had that stuff not hit home? He knew her, goddamit he knew he knew her. Had all that business with those two really knocked the stuffing out of her? How could it have done, she was as hard as nails, South American nails at that. He put his glass down.

"Well?"

"I don't know. I'm guessing - I don't know anything, I apologise. I think I know you, I know you would never have left Peter, not in the middle of all that mess with his niece and what it did to Michael, you're too loyal for that, it's just not you. Oh I know Peter's reputation, the things he's done, I even know some of them first hand. But you have a strong stomach you wouldn't have walked out, not the way you did, if you hadn't been in love with this other guy, this Steven Morris. Ruth Carrim doesn't change with the wind, and she doesn't make mistakes, or desert her people. For the Ruth Carrims of this world loyalty is everything, Steven Morris had to be the love of her life, and so Ruth Carrim is still in love now."

She wasn't listening, she could hear that voice, the voice of Steven Morris, that Gregory was suddenly so interested in. *Loyalty is more important than love; loyalty is higher in the hierarchy of human values than love, because loyalty...* stop it.

"I know Peter a lot less well than I know you Ruth, but I know his time is up, his day is done. And I need to know where he is, quickly. And I know he's gone looking for Steven Morris. And when you find one I'll have found the other. I admit I'm not trying to find Peter for the good of his health, more for the good of mine. I can explain."

"Don't," she held up her hand, not a ring, not a bracelet on it, the nails were red and short, the skin dark brown. "Don't bother."

"OK."

"If you knew anything about this, anything except whatever yarn Peter has spun you, I'd be extremely angry with you Gregory. Yes, very very angry. You come up here and lay this garbage on me, asking me to repay a favour from so long ago, that it's lost in geological time."

He attempted a gesture of protest.

"Don't say anything. I pay my debts, if they're seen as such. I thought this was long forgotten, long forgotten, after all that's happened since. You come up here knowing nothing about my previous relationship with this man. Pleading favours that barely exist, favours that my self respect would never let me ask for if things were reversed."

Gregory dropped his eyes in submission.

"For all you know this guy could be worse than Peter Barrow, worse than my own darling ex. He isn't that bad actually, but it's true what 'people say', he did steal Peter's niece, Michael's precious, oh so precious daughter, and then went on to steal, by that very act, the new career Michael had planned for himself."

Gregory looked up at her.

"And now that Peter is following Michael down the same slippery road you want to profit from his final ruin, now you come charging up here after three years silence to tell me news I don't want to hear. To tell me that one ex-lover is about to kill another. To tell me, after three years total bloody silence, to tell me, tell me, mark you, how I bloody well feel."

She stared at him. He looked up suspiciously, as if afraid the gesture would start her off again and this time he wouldn't get off so lightly. "I pay my debts, but let's get this straight. I am not, repeat not, going to find this man for you." She stepped closer to him, and eye-balled him more aggressively. "Are - you - receiving - me?"

"Loud and clear Ruth. Loud and clear."

"Good."

He nodded, she took him by the arm and walked him across the patio, away from the empty tables and towards the door. The party was continuing with gusto.

"Get the hell out of here Gregory. Go back to London. All of this is just meaningless history, like you. You're a fossil, nobody cares any more, you're a joke, I'm a joke." She hustled him towards the door. "Give me the key, I'm staying out here to think, I don't know why I agreed to come here tonight. It's over Greg, it's finished."

He did as he was told. Maybe he'd call her tomorrow, then again maybe he wouldn't need to. He stepped into the warmth of the house, it was stifling, there were people everywhere, on the landing, on the stairs, the new generation crowded against the walls, watching, as he slowly made his exit.

There was a howl of protest as Ruth immediately turned the key again and locked the door once more. Someone glared at her and knocked on the glass impatiently, she raised both hands as a stop sign and shook her head. "Not long", she mouthed at him, and pointed at her wrist as if to a watch. *'Go to hell' was what she actually thought, you pale pathetic imitation...* stop it.

Ruth walked back to the edge of the flat roof, it was cooler now, for the first time all day the lowering sun was hidden by a cloud, the breeze had sprung up again, an ice cube slithered from the table onto the ground. She leaned against the railing, watching the trees disturbed in the increasing wind, a few evening strollers, dog walkers, a lone runner, a young couple. She stared straight ahead, *you pale imitation of what we once were ... you nothing.*

"What do you think he was?" she said out loud.

CHAPTER 2
Steven Wakes

S teven woke with a start. His eyes rotated around the room quickly, suspiciously, quietly, without moving any part of his body. He listened intently, not even breathing. Why had he fallen asleep? He never fell asleep, not even at night when you were supposed to. He looked around, moving his body now, craning his neck into every corner of the gloom, he twisted back again, checking behind the armchair he was still sitting on.

Outside it was raining, a steady constant drizzle, blown in gusts against the house by the increasing wind. There had been a noise, there had definitely been a noise, not a rain noise, or a wind noise, not even a sheep noise. It was upstairs, there'd been a noise from upstairs. But why had he fallen asleep, that almost bothered him more, he never ever fell asleep in the day, never.

What time was it anyway?

He reached quietly over towards the table, moving slowly and finding the watch there amongst some other stuff. It was 8.30, not nightfall yet but it was nearly dark already. The clouds had closed in about teatime, across most of west Wales and it had been raining for a good two hours. Steven put the watch back on the table. It was in the window, to his left, off to the right was the remains of the fire, burned down low while he'd slept.

Why the hell had he fallen asleep?

He looked around again, with a puzzled distracted look on his face, as if the answer lay hidden in the room. He looked at the opposite armchair, facing him to his right, beyond the fire, just beyond that was the window at the front of the house. Steven stared fixedly at the old armchair, with a distracted and irritated expression, as if there was someone there, someone who'd asked a seemingly stupid, yet at the same time difficult to answer question.

Outside there was a drumming of sheep's hooves as they sought shelter from the intensifying rain. Suddenly he snapped out of it, the semi-glazed expression vanished. In front of him to his left was the door to the kitchen, to the right lay the door to the hall and the stairs. In one smooth movement, and in total silence, he pivoted up from the chair, took two strides, reached the door of the kitchen and opened it. Then he stopped and listened. Nothing... He reached inside, you couldn't go much further, his hand closed on the rolling pin, a solid chunk of wood with a handhold cut in one end. A club - he leaned back out. Watching the door to the stairs. Nothing happened. No strange creaks, no sudden clatter of noise.

Clubs are very underrated weapons.

Steven supposed professionals used guns or knives, Steven was an amateur. He'd once clubbed a ferret to death, the only thing he'd ever killed with his own hands in his life.

It had got itself trapped in a corner, a corner of the backyard of the house where he'd been born and brought up. It had been bitten by something, it was in a bad way - in pain, suffering but still far from death. He was damned if he could remember now what the hell he had used. He'd been fifteen years old and he could see the blur coming round, round and round, again and again. From behind his shoulder, over again, to feel it bang, bang to a halt, against the little body on the ground. Again and again, it was still moving, blood was oozing out of its mouth. Then suddenly whack, out shot something white, brains, innards, God knows what.

He could see it now, could feel how he had felt, sick. Pop, just like that, whatever it was had shot out, and that was the finish, the ferret was out of its misery. He still couldn't see the blur though. Something a damn site longer than a rolling pin, he hadn't been that close.

Steven had left it all day.

He'd heard it in the morning when he was ready to leave for school, there was no one else in the house. He'd gone out in the back and found it, trying to burrow its way into a corner, hiding behind some old paint cans. It was half dead, more than half, a lot more. When he knocked the cans aside it hardly moved. He didn't know what to do, it had sharp little teeth and an evil look in its eye. He'd poked it a couple of times with a stick. The ferret had pawed the end and revealed even more of its teeth.

Steven didn't really like animals, especially ones that bit. He poked it some more and then left. All day at school he'd felt guilty about it, when he came home he was convinced someone would have found it, and it would be either dead or gone. But no, no one was home, and it lay there still, about two feet from where it had been before. Its mouth was permanently open in pain, its blood a small stain on the ground beside it. Something needed doing, so he'd clubbed it to death, and buried it in the dirt at the bottom of the garden. He didn't tell anyone, it was his secret, he should have come home sooner, or done what had to be done straightaway in the morning.

He took three quick paces and had his hand on the door. What was on the other side? Peter Barrow…? He was a professional, but why would he be upstairs? He'd come through the front or in the back. Bursting forth like an avenging, modern day atheistic angel, with grey flecked black hair cut *en brosse*.

Why the hell had he fallen asleep? He listened again.

Silence.

Half-crouching Steven quickly pulled open the door and raised his club. *Only fools fight with the weapons the other side prefers. Fight to your strengths, make them fight on your ground.*

Coax them out, coax them out, out beyond their usual reference points, coax them out, coax them out a bit further. Coax them out to a place where they don't want to be, out to a place that they don't understand - a place they don't understand even exists. Out, out, out where their weapons can be swept casually aside. Out further, don't let them look back. Out, out further still. Out, out until they haven't a clue where they are, let alone what rules they're playing to - if any.

Fight to your strengths. Fight to your rules, never fight to theirs, always your rules, your rules. Never play their game, make them play yours, the game that's imprinted deep in your soul. Be yourself, be a special dark version of yourself when you fight.

You have no strengths?

You have no game?

Nonsense, I don't believe it.

Your first strength is that others do not know the inner you. None of them can predict which way you will go in any given situation, no one knows your answer - until you give it.

Don't give it.

Don't answer.

Make them wait, make them guess. Make them miss the point.

Nothing there, empty, no monster lurking on the stairs, he closed the door. Still vaguely disturbed he sat back down at the table. Better to write something down and steady his nerves, writing always did that.

Dear Ruth,

Long time no see. Or rather, long time no speak, and long time no apologise. Well here it is, I'm sorry, it was a mistake, if you can please forgive me. But to say sorry of course is not enough, I must offer some kind of explanation for my behaviour before I dare ask for forgiveness.

You know only too well all those ideas banging around in my head, well we must start with one of my theories.

I hope it will explain. It was around in a half baked form three years ago, but now it's fully baked.

First we must go back to those Six Great Threads that run through all human lives. This theory starts 2,000 to 3,000 million years ago, with the appearance of the first life forms. At this time the first of these threads commences, via the concept Pleasure/Pain.

1. PLEASURE/PAIN. Not Pleasure and Pain, because Pleasure/Pain are part of the same continuum. Tiny life forms move towards areas of their environment that suit them best; mild acid good -alkali bad, fresh water good - salty water bad, or for others vice versa. We are drawn towards Pleasure and at the same time are repelled by Pain: physical, emotional and intellectual. And this is the first and most basic of the Six driving forces that run through human lives.

2. POWER is next, as some life forms, conglomerates of cells consume others, swallow up the nearby single cell organisms, yummy, yummy, tasty. Being a successful predator is good, is PLEASUREABLE - I survive and you don't.

Then a gap in time ... 1000 million, maybe 2000 million years who knows, not me.

3. SEX appears next, umm double tasty, even more Pleasurable. Now if I am big and strong my Power keeps others off MY patch, where MY females are, double yummy, sex is double good - I procreate and you don't.

Then a another long gap ... let's say 100 million years ago.

4. KNOWLEDGE -- a bird learns how to drop and crack a nut, later a hominid learns how to make a tool, as chimps do today, or discovers fire, makes a spear, builds a hut, plants a seed, domesticates an animal, tans a hide, fashions a plough, invents the wheel, the printing press... Knowledge has arrived on planet earth, and it is good, for us humans it becomes as big as any of the three before, but something bigger still is coming soon.

In a while, in terms of geological time, another kind of Good is coming, a kind of Good so special we call it by another name, we call it Right.

Beware Power thy nemesis awaits thee, already hidden, where, where - like Herod you cry where?

Why hidden in thy loins of course where else could it hide? In your loins and in the loins of the object, and objects, of your desire.

5. MORALITY, from maybe 1 million years ago, covers all our feelings of Right and Wrong.

6. METAPHYSICS, from about 100,000 years ago, encompasses all our theories about what things MEAN. Abstract and theoretical questions have arrived amongst a certain life form on this earth, and the first answers are called Metaphysics.

Metaphysics covers all our theories about what our lives mean, all our ideas about what lies under the surface of things, why the Sun-God rises and sets, why the Rain-God sometimes comes and other times doesn't. Metaphysics gives rise to all RELIGIOUS and later to all SCIENTIFIC THEORIES too.

MORALITY and METAPHYSICS-RELIGION come tumbling after one another close together, these children of their four long lived ancestors. Predecessors that until recent times have had the field all to themselves. Why should they give ground to these upstarts called Morality and Metaphysics-Religion?

He stopped writing.

No this was ridiculous 3,000 million years was a bit too far back. This would keep for another time, no apology needs to go back that far, try again.

Dear Ruth,

They say that to be a philosopher, you must have a philosophical problem to solve, but there is one problem that haunts the whole human race, not just those with academic philosophical inclinations. It is the problem of 'doing the right thing', the problem of why Robin Hood was a 'Good' thief, but Al Capone a 'Bad' one. The problem of: abortion, injustice, euthanasia, infidelity, 'just' wars, blackmail, murder, theft, rape and torture, the problem of who started it, who reacted and who over reacted. Who was rich and had power and influence, who was poor and never had a chance, and what it means to say that such things 'are not right'.

It is the morning rush hour and the traffic speeds into London along two narrow lanes, there's not much room and the small red sports car is travelling as fast as the traffic will allow. The driver barely notices the heavy lorry as it comes around the bend up ahead, speeding, as if in it's urge to escape from the city, it will plough through those who are trying to get in. The car in front of him actually slows, as if in alarm, and he comes tight up behind it, before slowing himself.

That moment of irritation is his last coherent thought, as five tons of steel crosses over to join his side of the carriageway.

Suddenly it is there, battering aside the rear corner of the vehicle in front in its urge to annihilate the sports car. Driving the car back, diagonally back across the inside lane, carrying it towards the wall of the underpass beyond. Back, with it's bonnet already crushed into the front of the lorry, mercilessly back, inexorably back, back with the driver impotent, helpless and maybe already unconscious behind his useless steering wheel. Back, back, back to be swept, two vehicles locked together, a grinding screaming mass of crumpled steel and glass into the side of the concrete wall.

Remember that little car of Marc's?

And driving that lorry, was it any old human being behind the wheel? Or was it something ... Evil?

That was how it was, more or less, and he's dead, Marc's dead for sure. And you can't talk to the dead ... or so they tell us.

No, no, stop. This wasn't right either. Marc's death was too recent, only 4 years ago. No this letter had to start somewhere between 4 years ago and 3,000 million years ago. But where exactly? Evil is such a vague word, where should we start. You want precision? I like it too, I must explain exactly what I mean.

CHAPTER 3
Ruth Carrim in love

"What do you think he was?" Ruth asked herself, the same question she'd asked Greg Allen. *Don't answer don't answer. Don't answer! Keep control, keep control.*

"He was a shooting star, a super-nova, a being descended from another planet, a creature not of this earth, a burning sun, a galaxy about to burst, he was one of us, he was one of them. He was a sun, and he shone on me, and I basked in it.

"I basked in it and I loved it."

She laughed.

Threw back her head and laughed, standing there against the railing. Holding onto it for support and laughing, at Greg Allen, who thought he could manipulate this, that was funny, so funny. Gregory Allen MP, so clever, so sharp, so fond of putting two and two together, and ending up with five aces, so anxious to become involved. She should have said yes and dragged him into it. Later on he'd have had to be dragged out of it again, screaming and kicking the other way round. Gregory who thought five aces made you a winner.

It does, provided you know what game you're playing.

Gregory who was always looking at her tits, who thought he could predict. Predict the actions of others.

Gregory, an old man who loved breasts.

As all old men do, she thought, they find comfort there, no matter their inclinations when young, but breasts are no use with old men, they work only on the young, other weapons are needed for old men. *Long held illusions suddenly shattered, worlds once thought sacred turned on their heads, holy cows slaughtered mercilessly and untouchable ideas beaten to death with a club.* These are the fears of old men. For old men are past sex, their sex drives are now impregnable, fear of change is their weakness.

All philosophies are formed in youth, there are no old philosophers, only old men who once upon a time philosophised, and who now refine, refine, refine. Ruth shivered … she could hear his voice, for the first time in three years she could hear his voice.

Hear it clearly, as if he was standing next to her … *loyalty is more important than love, for loyalty and trust are the permanent steadfast entities that underpin all human Morality. Whereas love, love is much overrated, it is a transitory multi-faceted will-o-the-wisp, meaning many different things to many different people* … what a chat up line. What a chat up line that had been, what a perfect chat up line to approach her with.

Later she knew why - he'd done his homework, but she didn't care. She liked it, liked being a subject of his "homework". She could hear his voice, could see his face.

Ruth turned her back on the house, faced onto the road and the green of the park beyond, took a deep breath to fill her lungs, then opened her mouth wide and screamed.

Screamed in triumph. Screamed in relief, and screamed again … and screamed again in joy. Here was the proof he wasn't dead.

She stood more upright, and admitted wonderful defeat, she couldn't shake him off as she had done so many. The love of her life was waiting, waiting round a corner somewhere along the road up ahead. Ruth

See p. 7 –
Italics =
Steven
Morris
speaks

steadied her legs in a wide solid stance, took a deep breath, opened her mouth wide again.

And then one more time…

CHAPTER 4
Steven Morris

It was almost dark, but Steven continued to stare at it, absently watching an unmoving silent shape, a trick of the fading light. The club was dangling almost forgotten in his left hand. He'd been here a long time, standing rooted at the front door, staring at the spot where he thought he'd seen a figure, now disappeared. It was absurd of course, there was nothing out there, only shadows, cloud and rain, plenty of that, hiding the mass of mountain out of sight to his left.

He closed the door, there was nothing to see, he leaned with his forehead against it, as if in friendship, as if seeking moral support. There was nothing out there, he was a thousand feet above sea level, to his left was a mountain range, stretching away towards Snowdon. Somewhere to his right, miles away, was the flat coastal plain of North Wales, down there it would still be light, it might not even be raining, he was safe in the clouds, hidden, whereabouts unknown.

Up here was another world.

That was fine, it was a world Peter Barrow was unfamiliar with, down there was civilisation, up here was a world for renegades. It had been that way since the Romans first passed through. It would be that way forever. The buildings up here are grey, they drip in the soaking mist, the sheep shelter in the lee of grey stone walls, as they are doing now along the side of this very house. Nothing is flat, each small field slopes, the roads slope, every tiny garden runs along a hill, the mountains loom behind everything and inside the clouds it rains, rains sometimes from dawn to dusk, and then other times from dusk to dawn.

There was only one road into where he now stood, on one side lay the chasm of an abandoned slate quarry, on the other a mountain, while his back was guarded by a giant heap of discarded slate.

High, high above this house, lying in the rocky arms of the mist shrouded mountain lies a glacial lake, flat, calm and mysterious, being topped up even now by another night of rain. Steven's special place, scoured from the rock, a sheer cliff face climbs above it, cold and forbidding. On this southern face the summit seems inaccessible, but summits often are by routes that at first seem the most direct.

Steven laid down his club, leaning it against the back of the door, and as he turned caught a glimpse of himself in the mirror, hanging on the wall at the bottom of the stairs. His face was pale, that's fear, he said to himself, and placed a steadying hand on each side of the mirror, to look at the face that stared back, willing it to stay calm.

The black hair was a bit long, too much living alone and not looking much in this mirror, the dark blue checked shirt made the face look paler, and thinner than it really was. We see faces like this on the street each day, tired looking, lack of sleep, starting to look more middle aged than young, but not with eyes like these, none of those faces have eyes like these.

The eyes were the opposite of haggard, so alive that they burned, and so dark brown as to look nearly black. The pupils almost as dark as the irises, black, black like holes that led to his brain, led straight into his mind, and thus into *their minds too.*

How can black be so alive?

He turned away, trying to calm his thoughts, his nerves and his heart beat - he closed his eyes.

Darkness…

So he felt it rather than saw it, something different in the air.

Then that same noise as earlier, it was the second stair, right in front of him, it was right in front of him, a face, a bald head, it turned slowly downwards, as Steven eased his back off the door.

Seeking for him with its eyes - a gleam of teeth, a predatory smile, a nose, a huge bulbous nose, and beady close set eyes in an ugly old face. Steven smiled, "you" he said. *He started forward, stopped, and then he continued … into the arms of an ugly old man, into the arms of a god, into the arms of… one of them.*

There was no need for fear now. No need for anything to be said, he was suddenly at peace, safe in the arms of a god. You can't lose when they're with you, once they underpin your actions, once they join you in your battles, and add their strength to yours. Once they have done this, you are invincible, indestructible, one with all that is human, one with those, all those, who have passed this way before you.

He hugged the figure, that swollen face touched his, he was safe, he could feel the face smile, a huge domineering smile, a smile that unseen has dominated over two thousand years of human history. The smile of a face that has been dead all those years, but so what, who cares, because being dead hasn't stopped its influence.

You don't really think that we can't talk to the dead, do you?

For you have heard them too, the voices of the dead.

The voice that wrote the Koran, those that wrote the Bible, the ones that wrote the Rig-Veda, the Upanishads and the Tao Te Ching, how else do we communicate with each other, and with our past, but via *them*?

Every fossil we look at, every tomb we open, every flake of every morsel we dig up and examine under every single microscope, every dialogue we have with our own history, is talking to the dead. Oh what things we find there if we look and do not flinch, oh the treasures we find hidden there … *The Origin of Species by Means of Natural Selection, On the Revolutions of Heavenly Spheres, The Republic…*

I went down yesterday to the Piraeus with Glaucon, son of Ariston. I wanted to say a prayer… and oh my God, it sounds like yesterday. It sounds like yesterday even though Plato wrote those words 2400 years ago. It sounds as though he just went down there yesterday, *well it does to me.*

I went down yesterday to the Piraeus…

That cheek touched Steven's cheek, those thick Greek warrior arms encompassed his thin body, that face, that giant nose, those piercing eyes, that human smell, the smell of…

There were some chairs standing round about, so we sat down beside him. As soon as he saw me Cephalus welcomed me and said, "You don't come down to the Piraeus to see us, Socrates, as often as you should." The smell of an ancient Greek, the smell of history, and … the smell of living flesh.

CHAPTER 5
Goodbye

Ruth was sitting on an old wooden seat, against the wall of the house in Paul Dearbourne's long front garden, she sat facing the traffic sweeping along the drive on the other side of the hedge, watching the dusk turn to darkness. He was in there, the lights were on inside, she'd say goodbye to him in a minute. It was only a formality, Ruth and her Art Historian had been saying goodbye all year. He'd been a soothing balm, a refuge, he'd been too soothing, too restful, he'd healed himself out of a job.

The traffic had built up quickly, a half-hour ago there'd been nothing, now there was a long queue, tailing back from the lights on the next corner. Two lanes full, but the breeze was blowing away from the house and towards the road, it was still quite warm so out here would be better. Ruth got up, rapped on the door and waited, out here would be fine, she had a few things to say but out here would keep it short.

He'd know it was her, even though she had a key, he'd put down the book he was reading about the Art of somewhere or other, gather his dressing gown around him, that was his style, shirt and trousers underneath like something out of a Noel Coward play. Not that she'd ever seen one, but Ruth had heard of such things. Smoothy smoothy let's have fun. Where the hell had Gregory got that one from? Who was writing his speeches these days? Did he make that stuff up himself?

It had been fun with Paul, smoothy smoothy fun. What was wrong with that? Nothing and everything.

"You're earlier than I expected, I was imagining you at the centre of a group of intense young men, discussing the kind of things intense young men discuss."

"Let's sit over on the seat, I've something to say to you Paul," she cut across him, no silly banter, no more silly banter ever. "I met an old friend tonight, no one else, just an old ex-comrade, no intense young men." Ruth moved over towards the seat, motioning for him to join her, she quietly laid the key on the wooden arm by her side. "His name is Greg Allen, he was an MP once, a long time ago, you won't remember him. Anyway he did something for me, back when I first arrived in this country, and now he'd like the favour returned."

Ruth sat down, and Paul followed suit.

"He came to tell me that Peter Barrow has suddenly left London, apparently with information that could help him find Steven Morris. Gregory wants me to help him find Steven before Peter does. He'll bring along his private army and save Steven from a fate worse than death, or so he says."

Paul said nothing, he knew those names well enough. Even though they were mentioned only occasionally they hung as a backdrop to their life together, for as long as it had lasted. He knew what was coming, his frivolity long gone, Paul leaned forward next to Ruth, but he didn't look at her.

"I never really expected us to stay together, oh I hoped, but we both know what's been going on lately. I can't remember what I expected to happen in the end, but it wasn't this, for you to go back, back to what you were running from when we met."

"Not running, I wasn't running."

"No, sorry ... walking in a daze."

"I won't be returning his so called favour, but I need to find Steven."

"Can you find him? Just like that?"

"I can find his friends from three years ago, I've already found one, Denise, she was with Steven before me, she's that gallery owner we visited..."

"Yes, I guessed as much."

"Another, I found more recently, his name is Richard Hegan, and he confirmed something that I'd been wondering about. For that matter so did Denise in her way."

"What something?"

"That thing I told you Steven Morris did?"

"Yes?"

"He didn't do it."

"What?"

"He didn't seduce a fifteen year old girl and run off with her the way I said he did."

"But you…"

"There was no way the man I knew could mess about with a kid."

"If you say so, but you didn't used to…"

"I was angry, and it suited me to simply repeat the accusations and counter accusations made at the time. I never really believed it, Steven lied to me and he used me to get to Peter's niece. But what really angered me was that I never noticed how unhappy she was, never stopped and really looked - so stupid of me."

"How unhappy Hope was, the niece?"

"Yes, very unhappy, that's how Steven got to her. I was so damn busy as her father's Personal Assistant, we were all so wrapped up in his new career as an MP, that I didn't notice. What a name to pick for a child you're going to force to play a role she doesn't want, a role she hates, how stupid of me to have colluded in that."

"You didn't collude…"

"Yes I did, by not seeing it and stopping it. Anyway that's history, and there was some anger at Steven too, he lied to me. The only man I ever loved lied to me."

"The only man you've ever loved." He repeated it dead pan, as a flat statement, it was a fact. He knew Ruth and the directness that had first attracted him to her, it was too late to start complaining now.

"You told me…"

"I told you what happened on the surface of things, I told you what others saw. Should we judge by intentions or results?"

"Don't start with that stuff."

"Do you trust me?"

"Yes I do, but…"

"Why? Why do you trust me, on what basis?"

"Because I've seen you up close, because I know you."

"Anything else?"

"I know your history, what you've been through. How tough you are, what integrity you have."

"You know that I killed a man once, and you know how old, or rather how young I was when I did it?"

"Yes."

"And you don't condemn me or think I should go to prison for it? Even though you know only my side of the story?"

"No."

"Why?"

"Because I know you."

"And?"

"I trust you. Is this getting us anywhere?"

"I trust Steven Morris, and his motives, I trust his intentions in exactly the same way you trust me."

"But you could be wrong?"

"Yes of course, when we trust we take that risk. Something happened, something happened back there that I didn't see coming, that no one saw coming. I have to go back and take another look."

"We've been here before."

"Yes, but now I understand why he did it."

"Go on."

"He deliberately took that girl. Took her away from her father and her uncle to punish them."

"What?"

"They were criminals you know. We don't talk about it but I was in bed with a political enforcer, someone who has killed people, to order, and acting as PA to his politico brother."

"As a punishment? Abduct a child as a punishment?"

"She wasn't a child, she was sixteen by the time it all happened. Hope was important to them both; to Michael obviously she was the daughter he'd fought his former wife to keep. But to Peter too, Hope gave them an aura of a happy little family, which on the surface they were."

"A punishment for what though specifically?"

"I don't know specifics - yet. It could be many things, things I don't want to talk about, things I closed my eyes to."

"I don't know what you're saying."

"Things I'm ashamed of Paul. Things I should have … come on damn it, I've told you. I've told you what Peter was, at one time he was employed by the Russians, do you know how unusual that is? For them to employ a national in his own country? He was that good, he was that good at … he was that good at what he did. The Russians never normally let foreigners in so close, never, he had an appetite for it, he was good because he enjoyed his work. And his smoothy smoothy brother Michael, well he was no Peter Barrow, but he was no saint either."

"If you say so."

"I do."

"I'll take your word for it, but I still don't know what you're saying."

"I know you don't. One or both of them crossed his path, they crossed Steven in some way, I don't know how. They crossed him, and he made them pay."

"But … oh you've lost me."

There are two ways of getting even with someone who has WRONGED you, one is to knife them in the back when they least expect it, and there can be a great PLEASURE in this, it can feel GOOD. The other is to knife them in the front when they least expect it.

With the first you don't want them to see who's hurt them, but with the second you want them to know, it's important they know, just as you slip out of reach.

She looked at him.

"No, I'm sorry Paul but actually … you've lost me."

She stood up.

"A month ago I found Richard Hegan, he's more like a film star than a Civil Engineer, but those startling blue eyes clouded over when we got onto Steven. Back three years ago he was on the same construction project as him. Hope went with him that's where she disappeared to, she didn't stay with Steven, except for a few days. And those few days that girl spent with Steven - Richard was there too, the whole time. It was Richard who slept in the same room as Steven, not Hope."

"And so what?" Paul asked.

"You know so what, the whole thing was planned by Steven to get at Peter and his brother, it was nothing to do with sex at all."

"Nobody would do that to someone like Peter Barrow, not the way you've described him."

"Nobody you know would."

"You have an answer for everything."

"This nobody I know, he did that and then let the world think he'd abducted her. This nobody I know had to go into hiding for three years, for fear of his life, for fear of vengeance."

Ruth stopped and looked at him.

"This nobody I know," but then she stopped. "You remember two months ago, when we went to that gallery in Bradford?"

He nodded, he'd chatted up the woman on the phone first, made it seem like he was eager to buy. "Denise still doesn't like me much, she took pleasure in telling me how Steven planned our first meeting, planned it because I was close to Peter and Michael. According to her Steven betrayed us both." Ruth sat down again. "It was all carefully planned. There were reasons and I have to go back and unearth them."

Paul had given up replying he contented himself with a nod, and suddenly slumped back with an exasperated sigh.

She looked at him.

Hob nail boots are stamping on cobbled streets, through an open window somewhere a woman is cursing loudly in Spanish.

"It's night, I'm fifteen years old and we're living on the top floor of a twelve storey block. It's still so hot you can't breathe and outside it's suddenly quiet, there's a curfew, and all you can hear are troops moving through the silence. Inside the telephone is ringing and my father is answering it. There's muffled whispering and movement, always a bad sign, the ornamental flap on the back of the letterbox jingles, he's going out - and he's never coming back."

Mi padre es muerto.

"Ruth I..."

"My father is dead. Dead for talking too much, too loudly, dead for being left wing, dead for being ... an intellectual." She looked at him. "Dead for nothing. For nothing at all if I were to stay here with you instead of going back, *to them*." Ruth stopped again. She was staring at him, but looking into a world that Paul wasn't in, and never would be. It was over.

"In countries like mine everyone is scared, and the world doesn't care, doesn't give two hoots." She smiled at him for one last time, they'd had some good times. "Well I don't give two hoots for the world of smoothy, smoothy lets have fun. I don't really give two hoots for anyone who doesn't care as much as I do, preferably more. I can't coo and goo about art, or aesthetics, or beauty, or this or that while filth, lies, hypocrisy and deceit surround me.

"While drugs, murder, torture and rape rule a continent. I can't play bridge, or squash or golf, while the world goes to hell in a handcart. I only fall in love with heavyweights, men who can't be still. Men who are stupid enough to think they can change the world, if necessary change the whole of humanity, break it apart and start again, afresh from the beginning, the way it should have been."

"And he's like that is he?"

"Oh yes," she stopped, and looked at Paul again, before turning away to face the road for a moment. "We're too different, it was fun, I stayed longer than I thought I would. Go and find yourself someone 'normal' and make a life with her Paul, you deserve it."

She turned back and they looked at each other one last time. It wasn't just over - it had never happened.

CHAPTER 6

Peter Barrow sleeps

The small hotel was quiet, the season not yet underway, a heavy set creature stirred in its sleep - a human male. It grunted, surfaced and then dropped away to be smothered in the depths again, it snuffled and soon began to breathe more slowly, in a great heaving rhythm that drowned out the sound of the sea. He is at rest in a tourist hotel on the west coast of Wales, just before the start of the season, the wind whips straight off the sea, cold harsh and merciless, blasting the coast with its rain.

Peter Barrow stood six feet two inches in bare feet and weighed two hundred and twenty pounds, about ten pounds more than he had in his youth. In sleep he appeared a little too big, even clumsy, but despite the lost years his size was still mostly muscle and the clumsiness all illusion. At forty six he was still able to dominate those young enough or foolish enough to occasionally challenge him. What had changed though is the animal magnetism that once went with that power, still majestic five years ago when he'd first met Ruth, it had hardened now into something bitter edged.

He was born in Belgrade, where his mother had had time to produce only two children in between her work for the Party, two sons of a soon to be absent English father, brought up part of the time in England, but destined to follow closely in their mother's footsteps. Peter was the elder by a couple of years, he flew the coop at an early age, for a time he worked in the construction industry, another family tradition. A big, brash teenager holding down his first job, and at the same time haunting the fringes of his mother's world, he had soon found his calling, soon understood that every cause claiming itself intellectual, academic, respectable, has its seamy side too.

Picked out as the son of an English father, he was sent to London to renew his family ties, and in London he stayed, working by day in his father's building business, sorting out sub-contractor, and other labour problems. While at night ... *one night he was leaving a meeting where he was looking after the guest speaker, a local communist. Peter had left him shaking a few hands and had gone to fetch the car.*

He returned along a poorly lit side road and saw the scuffle as soon as he reached the main street. His charge was under attack. There were three of them armed with something like baseball bats, the last of the crowd had been scattered. Later he could recall no conscious thought process, he just swung into action, and headed towards them, driving down the wrong side of the road and keeping close to the kerb. As one stepped clear of the melee to raise his arm for a full blooded swing, Peter mounted the kerb and accelerated sharply. It was still raised when the car hit the would-be assailant in the hip, he bounced off the bonnet with a thud and landed in the middle of the road as Peter braked to a halt.

He'd barely hit the tarmac before Peter was out of the car, the closest assailant had turned, only dimly aware of the distraction, another loser, he still hadn't realised the cavalry had arrived. The straight right was so hard and fast that his head shot backwards and then catapulted forward again when it bounced off the wall behind him, the third loser panicked and ran - the only one with brains, but still too slow. Peter quickly examined his charge, a nose bleed and a swelling above the right eye. They wouldn't hamper his movements, he'd stopped them early. "Come on", he bundled him in, revved the car and then took off down the side street after the fleeing figure. It was a dead end, their path was blocked by a series of concrete bollards, up ahead stood three blocks of flats, the loser ran for the farthest.

This was the moment, the time when any other big kid, even if he'd gone this far would call it off, but this was a bad luck night for the baby fascist up front. This wasn't any big kid, this was a predator, this was a beast with no nerves, a beast whose heartbeat was virtually unchanged by the chase, its brain merely heightened, hard and clear as a diamond, its brutal logic closer to instinct than reason. Without knowing why, he knew two things, first that the runner lived there, and second that he'd use the stairs.

Later, at leisure he'd explain to himself that the man had passed two blocks, and chosen the third for safe refuge, and that no one would wait, standing still in fear of pursuit, while a lift came slowly down, with the enemy on your tail, you'd want to keep piling up distance.

Peter pulled his charge from the car, a handkerchief covering his nose and walked him quickly to the flats.

"I'm going in below. Stay on this side and watch for lights coming on in the minute or two after I come out again - I'll watch the far side."

Peter ran for the flats, if he lived low down they'd lost him already, each block was about sixteen or more floors high.

He raced into the lobby and made for the stairs. Someone was still crashing upwards, Peter waited in silence. A final crash and the stairs were empty; he'd gone through a door, maybe seventh or eight landing. Peter dashed back outside to cover his half of the flats, now everybody sit tight, he whispered as he watched the windows. That looked good, ninth floor as far as you could get on the left, he waited two minutes before walking round the other side.

"What have you got?" Peter asked.

"Half way along on the fourth, nothing else."

"We'll try my side it seems about right. You can stay in the car if you wish."

"No, I'll come with you."

A frightened young woman came to the door of the flat, a safety chain limited the strip that was opened.

"Is he here? Is he hurt? Is he? Those red bastards are everywhere."

She wasn't so stupid as to let them in, but a flicker of relief reached her eyes. Peter stepped back and kicked the edge of the door by the lock twice, the chain broke out of the timber and the door burst open, knocking the girl to the floor. The light in the lounge had been on all evening, but a new arrival usually turns one on somewhere, bathroom, bedroom, kitchen, the desire to scurry away, to find a mirror and see if one is still in one piece.

They found him hiding in the bathroom, he'd heard the door break open and was cowering down in the bath behind a shower curtain, gibbering. He was even younger than Peter, who was casting around for a weapon, punch bags like this one were hopeless to hit. A safety razor lay on the window ledge, he took it down, paused a moment, and then unscrewed it, loosening the blade in the end.

The razor was no longer safe. He stepped forward and pressed down at the protective forearm, then whipped the razor downwards, blood appeared by magic, pouring out along the arm. The victim squealed in horror as Peter slashed again, then again, and again, the thin slither of metal rattled in the top of the razor. He pushed its head against soft yielding flesh then pulled fast and hard, blood spurted from the loser's cheek, this was good, this would leave a lesson behind. He stepped in again grabbing his shirt front, ripping it open.

Having been in the building almost ten minutes, they used the stairs to go down, no one uses the stairs in blocks like these at night.

The muscled body thrashed suddenly beneath the covers and a strong square face turned from one cheek to the other, dreams, memories. The features were heavy, and the lines cut deeply into weathered brown skin, all beneath greying hair cut *en brosse*, his dreams, though apparently troubled, were not enough to wake him, a predator asleep. No wait, not a predator, something else.

Something that preys on its own species, a beast that preys on others of the same species, one who gains PLEASURE from the exercise of POWER over others. But not for sexual dominance as with so many beasts, instead for an idea, for the prevalence of an idea, for the ambition that an idea should be put into practice.

An idea mark you.

Don't bother about whether or not animals do or do not use tools, it is METAPHYSICS-RELIGION - hypotheses about that which underlies the surface of our lives, that separates us from the other animals.

The rain closed in, lashing against the window, the tempo of the storm increased, it battered the coast, soaking the hills, and soaking the roads, soaking the castles that guard the roads.

CHAPTER 7
Socrates

H *e sees them bidding farewell, one stood back from the rest is crying, kneeling alone in a corner. All of them are noble young men in loose, white tunics, bright early evening or maybe late morning sunshine, streams through the open shutters.*

Despite this, there is an air of gloom - a god is about to die.

The occasion seems a private affair, the mob is not present to witness the execution of sentence. In the centre of the room an old man lies flat on a bench, his tunic is grubbier than the rest. It was always that way with him, and he has not dressed for this final ceremony. Up until now he has lain with eyes closed, but here he tries to sit up and one of his entourage rushes forward to help him with eyes that are dry but vacant with misery.

They speak briefly and the old one, who can now raise only his head, surveys each of them with that huge domineering face, he looks as ugly as sin, it is the same face Steven hugged only five or six hours ago. Sharp, beady eyes hover above a great fleshy nose, he is as bald as a coot and running to fat, a warrior grown old. His head now shakes as he admonishes them for their gloom laden faces, he's right, they are a miserable bunch, handsome, unhappy young men, gathered to witness a murder.

Even the greatest of souls must die.

He suddenly smiles at something the one closest to him says, his eyes coming alight as he turns his head round to ask another one something. He stretches out his neck as he whispers a question, and then, before the answer can come, he passes quietly away. His last act then is the act for which he is famous - the act of questioning, questioning, questioning.

The king is dead, the king is dead, long live the dead, the king is dead, long live the dead.

Steven sat up in bed, listening, no funny noises now, and even if there were, so what, he knew where they came from - from human history.

We all talk to the dead, their words, we live by looking back at their words as we urge ourselves forwards, and try to improve on their efforts. They speak to us of science, religion, philosophy, politics, morals and we answer back. Their words and our response are the measure of our lives - the messengers of time.

Once you're dead you're dead my friend.

Really?

Well yes, but this interests me, why does every world religion claim,

in their different ways, otherwise? And whether or not you agree with
them, what is it that they succeed in keeping alive, generation after
generation?

It seems to me that … surely we keep alive *their* spirit, we share *their*
thoughts, we try to understand *them*. And by so doing ourselves too.

Without you Plato never lived, without me Jesus never passed this
way. Without us, without our emotions, efforts, values and beliefs, the
Buddha never was, his wisdom, words on paper. Empty words on paper
unless you use them, unless you live by *them*.

Do you feel them?

Do you feel their presence?

Relax into their arms, there are few better places to be. Has Plato gone
forever? Is Socrates still with us?

Do you feel them? Of course you do, listen...

*"I went down yesterday to the Piraeus with Glaucon, son of Ariston. I
wanted to say a prayer to the goddess and also to see what they would
make of the festival, as this was the first time they were holding it."*

This was hopeless, he was never going to sleep, time to get up
whatever time it was. Steven went downstairs, still night, he got himself
a drink and sat down in the armchair, legs folded beneath him, in the
posture of the sage. He settled back, it was time to get on with his letter
to Ruth, and this time he must get started properly.

Dear Ruth,

I don't think this letter has to explain everything, but it must start from
first principles, because these things are so important to you and I. The
historical details, the mechanics of how, why and when I did what I did,
these can come later.

I remember a moment, I'll never forget it, the moment when I was
no longer a child in a limited world. I saw myself as if from a distance
and asked for the first time the question all philosophers ask, what is the
good life?

*"You don't come down to the Piraeus to see us, Socrates, as often as
you should..."*

"As a matter of fact, Cephalus," I said, *"I enjoy talking to very old
men, for they have gone before us, as it were, on a road that we too may
have to tread, and it seems to me that we should find out from them what
it is like..."*

I've started this letter many times.

When I first played as a child in my little social group; did the question
of Morality plague me then, before adulthood and my first philosophical
idea?

Oh yes, I can remember people hurting little me long before I was even in my teens, and I can remember little me doing things to others that were wrong; selfish things, hurtful things, spiteful things, cruel things. Oh yes I remember Moral questions as far back as I can remember.

Moral dilemmas prey upon us even from our childhood,
When we tell tales on a playmate - to tell is to inform trusted authority that a Wrong has been done, but to tell is also to betray a trust, to betray our little friend.
What lies hidden here?
Clearly something more important even than simply 'telling the truth' is at issue.

"That's fair enough Cephalus," I said. "But are we really to say that doing right consists simply and solely in truthfulness and returning anything we have borrowed? Are those not actions that can be sometimes right and sometimes wrong? For instance, if one borrowed a weapon from a friend who subsequently went out of his mind and then asked for it back, surely it would be generally agreed that one ought not to return it, and that it would not be right to do so, not to tell the strict truth to a madman?"

"That is true," he replied.
A young child has been naughty, she has been bullying her little brother, and the mother or father is angry and scolds big sister, and big sister cries. For a few minutes the parent leaves her alone, so that the lesson sinks in, but within a very short time, Mum or Dad is picking the child up to console and comfort her.

In the space of only minutes discipline has been administered, hopefully useful communication made, and love provided as a balance. What has happened there? It is the speed I'm interested in.
Why does the speed seem so impressive?
Why I wonder does the speed seem so important?

What changes in the world of Moral judgements so quickly, that one Moral reaction turns on its head within minutes, seconds even?
The little brother was a victim of his bigger sister, but now the sister is the 'victim', of the parent. We humans rush to the aid of the one who is hurt, and vent our anger upon the aggressor, and then, hey presto, the circumstances change.

At speed this response judges a situation and acts, because of the action the situation changes dramatically, it judges again and acts again. This time the exact opposite response - supportive instead of critical, loving instead of censoring.

Instantly reversing a Moral decision, the parent takes pity, and forgives, and sustains an ongoing relationship. Sends a message of admonition, and at the same time the message that all the little person in the WRONG needs to do is to mend her ways, to behave more considerately towards her little brother - behave more Morally, stop bullying him, and all will be well.

No wonder the various lumbering summaries made by the many well-intentioned and less well intentioned kings, politicians and law makers can't keep up. No wonder the law is always so full of holes, loose ends and iniquities for slimy lawyers to exploit.
No wonder we are often confused, angry and puzzled over injustices and WRONGS not RIGHTED.
No wonder we talk of the spirit compared to the letter of the law.
   "Well then," I said, "telling the truth and returning what we have borrowed is not the definition of doing right."
   "Oh yes it is," said Polemarchus, interrupting, "at any rate if we are to believe Simonides."

The 'spirit of the law' is the **Individual Morality**, it emanates from inside each one of us, we want things to BE FAIR, we want things to be DONE RIGHT.
The law, the **Codified Morality** could administer discipline, and then it would simply watch while the child cried, unable and unwilling to do anything since the child's reaction to being disciplined was resentment, which is logical and therefore there's nothing further to be done.

The parent, acting from their **Individual Morality**, does something far more sophisticated, it forgives, and forgives at speed.

These are Moral issues, complicated issues about relationships between human beings; when does the parent stop being an administrator of justice and become an overbearing ogre instead? Difficult issues, for until that moment it would seem that the **Individual Morality** is actually the **Primary Morality,** a superior and more fair Morality than the slower **Codified Morality**.

Yes, until the moment that the parent steps over this hidden boundary, the individual is in possession of a **Higher Primary Morality**, with the **Lower Codified Morality** left trailing behind, the law is an ass. Only at

this tipping point does the law come into its own.
What is this tipping point, this boundary?
I suppose that…
It, it must be the moment when the parent becomes overbearing?
The moment when the parent goes so far that it itself becomes a bully?
Wouldn't you say?

Is this the something, the basic ground that does not change yet around which dilemmas and difficulties seem endlessly to revolve?
Is this what is hidden behind the stark fact that even 'innocent' children face almost daily Moral dilemmas?
Is it this that lies at the centre of the peculiar dichotomy between the rapid response of the **Primary Morality**, able to decide that it's right to kill our own mother to spare her from further pain, and the clumsy slowness of the impersonal legal system that is the **Codified Morality**?
Are we getting closer now?
Is there something hidden here?

If all the rules, from whatever source, are sometimes inadequate to meet real life issues, then it doesn't mean we don't need those rules. We most certainly do need rules, what it does suggest though is that the rules are derived from inside human heads and not from 'out there' somewhere in the ether.

    "Well," said Cephalus, *"I bequeath the argument to the two of you, for I must go and see about the sacrifice."*
    "While I take over from you?" asked Polemarchus.
    "You do," said Cephalus with a smile, and left for his sacrifice.

There is a rage at injustice that we all have even from childhood; "it's not fair", shouted with such self-righteous indignation. Most of us for most of our lives still feel that deep hurting resentfulness whenever apparent injustice touches our lives. We feel it even when the incident happens to someone else and maybe we only read about it, or see it on a screen.

It still makes our blood boil.
We feel for the victim of whatever form of unjust treatment it may be, from the jilted lover or cuckolded spouse to the person convicted of a crime they didn't commit, or just someone accused of making an error that was actually someone else's fault.

Oh how we hate injustice, perhaps this is the place to start? After all it is Morality that has turned the logical truism that, 'all philosophers are human', into the far more astounding statement that: 'ALL HUMANS ARE PHILOSOPHERS'.

"Well then," said I, "as heir to this argument, tell me, what is this saying of Simonides that you think tells us the truth about doing right?"

"That it is right to give every man his due," he replied...

Give every man his due, but is that possible, even with a relationship as close as a mother and child, to always administer perfect justice, even to one's children? Surely that's the whole problem?

Why is this so hard to figure out?

Why does injustice hurt us so much?

After all no other creatures react this way.

Or do they?

Outside the night lay silent over everything, but dawn was on the way, no more sleep tonight. He stopped writing, long enough to put the kettle on, and then...

CHAPTER 8
Doing Right

Dear Ruth,
I'm sorry. I apologise again and I hope that somehow you can forgive me. I'm here to take my chance with you, to throw myself at your feet, I'm writing to plead for forgiveness, to plead my special case.

When we look back to our pre-human ancestors a million or so years ago, and at how life is played out in the raw animal world around us now, we see that the "bully" is king. The most powerful rules and those who are less powerful must be well camouflaged, or fast; the prey must flee the pursuer, must run, run, run to avoid becoming a meal for another.

In this world the strong, the bully, rules in a natural order of things that has existed for millions upon millions of years. When the pack makes a kill, then the biggest of the bullies, the bully amongst bullies, eats first, eats best, eats longest. In the mating season he mates first, mates many, mates longest.

From time to time a young male challenges the top bully.

When the pack leader trounces him he has to slink off disgruntled, disaffected, pride hurt, hot and angry. He was a contender and he's had a crack at the title, no good complaining, maybe he'll get another shot, or maybe not. Either way he still continues to tag along at the back of the group, because without the pack he'll die.

In this context the word bully is meaningless, because bullying is the only order of things. One shall rule, the biggest, fastest, most aggressive, most POWERFUL shall rule the small, the slow, the weak. There is no question of morality because this is all there is; God is on the side of the big battalions, and if there were such things as words, then the word 'moral' would be the same as the word 'strong', the word 'bully' the same as the word 'right'.

All this has occurred over and over again, for millions upon millions of years of evolution. It is the story of life and the way it has evolved on this planet.

And then, one day, something different happens, and evolution takes a turn down a different road.

The first hint that human Morality is about to appear, is about to impinge upon this norm of evolution, is when someone, or rather some pack member, first complains about rough treatment.

Maybe he complains about the leading male, or maybe he complains to him, we'll never know.

However it happens, harsh treatment at the hands or teeth of another, is resented and labelled unfair, is called out loud, for the first time ever - UNJUST! NOT FAIR!

Watch out, here it comes, a change is coming.

The first time the concept bully appears on this planet, is the first time that some creature, some individual in a social group, a vanquished rival for pack leader status perhaps, or an out of favour youngster denied a share of the kill. Instead of cowering back and QUIETLY returning to his allotted place in the pecking order to await a further opportunity, still goes, but as he does whispers to his neighbours "not fair". Then soon afterwards cries out; "FOUL PLAY! INJUSTICE! STOP. STOP! STOP BULLY STOP!"

From here commences the whole of human Morality, all sense of just and unjust, fair and unfair, right and wrong.

I see before me the whole of human Morality - a cry for help from the dominated against the dominator. I see Moral issue after Moral issue and every single one has on one side the oppressor and on the other, the oppressed.

I see no good spirits versus evil demons, only human behaviour, only right versus might, the two extremes of human nature. I see freedom versus repression, the dominated and the dominator over and over, and over, again and again and again.

That's the seed, but there is something else that seals it. After all a whole series of creatures suffer such humiliations endlessly, for thousands maybe millions of years, there must be another factor as well, something that imparts the final impetus that produces … Morality.

The 'moment' of NOT FAIR plus something else…

The moment when SOMEONE ELSE AGREES WITH THE ACCUSER when another being says, I AGREE, that wasn't RIGHT, you have been treated badly, you have been, you have been WRONGED.

Only at that moment, the moment of AGREEMENT, that is the long, slow long ago 'moment' in unrecorded history when Morality begins.
The word 'Wrong' comes into existence, and for the first time ever on planet earth, the word 'Right' sits in opposition to it.

Before this, creatures are preyed upon as food for others, many have the food they've found stolen by rivals, and many are defeated in trials of strength for sexual partners. It would seem a reasonable assumption that, in their different ways, and for differing lengths of time, these creatures feel bad about their defeats, but they have short memories. They put their disgruntlement behind them, and get on with their lives.

But when some with longer memories come:
All this changes, something fundamental changes the first time one of them cries out in anguish, cries out NOT FAIR and another AGREES.

They turn to other members of their social group, and some maybe most nod their heads, nod their increasingly clever primate heads in assent, we concur "you have been TREATED BADLY". Heads with special 'bigger brains' new upon this earth, now make a judgement, a new kind of judgement, heads with longer memories than this planet's ever seen before.

Prior to this moment myriad numbers of creatures nurse their sense of hurt alone, for however long, or short, it lasts, but from this moment, in some kind of pre-human social pack, that feeling is SHARED.

SOMEONE AGREES, or rather someones, and those someones gang together, perhaps drive off a bully and protect the weak, maybe they re-instate the vanquished one within the group again, or they stick together because their leader, their Alpha Male is too harsh, too much of a bully. For the first time in the history of the world thus far, being strongest or being fastest is not enough anymore.
Not enough on its own.

For the first time ever you now have to consider the FEELINGS of others.
For the first time fascism has been questioned, unknowingly politics has just been invented, Right and Wrong appear and are soon called **Moral and Immoral**.

What is Justice?
The great Socratic question, what is doing right?
Plato's question, the most famous question in all philosophy.
Justice is when the weak, the repressed, the Bullied, strike back at their oppressor, strike back at **The Bully**.

There is no justice throughout most of the animal world, only murder, rape and theft, the law of the jungle, the law of the Bully. He reigns supreme, reigns because there is no concept of bullying, no concept of an alternative. And when, for the first time ever on this little planet, some pre-human shouts, or rather grunts: FOUL PLAY!   NOT FAIR! CHEAT! STOP BULLY STOP!
Shouts out "I have been WRONGED".
And SOMEONE else AGREES.
Then, then it is that MORALITY is BORN.

Of course Morality starts as a negative, Morality is so strong, so sure of itself in the negative; **thou shalt not**. 'Thou shalt not' is so much easier to sum up than 'thou shalt'.
Why?
Because MORALITY is a cry for freedom against repression.
'Thou shalt not' is actually always THOU SHALT NOT BULLY.

Every time - no matter whatever else is also said at the same time. It is really thou shalt not bully by stealing, by murdering, by raping and so forth. It is ALWAYS THOU SHALT NOT BULLY.

Theft - I oppress you by stealing some of your resources, your survival kit, your store of food in the animal world.

Sexual infidelity - I oppress you by the use of a lie, I manipulate you to my desire.

Blackmail - I oppress and manipulate you by the threat of exposure.

Rape - I oppress you by forcing you to have sex with me.

Murder - I oppress you by taking your life.

Torture - the ultimate repression, I repress you by holding you at my mercy, to do with as I will, ultimate POWER, ultimate repression, the definition of EVIL.

We all have to die, but we don't all have to be tortured. Torture is worse than death. If it weren't then there would be no such concept as a fate worse than death, no such thing as a mercy killing, a release from misery and lingering pain by death.

We never torture as a favour, but we do kill as a favour. Torture is the ultimate crime, the ultimate oppression in the great and endless battle of freedom versus repression.

Torture, something so cruel, something so bad, we call it EVIL.

To hold another in your POWER, to do with them as you will, to inflict pain, to desist, for awhile, then to inflict pain again. Pain, fear, rape, to force entry, to hold another at your mercy, and to have no mercy, to enjoy, the feeling of POWER MISUSED, to enjoy the helplessness, the suffering of another, to inflict more, more, and then a little more.

I put it to you that good and evil are derivative terms, that the root terms beyond these surface labels are the basis of all human Morality; Right versus Wrong is freedom versus repression. Good and Evil are words from old time religion, they have no existence except as freedom and repression, bullied and bully, right versus might, MORALITY versus POWER.

Tell me, does this not accord with the facts? Does this not accord with the human behaviour you see around you, amongst your friends, and amongst other humans you deal with, and out in the wider world, in other countries, in other places, now and throughout our history?

Bullying is not one face of bad behaviour, it is THE WHOLE OF BAD BEHAVIOUR. Bullying is not one mask of immorality, it is the face behind the mask, the hidden face behind all the masks, the face behind every mask that immorality wears.

The HIDDEN FACE OF IMMORALITY in all its naked ugliness is the face of POWER MISUSED.

CHAPTER 9
Ruth Wakes

R uth couldn't sleep, a pale grey light was peering around the edge of the window, she rarely used the curtains. Ruth liked to see the outside world, she liked things clear and open.

Denise had been open enough, despite their history, maybe because of it, they had sat in a little glass office near the entrance to the gallery. There'd been an element of triumph in her description of how Steven had set about, very quietly, very gently, very all round the houses, gleaning information about Ruth, or rather about Ruth, Hope, Michael and Peter Barrow.

Pumping people, she'd said, when Ruth had seen her three months ago, all very subtle, God knows he was subtle at everything, but he'd been especially so over this, never talking to one person in front of another, except for Denise, which had been unavoidable. Gradually zeroing in on Ruth and Hope, and then one day, hey presto, he had a new girl friend, her name was Ruth Carrim, and she was a means to get to Hope. Denise had finished with a flourish, and Ruth, had let the silence run on, a shiver running through her, a shiver of pleasure, a shiver of recognition at hearing something she'd already known, confirmed by Denise - a star witness.

He'd used her.

She'd dropped her head a little as Denise stood up to make tea, and at the same time administer a consoling pat on the shoulder. But Ruth's head had not dropped to cover a frown, much less a tear, her head was dropped, her hand across her mouth, to cover a smile.

The full meaning of it sank deliciously in - he'd used her. He'd used her and how good it felt, he'd picked her out and used her as a means of getting to Hope, and picked out Hope as a means of getting to Michael and Peter. He'd used Hope to bring Michael Barrow crashing down. It had all been carefully planned, since way before they'd met. She'd never really minded the being used - by him, it was the not seeing that Hope was so ripe for it, that had irked her so. The anger had been mostly with herself.

Especially afterwards, when all the tell-tale signs were so obvious, Michael parading Hope around like a wife, a loyal little MP's wife, and worse, there was a sexual element to it, the way he fussed her, almost courted her, and him with no woman in his life. There is nothing worse for a new MP, or any MP, than the whiff of scandal; a runaway daughter, Steven's letters, and the claim he wasn't abusing her, he was saving her from abuse. A runaway daughter with a reason to run, a runaway daughter that never came back.

Steven had used her and she was smiling, he'd used her and she didn't care. Far from it hurting, it felt good, it was a pleasure to be used. It didn't matter what he'd done, or what he'd intended to do, she knew that she could trust Steven Morris, trust him like no one she'd ever met, like no one she'd ever known in her life, or ever would. *Come on, come on baby please, come back here, use me again, come on baby, please, please use me again, come on back and use me some more.*

Wave after wave of it had washed over her, all the way from Bradford back to Liverpool; *use me again, come on back and use me some more. Please baby, come on back and use me some more, please.*

Time to get up, dawn was on the way, she watched the grey light slowly fill the room. Ruth was usually an early riser, she rolled over onto the empty side of the bed and looked out of the window. Was that a movement in a car on the opposite side of the road, hadn't there been a car there yesterday? She stared at it, peering about amongst the shadows cast by the trees, maybe nothing. Ruth lived on the top floor of a house very similar to the house of the party, but on the other side of the park. A fair sprinkling of weirdoes were to be found hanging around, but that was at night.

Beware weirdoes keep away, a killer's eyes raked the car again, trying to see if ... from her window the fading street lights were lost, below the tops of the trees, the park stretched away, still hidden, the grey light not yet strong enough to see clearly.

She got up, made herself a coffee and sat down to the paperwork left in neat piles on the table in her living room, in front of another window, next along from the bedroom. She looked out again as she settled down to think things through, for one last time, but there was no figure and no car there now, just the park, green and dripping in the early morning light.

The top piece of paper held some names and other notes; she had set out to find them in the same way she would undertake any other piece of research, write down what you know, then check and extend it by searching the archives for whatever you still need. That's why they call it research.

A search of Art Galleries for signs of work by Denise, Karate organisations for Jeffrey, Civil Engineering ones for Richard, and... And Jim was a problem, as she'd half expected he was no longer a registered seaman. Maybe he was still working as a labourer in the construction industry, and then again probably not - that had to have been a passing phase. She looked at her list again.

The friends of Steven Morris:

Jeffrey Vardan - from Hong Kong, Karate organisations, UK, abroad?
Jim Kemp - from Cornwall, not on any list of seamen. Where?
Richard Hegan - Civil Engineering organisations, crossed off seen.
Denise Trentor - Art Galleries, sculpture for sale or was that sculptress, already seen.
Iain Black - from Glasgow, now wealthy and married to Denise.
David Todd - crossed off, nothing, no clue as to his whereabouts.
Maria Lynch - crossed off, easy to find but not worth the effort.

There had been others, kids, drifting along, wandering through their early adulthood, all with problems of their own. Maybe that's why she'd written down these seven, they'd had more direction than most, and that summer they were a crowd who hung out together more than most. Something formed them into a group and then held them together.

Him - for that one summer they were all sitting, if not at his feet exactly, at least around the same table as him, in the same series of bars with him, their one-summer guru. Except for David and Richard they were all too old to be students, and that was the other thing that set them apart, they were the same age as Ruth, early thirties, or thereabouts, her contemporaries.

On the following sheets of paper were her results to date, all laid out in the same order, in order of how long they had known Steven, in order of the longevity of their friendship. Funny how she'd ended up seeing them in reverse, partly due to the difficulty of finding Jim, and partly her being in no rush to renew her acquaintance with Jeffrey. Somehow they'd never hit it off. With the rest of them she'd made a big hit, even Denise had grudgingly accepted Ruth eventually, especially after Denise had fastened onto Iain. Maria she'd fixed up with a job, and Richard, well Richard was just young and lovely, ten years younger than the rest of them.

But not Jeffrey, it was he, ostensibly as a joke, who had come up with the summer's in-group description of Ruth - 'our very own little USSR, our ugly-spic-socialist-refugee'. She was in love that summer for sure, to have let him get away with that.

It was Richard that Ruth had seen next, and only a month ago. He was far less pedantic about Steven being in the wrong than Denise had been, but surprisingly reticent to talk at first, considering as she'd suspected, the part he'd played in the drama. It had taken a little persistence to extract the facts from him. Once she'd got him going it all came tumbling out, as if a part of him had been bursting to break his vow of silence.

The job Steven had wanted him to do had been to 'befriend' Hope. He befriended her all right. She disappeared from London one dark night, and went to live with Richard, in the guise of his stepsister.

They lived as brother and sister, and he had kept a brotherly eye on her as he'd agreed to, it was mostly a pleasant duty apart from some tears early on. He'd kept his hands off her, Richard came by women easily, which is why Steven chose him he now suspected.

At first he did it because Steven asked him to, as simple as that - just like the rest of us. Now he wasn't so sure if he hadn't been taken for a fool, made a sucker of, manoeuvred into something he should never have agreed to. 'Uncle Steven' paid them regular visits, but no, neither of them was ever told where he was living.

"So I could be trusted to do his dirty work," he'd said "but not with information like that." To which she had responded "for your own safety surely?" To receive a grudging "I suppose so" in return.

They went to live in Bangor, to distance themselves from London, Richard was still there when Ruth found him, he'd been employed for almost three years on the new road across North Wales, and it was still employing him now. The brother and sister act worked fine, everyone believed them, Hope was now Emily, with a cast iron surname provided by Steven, a new set of friends and a new big brother to look after her.

It had only been for a couple of years, she'd finished off her education in that little University town and had a high old time doing it - as free as a bird. Yes Richard had had a couple of girl friends, but no one ever suspected a thing, until finally almost a year ago she went back to London, to drama school, where she seemed to be doing fine, as far as her brother could tell.

And that was all there was to it really, so easy for someone to disappear, especially when popular opinion thought it was probably an elopement not a kidnapping. Richard warned Ruth against finding Steven, he was uneasy about those letters and the downfall of Michael Barrow, he'd had to watch Hope go through it close up.

She was a good kid, and she'd needed to escape, and Steven had been around a lot back then to help Richard talk her through it, "you can tell she's OK because she still hasn't gone running home to Mummy, or God help us Uncle". But … but he saw himself now as having been used, and unlike Ruth, he obviously didn't like the feeling much.

After a long lunch she had left him late one afternoon, in front of his work place, one of the large contractor's compounds spaced along the new road.

She started her engine in the fading light and the huge site gates swung magically open for him as he turned away from her, as gates always would do for Richard. A breeze stirred his dusty suit, and his boots scuffed the ground, already walking away he waved a sketchy salute, either to her or to the hidden gate mover it was difficult to say which, maybe both.

She somehow doubted she would ever see him again, it was a pity, but as she'd said to Gregory 'no one likes to be used'.

Her plan had been to see Jeffrey next, but she'd hesitated. These two she had seen, they were safe, they weren't like going back, they were a kind of half going back. You could go and root around a little and see how you felt, and then you could withdraw again if you wanted to, which she had done briefly. But Jeffrey Vardan wasn't like that, Jeffrey Vardan acted as though, as though … Jeffrey Vardan, Jeffrey Vardan understood about loyalty, he - *Jesus Christ of course he did, of course he did, Jeffrey Vardan was a Samurai, they invented loyalty didn't they?*

Well no they didn't invent it, but they certainly carried it further than most, including making it part of a special Warrior Religion they called Bushido.

CHAPTER 10
The Council

Dear Ruth,
So Morality commences as a response to being bullied, the first Moral judgement is a cry for freedom. What happens next?

To see that let's move to an early human or pre-human community of some description.

At first such communities are little more than family groups, but gradually they band together and acquire a Leader, the strongest the most resourceful, the Alpha Male. Not much different to their animal neighbours at this stage, but things are beginning to change.

Alongside this main Leader or Big Man as the Anthropologists call him are the lesser leaders of each family, and from time to time the Big Man finds that he is approached by individuals who wish to air grievances against the head of their particular family.

Fair enough he thinks, where else can they go, but it may seem unfair if I handle this alone, I'll ask the other household heads to investigate and report back to me. I could even get them to recommend a course of action, then it won't seem as if I have a personal motive in all this, after all they are the Council I call on in times of war, why shouldn't they have duties in times of peace too.

Thus are human rights codified; a complaint of not fair, followed by a hearing, a judgement, and a penalty or resolution of some kind.
And next?

THE LAW
The Council and the Big Man find it simpler and more convenient if they make some general rules, guidelines for behaviour, but also to guide those petitioning the Council, complainers and complainants, plaintiffs and defendants, the bullied and those-accused-of-bulling.
They find this can nip many cases in the bud, because not only do these rules ease administration, but they also prescribe the Rights and Wrongs of group life.

Thou shalt not kill ... your fellow group member.
Thou shalt not commit adultery ... with the spouse of a fellow group member.
Thou shalt not steal ... from a fellow group member.
Thou shalt not tell lies ... about a fellow group member.
Thou shalt not rape ... a fellow group member.
Thou shalt not torture ... a fellow group member.
Just six commandments in these early days, the others will come later.

This is a great idea, it eases administration of the group, and is an improvement upon the rule of the bully. It seems a good thing, and I think it is, but it hardly matters what you or I think, because it's here to stay, this dislike of injustice is born in each of us.
In later life we are more able to exercise some adult self control, but we still hate injustice, as neutrals we always tend to side with the underdog, we take the side of the bullied against the bully.

This is the basis of all human Morality, and we're stuck with it, even if one is sometimes forced to wonder whether or not the animal system (a POWER system in which the strongest is almost always 'right'), is not far more straightforward in operation than our constantly disputed and argued over confusion of claim and moral counter claim.

We can wonder as much as we like, it doesn't matter, doesn't matter a damn that Nietzche thinks our moral system is for weaklings and softies. Doesn't matter because his much vaunted superhuman is the Bully, the *Über-Bully*, the Dictator, the Alpha Male the strongest of the strong. Of course we are opposed to your superman you clod, he is the dominating bully of bullies, he is that which Morality sets its face against, he is its whole *raison d'etre* you numbskull.

Tough luck Friedrich, your 'superman' was on the run from the first day of the very first *ad hoc* Council Meeting, the meeting that agreed "you have been treated badly", and he will never reign unchallenged again. For we, the average, the silent majority - the whole damn human race apart from the would-be dictators and their henchmen - we hate to be oppressed.

But it's a never ending battle, because inside each and every one of us, are the seeds of the bully, the desire to dominate, the desire to be the best, to have the best, food, clothes, house, money and mate. After all, one of the most certain ways to be free of repression by others, is to dominate those others before they dominate you - behold, the moral response of the fascist, the response of Machiavelli.

Here is the primary reason that our Moral system becomes so entangled compared to the much simpler Power system of the bullies. So often in any dispute it is difficult for even the neutral to decide who it is that is bullying whom, let alone for the protagonists.
"He started it, he hit me first." Or "oh no it was her that did such and such, and that's what I'm protesting about, I'm the one who's being badly done to, I'm the one being wronged not her."

But we ALL AGREE about one thing; that TO BULLY IS ALWAYS WRONG.
In any situation what we frequently DISAGREE OVER is...
WHO we think IS BULLYING WHOM.

He stopped writing...

Savour that for a moment, feel it, smell it, nestle up to it.
It is the basis of all I have to say to you my friend.
It is the very core of the single greatest idea that I have ever had - it's the only idea I've ever had.

WE ALL AGREE.
Before another word is spoken, WE ALL AGREE ON THIS.
We are all Moral Beings in EXACTLY THE SAME WAY - the Moral Mechanism is the same in every last one of us; black, brown, white or yellow, male or female, young or old, Religious, Atheist or Agnostic.

Recall in the disputes you have witnessed in which you were neutral, how difficult it was to decide who 'started it'. Then pass on, to those disputes in which you were a protagonist, rather than an umpire; the difficulties sky rocket - now you are PREJUDICED, hence the LAW and the need for rules.

Nestle up to that; rest yourself against this central TRUTH of the human condition.
Feel its presence, feel its influence over all your relationships - with others. ALL OTHERS, every single one of them, from the most loved to the most disliked.

This is the great question of Morality, the great question at the centre of all our lives. "He's just pushed in front and knocked me out of the way. Is he trying to bully me?
Or am I being too sensitive, maybe it was accidental? Or maybe not…"
There is a Moral question to judge; some situation has arisen. And how do we judge? We ask ourselves: WHO IS BULLYING WHOM here?

Then, as if that weren't tricky enough, the Council unwittingly adds a further layer of complication.

THE COUNCIL
What is it that the first Council of household heads actually does when it formulates those first six commandments?
It takes each of several individuals' feelings as to what is fair and unfair, and pulls these together into a set of rules.
The FEELINGS of each individual about what is right and what is not right have been aggregated to achieve a consensus - thus are laws made.
And if the whole thing had been done by referendum, with every group member taking part, pretty much the same laws would have been made, no problems on that score. After all these are hunter-gatherers, no one has any great wealth to protect; they all share the work of the group, and need its protection.

No, the problem, the really fascinating thing that has gone completely unnoticed, is that Morality has just been REDEFINED.

And at the same time the origins of human Morality have been hidden from view.

Now Morality has become the response of an individual to a SET OF MORAL RULES, and this accidental obfuscation hides forever the true face of the Moral order.

Hides Morality's real Origin the RESPONSE OF AN INDIVIDUAL to ACTS of BULLYING.

Hides for all our history up till now, the TRUTH that Morality is the response of an individual to various acts by fellow group members.
In particular, acts of ... UNPROVOKED AGGRESSION.

Remember that phrase: 'fellow group members' it's important, we are not considering provocation from those beyond the Group, for aggression from outside the Tribe is not yet a Moral question, that issue will come later.
To take advantage of anyone outside our Group is at this time still FAIR GAME, the concept 'to bully' applies only within-Groups, not between-Groups. Between neighbouring Groups there exists either an uneasy peace, or a constant state of war.

But even now, this early on, Moral dilemmas, the problem of deciding who is bullying whom, have been suffused with an extra layer of complication. It wasn't easy before this First Council, but it was a straight choice, he just elbowed me out of the way, is he 'trying it on', and if he is shall I let him off with a warning or shall I hit back - hard?

Unknowingly the household heads, in pooling their ethical feelings to bring into being the first description of what constitutes bullying, using everyday terms of group life, have produced what is soon taken as an IMPARTIAL MORAL STANDARD.

A standard whose existence is somehow separate from relationships between individuals.

The Council is the guardian of a Secondary Morality, the **Codified Morality** (the LAW), but they think, the whole community thinks, that they are the guardians of the only Morality. *The Codified Morality is the aggregate of our individual Moral judgements.*
It tries to judge, as we've just considered, whether the scolding parent is bullying the child it chastises, or if the child deserves it.

Thus is the **Primary Morality**, the MORALITY of BULLY versus ANTI-BULLY, hidden from view by the first consensus, lost before antiquity, lost in the darkness of pre-history.

It is primary because it is the First Morality, the underlying basis from which the **Codified Morality** springs. It is the basis of all our Moral FEELINGS, the basis of why we say this or that is WRONG, or that someone is EVIL, the basis of why we say that such and such, 'is not RIGHT'.

But from now on, whenever we mean to remind members of society not to bully, we actually say don't lie, don't steal, don't kill, don't covert thy neighbours spouse, we talk specifics, and we never again say; DON'T BULLY - until now.

The Council metes out justice, without prejudice, to individual bullies within their community, but their accidental elevation to font-of-wisdom status, is an innocent step towards disaster. Set soon not to be quite so innocent.

Morality has gained it's first Codified foothold, and this foothold is itself the first formal framework of the first SOCIETY. Before this, pre-human Society is little different from other ape or even wolf groups, a constant jostling for position, a never-ending backbiting for one-upmanship within the pack.
Now ... for the first time ever, there is a framework, a formal basis of dos and don'ts, and along with the advantages this structure brings, come certain disadvantages too.

There are two immediate dangers:

(1)
Firstly that the extra POWER given to the Council results in it itself becoming a bully and a worse bully than any individual alone could ever be.
This is the ongoing battle of government, the battle of dictatorship versus democracy, now in institutional form. Will the commandments be used for the benefit and protection of all, or will they be twisted by an aristocracy, by a ruling caste, to bully a whole group and later a whole country?

Despite the battles we have had, and still do have to control the bully of bullies, the dictators and their willing henchmen, this is actually a relatively obvious danger compared to the subtlety of the second.

(2)

Secondly it sets the scene for a takeover...

The laws and edicts of the Council become the SOURCE OF ALL MORALITY.

This happens despite the clumsiness of their generalities; despite what a cumbersome ass the law is, despite the fact that they see only results never motives. This subtle change occurs because we, the individuals **from whose brains Morality really comes,** in large part agree with the rules of the household heads.

As generalities they sum up pretty much what we ourselves feel to be Moral behaviour. Of course they do, that was their original purpose - A SUMMARY.

Now instead these same generalities have become THE SOLE and ONLY DEFINITION of RIGHT and WRONG. Little wonder that later on we become puzzled and confused by the increasing subtleties and complexities of Human Moral Questions.

Little wonder - it is because the underlying principle has been lost to view.

Wait though, wait, the worst aspect of this is yet to come.

Complicated as things already are, later still the Council takes one last step, a step that makes the laws far more than any aggregated opinion, a step that makes the laws irrevocable, laws now cast in tablets of stone.

CHAPTER 11
Medicine Man

He looked outside, the sun was up, and had been for some time by the look of it. Time for some air. Steven swung a small rucksack onto his back and slammed the back door behind him.

He walked past the first quarry, and then on over the next hill to a second. The silence enveloped him as he reached the upper gap in the mound of slate waste, and began a scrambling descent to the base, leaving the noise of the wind behind, walking and running by turns into the deserted hollowed out heart of a mountain. The bottom was still lost in shadow, the morning light unable to penetrate its full depth, somewhere below him a lamb bleated plaintively, lost in the opened earth. Its cries were puny compared to the silence, nothing could disturb it, death would be noisy by comparison, and then the bleating stopped.

Silence.

The wind disappeared with his descent, somewhere, way overhead, a single gull called once. Then silence again, even deeper than before.

Running and sliding down one of the slopes he finally trotted along the bottom of the quarry and came to a stop. Gulping in air, he basked in the silence and looked around as his breathing calmed. Off to his right lay old rusting machinery, barely recognisable after all the years of decay, he smiled at it, sat down and closed his eyes.

His Welsh grandfather sat on its corroding old seat, the stories he'd been told, a few memories of his own, one old photograph, a memory of being picked up and swung round by him somewhere. Swung round laughing, slightly scared by the strength in the eyes of the man of stone, as his fellow workers had called him.

What could be more natural than to talk with your ancestors, what more normal than to have them by you? The man of stone who survived explosions and rock falls, and eventually succumbed to despair, who couldn't be killed except by his own hand, a quarter of whose genes are sitting here today, alive in Steven Morris now.

After a while, he got up, waved goodbye to his grandfather, turned left and began to follow the central track once again. Raising a hand to salute him is evidence of a Metaphysical Belief, and Metaphysics is the basis of all Religion, the basis of everyone's Religion. It is a word that is unfamiliar to many of us I know, think of it as beyond-the-physical, that is all this ancient philosophical term means, the realm of abstract ideas, as opposed to concrete reality.

The Greeks had their beliefs and I have mine, invented by me just for me - and surprise surprise - they fit me like a glove.

He rounded the dog leg turn, to seat himself quietly down in the middle of a vast and silent auditorium, grey-black rock and purple slate towered up on every side, neutral, ominous and silent. Steven listened, and he heard his father's father calling him and then his uncle, he heard his mother's father, that miner of slate, their voices calling him, calling him

And then he heard a different voice…

"JE HAIS VOS IDEES, MAIS JE ME FERAI TUER POUR QUE VOUS AVEZ LE DROIT DE LES EXPRIMER. I do not agree with a word you say, but I will defend to the death YOUR RIGHT TO SAY IT." I do not agree with a word you say, but I will defend to the death YOUR RIGHT NOT TO BE BULLIED INTO SILENCE.

It was the voice of one of THEM, ringing round the vast empty chasm, one from further back in time than his forefathers. It was one of his all time favourites. "I understand your message Francois Marie Arouet,

Voltaire, spirit of freedom, now I understand it to its core. Now I see, now I breathe, the beauty of your famous Anti-bully principle."

"THANK YOU GREMLIN", he yelled. And heard in reply "YOU GREMLIN, Gremlin" come echoing back. One of his favourites not generally considered a proper philosopher, but that was fine, Steven wasn't very proper either. "Thank you spirit of freedom, thank you Gremlin", and the quarry answered him back. "Thank you spirit of freedom, thank you. Thank you spirit of freedom," echoed around him.

Feeling refreshed he settled himself down and got back to his letter of apology.

Dear Ruth,

As the big human brain increases in size and complexity, it seeks for what things MEAN. Theories about meanings, about what may or may not lie beneath the everyday surface appearance of things are called Metaphysics.

On the Council sits the Medicine Man, soon to become the prophet, the high priest, the theologian, and who now adds a METAPHYSICAL EXPLANATION of where the new laws have 'REALLY' come from.
And the laws become God's laws, UNALTERABLE, SACROSANCT, FIXED FOR ALL TIME.

And the penalty for transgression?
The ultimate penalty of course - Eternal Damnation.
And how useful this is for putting a little extra pressure on us to behave Morally.
And I'm not knocking that aspect of this turn of events. Oh no, anything that encourages us to behave more Morally, by which we can see we mean more considerately, less selfishly, being less of a Bully towards others, can only be a step forward.

Ye shall have no other Gods before me.
Ye shall not make for yourself a graven image, for I am a jealous God.
Ye shall not take the name of the Lord your God in vain.
Remember the Sabbath day, keep it holy.

These next four commandments arise as a result of metaphysical and in due course religious speculation, ideas about that-which-is-beyond the everyday physical world. And therefore inevitably, the 'explanation' of these thoughts, also invokes the visualisation of entities that themselves lie beyond the physical surface of things. Furthermore, though they are quoted here in second place, in fact in the Bible, even in the order of the commandments - these come before the Moral instructions.

Thus does Religion REDEFINE Morality.

Yet we can see, in the social lives of our primate cousins, chimps, bonobos and even monkeys, alive and living next to us today, how the opposite is true; Morality precedes Metaphysics. It is Morality that walks first upon the surface of this planet, and Metaphysics-Religion that appears later.
Morality appeared on this earth before the Metaphysical concept God, not vice versa.

I say only this and no more.
I do not say that God only comes into existence along with the human mind. Along with the increasing size of the human brain, though I grant that an atheist might say that; but what I say is only that no creature before us can **conceive of the idea** - GOD.
And thus cannot have any possible hope of communication with, or recognition of such a thing. For all the creatures that precede humans have no concept of, or concern about TOTALITY, and they are thus INCOMMUNICADO.
They see only daily life. They never speculate about what lies beyond.

Remember that the existence of God is not the question before us. We shall leave that argument to the atheists - to those who believe in that other view of Totality.
Only the time in history, the point at which no living creature had DEVELOPED A BRAIN that could be aware of the CONCEPT 'God' is at issue here, since until this time no one could be capable of a dialogue with God.

At this time it seems reasonable to say that pre-humans, in not yet grappling with Metaphysics, have not yet produced the First Religion.
At a glance this might seem an irreligious thing to say, a statement prejudiced in favour of the atheists. It isn't, because I did not say 'produced God', I said produced their own particular vision, their own particular way of 'seeing' God/Totality.

So in effect the no-group-member-shall-bully-another issue exists, but God 'does not', because we are INCOMMUNICADO.

I put it to you that Metaphysics-Religion cannot possibly define

Morality, that Morality arrived on this earth long before Metaphysics, that Morality is in fact thousands, maybe even a million years older, than Metaphysics-Religion can possibly be.

I've rushed that. I've said too much, you're no Believer in God I know darling, but some of my other friends are.
You are a believer in Truth, in Science and in one step at a time I know.
Either way I've gone too quickly, we must back track.

He got up, he was getting cold now, better head home and put at least a little bit of evidence down on paper.

Dear Ruth,
The evidence for the timing of the dawn of Morality amongst us is thin. Our cousins of course, primates and other animals who live in packs seem to have rudimentary moral relationships, that is individual group members seem to have relationships to each other. How long ago must this phenomenon have started to be present in wolf packs, as well as in chimps and monkeys? Not to mention elephants, dolphins, whales and indeed all those who travel in small groups, as opposed to the solitary or those in large herds?
A long time ago... We humans split from our common ancestor with chimpanzees 5 million years ago. A long time, a long long time ago.

SPEECH
Is speech an indicator?
Can one moralise successfully without speech?
To moralise one has to point out specific instances of bad behaviour, discuss them, gossip with others and compare notes regarding what shirking they too have noticed. What reticence in the sharing of work, what laziness or selfishness did others see on the last hunt, and how did it compare to previous conduct, right or wrong? One must come to a consensus and then organise the reprimanding of offenders.
The experts' estimates of how old speech is vary from 150,000 years ago to as much as 1 or maybe even 2 million years ago. A large range, no specific dates for us there. In part this is because there is so little evidence - no pristine vocal chords left neatly fossilised for us.
Speech and time, time to discuss, time surely is also paramount?

FIRE
Did we sit for lengths of time in groups, in group discussions, before FIRE? Time, night after night around the camp fire - fire gives time for increased social possibilities, time to talk in private, the privacy of night.

Have I not been wronged?
Brother am I not entitled to redress?
Speak brother speak!
Sister cast your vote!
Human control of fire is something that has left traces, thin layers of ash, and based on this evidence is thought to be between 500,000 to 750,000 years ago.
It's tenuous of course; we're trying to look back into the darkness of our beginnings, and utilising secondary necessities to do so.
We are looking back, so far back, back before *Homo sapiens, back* to *Homo heidelbergensis* or *Homo ergaster*, our immediate predecessors.

TRADE
Can a creature without a sense of fair and unfair possibly trade with others?
From stone and bone artefacts found in one area that can only have been produced from materials found in another, sometimes hundreds of miles away, trade is reckoned to be about 1 million years old. A pattern of exchange develops, regular meetings and discussions, about … business reputations, about who is FAIR and who UNFAIR in his dealings, in his or her relationships, with OTHERS.

Is it reasonable to guess that Morality is half a million years or maybe 750,000 years old? For now, to get us started after such a brief look, let's take Morality as being maybe a half million, about 500,000 years old, as a working hypothesis.

METAPHYSICS APPEARS
There is a general scientific view (contested by some), that the single most potent piece of evidence for the first arrival of Metaphysics-Religion is the ritual burial of their dead by humans from about 60,000 to 80,000 years ago onwards.
Assuming that the early evidence of such behaviour might have been missed and also that the idea comes before the action, in other words various ideas of God, Totality and worship thereof circulate for awhile before they coalesce into a formal ritual. Then 100,000 years ago seems a reasonable estimate in round figures for the first glimpse of the phenomenon known to us as Metaphysics-Religion.

This suggests that 100,000 years ago METAPHYSICS starts to appear amongst us, we are no longer INCOMMUNICADO, and this is then followed by the formal rituals of the first RELIGIONS. Our enlarged brain has begun to speculate about whatever it is that lies hidden beyond the everyday world.

There must be something, something behind all this, but what?

And whatever this something is, how does it effect me?

What does my life MEAN?

Religions can be thought of as the first hypotheses about what might underlie the everyday things that happen (good, bad and neutral) in the world-as-we-see-it. Each individual Religion is a Meta-system, a theory of what lies beyond, what lies behind the problems we come up against, what causes the difficulties we suffer in our daily struggle to survive and flourish. It is an effort to predict and if possible to avoid some or all of that suffering.

The brain of a primate is between 600 to 750cc (cubic centimetres), whereas the brain of a human is generally about 1450cc, twice as big, and not just different in size, but different in shape as well, different in the emphasis of its development.

Slowly along with this change and increase came Morality, followed by Metaphysics-Religion. The sciences of archaeology, anthropology and evolutionary biology amongst others suggest that it was this way round, not Metaphysics-Religion first with Morality following.

In summary:

Morality - 500,000 years ago

Metaphysical-Religious concepts - 100,000 years ago

Earliest current Mass Religions: Hinduism and Judaism - 3 to 4,000 years ago

Confucius, the old master - 2,600 years ago in China

Buddha, the agnostic prophet - 2,600 years ago in India

Jesus, the forgiving prophet - 2,000 years ago

Mohammed, the seal of the prophets - 1,400 years ago

Along with all the advantages of a bigger specialised brain comes one big problem.

The brain that is big enough to conceive of a concept such as Totality is big enough to be frightened and confused by this vast world from the moment it realises that it is only a tiny insignificant part of it. Thus for the atheist this brain, 100,000 years ago, comes up with the concept God, to reassure it. While for the theist, God can contact us directly for the first time once our brain is now big enough to receive a message.

I put it to you that Metaphysics-Religion can never DEFINE Morality, though it can ENCOURAGE US to behave Morally.

Morality arrived on this earth long before Metaphysics. Morality is about half a million years older than Metaphysics-Religion can possibly be.

I put it to you that the origin of HUMAN MORALITY is based upon something else entirely, is based upon the simple principle THOU SHALT NOT BULLY, and it is this, not Metaphysics-Religion, that is the bedrock of that which we humans call MORALITY.

CHAPTER 12
Jeffrey Vardan

She stood in the street outside the Dojo, it was evening, but there was still plenty of light in the sky. Ruth had been very clever so far, quick off the mark, putting Gregory off even though she'd already started the job.

Oh yes she'd been very clever, but how clever was it to go in here, Jeffrey Vardan was not Steven Morris, close as he once was to him, Jeffrey was uninterested in Ruth and her politics.

And in the orange corner, introducing, from Nepal in Northern India, the undefeated spiritual heavyweight champion of the world. Siddhartha Gautama, THE BUDDHAAAAA. The Buddha, undefeated ... undefeated even by death itself.

Taken and used by the Samurai - and oh how he loves to be used, to create a religion of their own. Because even professional killers, maybe especially professional killers, need a Religion.

This was out of her territory, a part of Steven she'd been in touch with least, a part that fascinated her, but when it came in the form of Jeffrey Vardan, could also repel her.

Ruth could hear his voice again, coming from inside her own head, the voice of Jeffrey Vardan, the voice of Steven Morris; *how can you right a wrong if you don't know what wrong is, don't know what right is?*

What?

She shivered at the once familiar sound, said usually in feigned anger, that or disparaging scorn, combined with a derogatory, almost pitying laugh at the utter stupidity...

These days there are many fine Dojo in bright gymnasia within modern buildings and new sports centres, the old ones though, the ones of our youth, are always in draughty old rooms in run down premises, hired at a cut price rate. The local church hall, rooms above public houses, or shared space in some other communal wreck, where there is always the smell of dust from the floor, and the stale smell of sweat in the air.

In winter the Dojo is cold, and you change behind a broken curtain, or a screen in a dirty storeroom. Then you go out to do press-ups on knuckles still sore from last time, and feel the bruising on your inner thighs, not from blows but from the sheer torment of stretching the legs to achieve the impossible. To achieve with the foot that which most people only expect from the fist - speed and laser like precision.

Afterwards you never shower, you go for a pint and then home on the bus, the same way you came after a skimpy meal so as not to throw up if you catch one hard in the stomach.

The Dojo Ruth arrived at was one of these, in a basement in a large old Georgian building, on the edge of Nottingham city centre, he had always said they were gloomy places, stone steps led down from the damp pavement through a street door and into the entrance area. Single doors were visible to the right and left, and straight ahead a double half glazed door let in a little light from the main hall. The Dojo was already in use, he'd be there all right, she could feel his presence and feel a shiver go through her in response, to go into that hall was to travel back in time.

The others, Denise and Richard, they were nothing, this was the real thing. Ruth pushed open the doors, and walked into the light of the Dojo.

It looked much as she'd always imagined two rows of white suited figures stretching away, one seated right and one seated left down either side of the hall. Most were kneeling, Japanese style, sat back on their heels, the youngsters who found it too painful were sat cross legged instead. A few chairs stood close to the entrance door, non-participants occupied two, Ruth sat down on the third. In the centre of the room three men circled, lunging and shouting, actually, she soon realised, two were combatants and the third the referee.

The contestants changed with those seated quite frequently, every three or four minutes. The Black Belted referee remained, constantly in attendance, explaining demonstrating educating those involved in the combat.

At the far end of the room, beyond the guttural cries, the punching, kicking, parrying flurries of movement sat another Black Belt. He was perched kneeling and immobile, he watched, he sat in the room, in all of it, in each and every last corner, his presence filled the Dojo. Everyone knew he was there, all the time, you were aware of it all the time. Attentive and straight as a ramrod, yet also totally relaxed, Sensei Jeffrey Vardan looked as though time had stood still. He may have been looking at her, it was difficult to tell from a distance, certainly his eyes encompassed her end of the room. The face was devoid of expression, except for watchfulness itself, those eyes were the soul of the Dojo.

After four or five more bouts, he stood to speak for the first time. A voice she didn't recognise, guttural, staccato, commanding, dominating even in explanation.

He demonstrated movements and kicks to several participants now re-seated along the walls. Then all those assembled were engaged in a hectic half hour of punching and kicking the air. Ruth couldn't take her eyes off him, prowling and pacing the room, a word here, an adjustment of posture there. She was back, something about Jeffrey's way of moving was the expression of a state of mind, no wonder Steven and he used to be as thick as thieves. With a surge of confidence, she knew they still were, they must be, they had to be, when you have troubles you keep your friends close, when you have trouble like Peter Barrow what better friend than a Samurai.

Finally all the figures were kneeling once more, this time in two long lines facing Sensei Vardan to the right. His closing words were a brief exhortation for constant practise and effort, the staccato tenor of his voice echoed powerfully through the Dojo.

"More and more effort. More concentration. No relaxation until black belt. Then relax a little, then work, work, work. More effort again, more effort, more effort, EYAMUU MUKSO". The guttural voice reached a crescendo with the instruction to relax, and all closed their eyes to look inwards. In profile the Sensei appeared more taut and hard than she remembered. A voice cried out from amongst the senior black belts at the furthest end of the room, "MUKSO YAMU. SENSEI MAI REI."

Everyone touched their foreheads to their hands on the floor, training had ended, they waited for Sensei Vardan to stand, and then followed suit and began to disperse. Despite having shown no knowledge of her presence he immediately walked over to her. The impassive face broke into a smile, at the edge of the room he stopped, turned, bowed back to the Dojo and then turned again towards her. Ruth, now standing, felt a ridiculous urge to bow herself, instead she leaned forward and kissed him, once on each cheek, she had better get him out of here onto neutral territory.

"Welcome to the Dojo, Ruth." Then a pause, "What took you so long? Another pause, "At times I thought you were never going to show up."

The voice was normal, more gentle if anything than it had been three years ago, the staccato quality had disappeared, but each phrase was short, with a longer than usual silence in between.

"How inscrutable", she responded, "I must admit you don't seem very surprised."

He put his arm around her shoulders and brought his head in close.

"They pay me not to be surprised," pause "it's a Japanese thing."

He pulled back and laughed, and faces turned their way from the groups still leaving the hall. Soon though everyone had disappeared and Jeffrey and Ruth were alone. "It's good to see you Ruth."

He sat down next to her, explaining the protocol that his ranking was now so high that etiquette didn't allow the common herd to get changed with him. He must be given the privacy his position deserved, he either got changed before them and they had to wait, or he waited till they were all done, usually the latter. So they caught up on some history, including her visits to Denise and Richard, everything but Steven, that could wait.

"Richard was OK, a bit young and naïve, but there's no law against that - yet. I never liked Denise any more than you did Ruth. Two kids and a nanny, you say?"

"Twins."

"It was pretty funny when you appeared and shoved her out, she'd have moved on of course, Steve was no good for her in the long run, but that type, they like to move at their own pace, not be pushed around. Dilettantes," he spat the word out, "tourists passing through life, very sexy of course, I like an hour glass figure and a mass of red hair as much as the next man."

"Ah, this is not quite so aesthetic as I expected."

"You're thinking of Christian aestheticism Ruth. Us Buddhists, we're a bit more flexible than that." He grinned at her. "It figures she would stick with Iain, he was dedicated to 'making it big', remember? Making it rich he meant, they're the same type, neither of them ever did anything for free."

You'll never marry. Men get married to hear how wonderful they are, you'll never need anyone to tell you that.

"Do you remember what I used to say about you and marriage?" Ruth interrupted him.

"Oh sure Ruth," but he didn't repeat it, he just sat there, hands clasped together in his lap, smiling at her, and she had to admit it, the calmest person she had ever met in the whole of her extremely varied life.

"Go and get changed Jeffrey, you make me nervous in that outfit, then we can talk about why I'm really here."

"OK, I've promised to go for a drink with some of the boys. It won't take long, it's just a few of the higher grades."

Over a drink the boys proved to be interested mainly in fitness, sex and their ability if necessary to beat the life out of anyone else in the bar. They were a pleasant enough bunch, but Ruth couldn't give them full concentration. When most of them had gone, and Jeffrey settled himself down next to her, Ruth mentioned that it all seemed a very long way from the Buddha.

He was now wearing a light grey pin striped suit and a pale shirt, the rest including his short crinkly brown hair looked much as it had. His face was strong but not heavy, the eyes rather narrow with prominent cheekbones. In his suit he looked like a middleweight, but at fourteen stones was into the heavyweight class. From across the other side of the Pub he looked like anyone, like no one, but he was someone all right, and she was glad to see it. Glad to see too, that when you got close, even out here in Civvy Street, he had a presence that others didn't.

"Well Ruth, most of my clientele hereabouts are from the rougher streets of this fine city, so a healthy and mature interest in the basics of life I consider to be quite a success."

Vardan surveyed those left in the bar, and then leaned closer to speak confidentially, conspiratorially. "The Buddha wouldn't expect more than that, he was always very realistic. You and your comrades demand far too much. As a result you end up with only the fanatics, while I cream off the real human beings. It's an arrangement which suits me fine I hasten to add."

"Very funny, but teaching them unarmed combat won't change their social conditions."

"I don't teach them to fight Ruth, I am after their souls. Yes I preside in the Dojo, but you'll notice I took no direct part in the free-style fighting itself. I'm a traditionalist, I stand back from such folly. All the competition in Karate is against yourself."

Know thyself says the oracle, know thyself.

"The kids love to fight, and one should never stifle a human urge, when to merely deflect it," he indicated with his right hand, "while it expends itself is enough. So in my Dojo they pay for their thrills. Most of the higher grades in here tonight are already Zen Buddhists, they just haven't put a name to it yet."

He smiled with genuine pleasure at his triumph.

"I've got them Ruth, and you have lost them forever."

"You don't help them, you make them happy as they are."

"Happy to be human, yes. Do you offer something better? I offer something most people don't have."

Ruth finished her drink. This was stupid, he was toying with her, she could tell. How many times had she tried to bait him, and how many times had his answer been a shrug, a laugh or a wink, never a word.

Tonight it was his turn - he was baiting her.

This was the side of Jeffrey she'd always disliked, a presumption of special knowledge, a kind of superior soul, he really thought he knew something about life that others didn't. Arrogant sod - he didn't, but he knew something about Steven she didn't, where he was for one. Fine she thought, whatever you say.

"Let's go somewhere private. I came to talk about Steven Morris."

"I know what you came for," he said, as he swilled the last of his beer around the bottom of his glass.

"Don't be so inscrutable, you know what I tell you."

"You kept coming back Ruth. Three years ago you kept on coming back. You were working yourself to death for your political causes, for that stupid MP, but you kept on coming to see us."

He waved to the last couple of his protégés leaving the bar, and then suddenly started to laugh, really laugh, which meant he was about to make a point, she remembered him surprisingly well. "Didn't you know we were after your soul? Baby we deal in souls, that's where we live, that's what we do. What did you think we wanted?"

"My body?"

"An ugly-spic-socialist like you?" His laughter came out as a snort of derision, louder than he had been all evening.

"Charming."

"Forget it. We wanted your soul for one reason, one reason only Ruth Carrim - because you have a great one. Welcome back, welcome back. Where else were you going to go? There is nowhere else - this is where we both live."

He stood up, still smiling. "This is it for you and I Ruth, you're not like that vamp Denise, or pretty boy Richard, you're the same as me." He leaned forward and whispered, "you're the same as me."

"Oh God I hope not."

"Oh yes, we're just different flavours of the same thing, you and I. We have no other home, this is home, we're sitting at home right now. We're at home whenever we're together. We're the same, we're like Steve, there's something gnawing at us, and it..."

Home, in that moment, as he stood by the table, draining his glass, gathering his clothes and his bag, talking his wonderful nonsense and making his preparations to leave *she knew where Jim Kemp was. She knew even though she'd never been there, Jim was a drunk, but a drunk whose loyalty to Steven was unquestionable.*

Home, Jimmy had told them where he would be, he'd described the place to them. He'd been born and brought up in a seafaring family, "when I've had enough, when we're done here when I'm ready, you'll find me on the mud flats back home, beach combing. Look for a place called Home Farm, it's on the Cornish side where we come from, just across the river from Plymouth. I'll be heading home, that's where I want to die.

A melancholy drunken moment, I'll be waiting there he'd said, I'll be waiting there with my ancestors, no matter how long it takes, I'll be waiting there - like death itself.

Outside the darkened streets were quiet, the quiet just before the bars close, a wet night, a drizzle had started while they were inside. The Karateka walked in front of her, travelling bag in hand and face turned up towards the rain, he stood there just breathing, just being.

Ruth wasn't impressed.

He suddenly banged the roof of a car with the flat of his hand, it echoed in the damp silent street.

"Your place or mine?"

"Yours."

He still didn't move, just placed his bag on the roof of the car, and stood staring into space with his forearms resting on top of the bag. Silence, absence of other traffic, absence of movement, absence even of thought, *absence of the thought of I.*

"I have nothing else to tell you. You of course are going to tell me to warn him, warn him that Peter Barrow is coming, I hear what you say, but I still have nothing to tell you. Where's your car?" He asked suddenly. "Do you want to follow me?"

"I'll ride with you."

"OK, hop in. I'll put my kimono on," pause. "We can get drunk on Saki, and talk about nothing," a pause. "Or old times, whatever you like," a pause. "You can check under the beds or wherever, for traces of our guru," pause again. "And I'll still have nothing to tell you."

Ruth drew closer to him along the side of the car.

"You know everything Jeffrey, you're so clever, you know so much don't you. You think you know everything about me for instance. You think I'm a good Catholic girl turned spic-socialist from Chile don't you? Silence - the sound of the Sensei breathing, and the gentle evening drizzle.

"Well? That's what you think isn't it?"

"Aren't you?"

"Get in the car, I'm getting wet."

He obeyed, and when he'd settled in his seat turned to face her.

"No. I'm not. I'm from Yugoslavia, I'm the daughter of communist spies from Eastern Europe. I'm not South American at all, Mr. Know-it-all. You fool, know nothing about me, nothing at all Mr. I'm-so-fucking-superior."

"Charming."

"My parents were sent to Cuba, and then on to Chile when I was a small child. You know nothing."

"Apparently not."

"You're getting into something you know nothing about. It took me an hour or two on the telephone with a list of Karate organisations to find the one that employs you, I could walk away from you now down this street, disappear, and it would be as though I'd never existed."

"I'm impressed Ruth, honestly I am."

"We, the we you don't even know exists, have a file on you big boy. You're an open book. Born of a Dutch father and English mother in Hong Kong, Third Dan Karateka, living, teaching, eating, drinking and breathing Karate, religion, sport and livelihood rolled into one. Peter Barrow has a file on you, I know because I put those entries on the file, he's never met you but he's interested in you, you poor fool. God you're so innocent, you're a bloody lamb to the slaughter is what you are," she offered him a pitying smile. His miscalculation was his business, but it could be Steven's mistake too.

"Met Steven Morris such and such, blah, blah, blah, his oldest known friend. Your first meeting's there, when he gave you that crazy essay to hand in for him. Then later that time I saw you in the University pool, kicking under water, that's there, far harder than kicking in air you said. We love our paperwork us reds, us nosey-spic-socialists."

"Yes, except..."

"Everything you said to me worth noting, every tiny scrap of hard information, is on file somewhere, if he was still alive we'd have a file on your precious fucking Buddha. So I hope you fight as good as you talk big boy, because my God you're going to need it."

"Except it's Sixth Dan Ruth, Sixth Dan nowadays," he held up one admonishing finger.

"You dummy you arrogant dummy," she shook her head. "Wake up to yourself, wake up to what you're walking into. You think I was with Peter Barrow because he and his friends were communists like me. You stupid know-nothing, I was with them because they were from my country, they were Yugoslav émigrés like me. I was with them because they could connect me to the homeland I never knew. I was with them because they were pragmatists, men of the world, not head-in-the-clouds semi-mystical mumbo-jumboists like you.

"I know everything about you, and you know nothing about me, and nothing about what you're getting into."

"So I see. And as I say I'm impressed Ruth. Really I am."

"Jesus Christ. The first time I met Peter Barrow, this guy I was with pointed him out to me at some social function or other, pointed with his eyes across a crowded room. 'That's Peter Barrow', he said.

"For the hell of it I played dumb, even though I knew who he was, I kept asking which one, but he wouldn't point, he was too nervous to point with his finger. And when finally I suggested he come over and introduce me, and he could see I was serious, when I continued to persist in trying to cross question him about Peter, and what it was he did that made people so afraid of him, that's when panic set in. I could see how much this pathetic creature, trying a minute ago to impress me, wished he'd never brought the subject up.

"He was standing there, safe across a crowded room but he was afraid, afraid because I was talking too much, too loudly, too openly, and Peter was moving closer. He actually tried to drag me out of there, he was ready to run, I could see him panicking more and more, like some kind of cornered prey. So I walked up to Peter to introduce myself, and when I turned to look back, my escort had gone, disappeared, vanished into thin air."

Ruth stopped, making sure she had his attention.

"This isn't some big lad in a pub, or some bouncer on a bar room door. This is a forty six year old man that killed his first human being at the age of twenty, and liked it, a man who learned how to torture others at the age of twenty four, that's twenty two long hard years ago. A man who didn't get tired of his chosen profession at thirty, or at forty, this is Evil personified coming looking for Steven Morris, tell him that, remind him, and learn yourself while you're at it."

"Evil?"

"Take it from me, this is the beast itself - and I've been close to it, I've slept in its bed, many times. Many, many times."

"That's close, I grant you that."

"What it is they're all so frightened of is being alone, in a darkened room, alone with a creature that gains PLEASURE from inflicting pain. Inflicting pain upon others, that's why they sweat, even when they're close to him in public.

"This isn't some game, some test of your phoney manhood, this is every person's worst nightmare, the Prince of Darkness - a torturer, a torturer who knows where you live, and knows that you live alone. And you're the one who is going to have to stop him, because no one and nothing else will. So welcome, welcome to my world."

Ruth paused a moment for breath.

"Welcome Mr. I-am-the-font-of-all-fucking-knowledge, welcome Mr. Know-it-all Mr. Super-effing-cilious you who know so much welcome." Ruth stuck out her hand, and without a flicker of hesitation he took it.

"I know, I know what you're saying. You're right I know nothing of your world, but I'm not a fool, even though I play the fool to taunt you sometimes."

Sensei Jeffrey Vardan, the Samurai in the pin striped suit, looked her in the eye, squeezed her by the hand and then kissed her on the cheek *but he still didn't tell her where Steven Morris was.*

CHAPTER 13
Inland Sea

Dear Ruth,
We can picture Morality as an Inland Sea surrounded by four shores, north, south, east and west. The waves lap backwards and forwards on these shores as the tides rise and fall, and it can often be difficult to see clearly where the water ends, and the shore begins.

Social and Personal Wisdom (our bad habits)

Limits of Bullying   MORALITY   Metaphysics

Responses to acts of immorality (Revenge)

Firstly we'll go West and explore the limits of the concept 'to Bully'. Can something as simple, and as commonly understood, as bullying lie at the heart of all human Morality?

TORTURE

It can, it is, it does, if just one thing is TRUE.
If torture, not murder, is the ultimate act of immorality.

Do you feel arrogant?
Do you feel proud?
Step into the torture chamber, the secret home, the very core of evil, and learn humility. Learn how small, frail and weak you really are, human, see evil face to face, eye to eye, and scream, scream, scream, and hear the silence.
The silence of no one listening, except your torturer.

To kill a human is an immoral act, a bullying act, to torture and kill is worse; to torture endlessly, for years and years is worse than murder.

Let me put it to you that the reason we regard torture alone as less bad than murder is that we assume that somehow, somewhere along the line, THE TORTURE STOPS, whereas you stay murdered forever.

But what if the torture were to last the whole of your life?

What if, you were destined to remain a prisoner for years, and were to be tortured every day, and finally killed, and that this was **a certainty**, that there was no hope of any reprieve, no respite, no glimmer of a chance of escape, no pardon, and definitely no mercy?

Surely it's the hope that one day this will stop, that helps sustain imprisoned victims of torture? But if you remove this, and guarantee instead **endless-torture**, then torture can be clearly seen as being worse than murder.

A fate worse than death.

Then Torture is seen for what it is…

ENDLESS-TORTURE is the ultimate immorality, is THE DEFINING END POINT OF ALL THAT IS IMMORAL.

It is the ultimate misuse of Power, the ultimate Bully and the ultimate victim. It is EVIL defined and personified.

If endless-torture, torture ending in death without hope of reprieve, **torture-unto-death**, is the ultimate form of bullying, it would appear that our condemnation of murder is based upon it being the next to worst form of bullying.

This is why we often pass a light sentence, or none, on the wife who, tortured and battered for years by a brutal domineering husband, hits back one night by stabbing him to death while he's drunk.

We abhor the crime of child abuse, we detest the policeman torturing his victim, for these, like the dictators who bully whole countries, are the ultimate bullies.

These are instances of those who are supposed to protect those in their care, turning from protectors into bullies, the ultimate betrayal.

The ultimate crime, and the ultimate immorality.

To be bullied by your protector, in secret, alone in a dark room, to be **tortured-unto-death** is surely a fate worse than death itself, worse than a quick death.

That is the ULTIMATE **EVIL**, THE FULL STOP AT THE END of those things we humans DESIGNATE AS **WRONG**.

Is there anything worse in this world than ENDLESS TORTURE?
Anything worse than TORTURE-UNTO-DEATH?
I don't think so.

Reflect on this, reflect on this as I do human, you who are so much like me reflect on this.

Suicide and Euthanasia

If endless-torture, not death, is the fundamental end point of our Moral world, then it would seem that euthanasia cannot be Morally Wrong.
Death is only Wrong when it robs someone of the most precious thing they have, life itself.

Bullies them by stealing from them something they want to keep.
Conversely, when someone pleads with us to take something, it is not stealing, it is the fulfilment of a trust - it is a PRIVILEGE.

Therefore to assist someone with a terminal illness (so bad that they wish to give up their life) to do so, cannot be a bullying act.
It therefore cannot be an immoral act.

Sperm

No one can bully or oppress a sperm because it is not a sentient being - it feels no pain.
Therefore catching a sperm in a trap of rubber is not a Moral question.

Trapping a small animal in a painful snare and leaving it in torment for days is a Moral question, not as serious as doing the same thing to a human being, but far more serious than trapping a sperm. Because it is an act of bullying, it is the infliction of suffering, an act of cruelty.
How can one be cruel to a sperm?
It is not an independent living creature capable of suffering, and any act devoid of a bully or a bullied, is a non-moral act.

Abortion

One limit of bullying must lie somewhere between a 23 to 24 week old foetus, capable (with hospital care) of independent life, and that same life as a sperm and egg, at or just before the moment of fertilisation.
Some say that all-human-life-is-sacred, but the truth is that all human life must die.
The truth is that what we believe is 'sacred' is the right to live and die UN-BULLIED.

Some say abortion is Wrong because all human life is sacred, but they are mistaken to call this Morality for this is a Metaphysical-Religious opinion.

If they were to say that abortion is Wrong because it is an act of bullying of a human foetus, the bullying of a POTENTIALLY fully-fledged human life, they would have a Moral point, they would then be making a Moral not a Metaphysical-Religious argument. Arbitrary as it seems, in practise we draw this boundary to differentiate between a blob of tissue so insignificant that we cannot bring ourselves to realistically apply the bullying principle to it, and a being almost human that we have difficulty not applying the principle to.

For the moment the issue is not where we draw the line, but that we draw it based upon the true source of Moral behaviour in the human race, not upon a metaphysical chimera, a religious dogma, an error.

Animals

If endless-torture is the ultimate immorality, then those who apply to us on behalf of animal liberation are right; the torture of an animal by its conditions of confinement, by vivisection, by the method of slaughter, is immoral.

They are wrong when they espouse the belief that we should give EQUAL consideration to animal life as to human life, since over the surface and beneath the waters of this world, species upon species chase, trap, kill and eat each other, under the pressure of evolution. It therefore seems strange to suggest that killing-a-member-of-another-species-for-food is contrary to Morality, to kill for food is common, death is a far more natural part of life than is torture.

And so it appears doubtful that death, or the sacredness-of-life, could be the foundation of human Morality towards animals, but torture, the ultimate form of bullying could logically be so.

I see a turkey, bred and bred to increase its size, so that it can barely walk, let alone have sex or fly, I see it kept in a dark endless warehouse, which it occupies together with thousands upon thousands of other similarly stunted and manipulated birds.

I see bullying.

I see endless-torture, it goes on for the whole of these creatures lives.

I SEE ENDLESS-TORTURE, TORTURE-UNTO-DEATH.

I SEE THE HUMAN DEFINITION OF IMMORAL BEHAVIOUR.

Animals do not have full Human Rights because they are not able to perform the DUTIES expected of members of the human team.

They therefore can have only a PROTO-RIGHT, a Right to a life free of torture, in particular endless-human-inflicted-torture, and the proto-right to a quick death when the time comes.

Homosexuality

Two persons of the same sex, a couple in love, go into a private space somewhere together to have sex, as we all do.
Two consenting adults, neither of whom are under duress of any kind, emotional or physical.

Who is being bullied?
Who is the oppressor and who the oppressed?
Let me think, stand back let me see, let me judge.

No one.
No one?
Neither of them?
Then we will withdraw the old law and make a new one, a MORE JUST one.

Shoving your penis into the anus of another male, who condones, co-operates and (so I'm led to believe) actually enjoys the act, cannot be immoral. It is only immoral if one party is coerced, pestered or bullied into taking part in an act he would not involve himself in voluntarily.

It may not be how you or I would choose to pass the time.
But, NO BULLY - NO CRIME.
And that's why we made it legal all those years ago.

No matter how odd their behaviour seems to us, the majority, since no one is being bullied we cannot designate their behaviour as immoral.
We therefore cannot and should not rule it illegal, between consenting adults, in private.
Sex is a private matter, just like it is for the rest of us.

Infidelity

By the definition of bullying, infidelity is clearly immoral, for it is the manipulation of another - it is betrayal, the breaking of a TRUST. And it is upon the concept TRUST that the whole of the first group co-operative is built, so those who betray that trust behave immorally.

The great force irrevocably allied to survival is the great force of SEX - the third of the six great threads of human life.
And as we look across the animal world it seems extremely unlikely that we are creatures created to be totally monogamous. If we were so created, would we really have all the temptations to have sex with so many others we meet, wouldn't we on bonding, truly bond for life as

certain birds do, with those having the urge to wander being as statistically rare as those undergoing sex change operations?

Infidelity, is a place where Morality meets a selfish urge, but not any old selfish urge, born solely of our own personal avaricious nature and therefore to some extent controllable, it is the urge of urges, the one imprinted in our genes. To describe it as selfish is not really true, it is the urge that underlies the concept "urge".

Then it is an exception to the rule?

No, it is not, and that's what makes it especially interesting, because we see that even in a secular society we disapprove of infidelity - because it is **the betrayal of a TRUST.**
It is bullying by misinformation, by manipulation, by the use of a lie.

Even here, where Morality faces the urge of urges, the urge for which the word urge was invented, even here faced with the most natural urge in the world, MORALITY WINS.

By which I mean that, despite all the temptations and even when we give in to them, the vast majority of us believe that infidelity is MORALLY WRONG. As opposed to serial monogamy, to which we have no Moral objection.

Yes even here B/A-b Morality wins, going head to head with the urge behind all life, THOU SHALT NOT BULLY transcending THOU SHALT SCATTER THY SEED.

Quod erat demonstrandum

CHAPTER 14
On the Road

A misty morning, with a large red sun burning above the horizon, beads of moisture still hang and glisten on the long wet grass at the edge of the park, soon the day will clear, to reveal a blue summer sky. Ruth had packed a suitcase, she knew where to go next and would be away at least two nights.

There was a car in the lay-by again, but even now the shadows made it hard to tell whether or not the vehicle was occupied, it was different, she thought from the one she had seen two nights ago, a dark brown foreign looking sports car. *Always give yourself the benefit of the doubt, never waste it on someone else, if you have a suspicion, treat it seriously, stop it from niggling, try to prove or disprove it one way or the other.* Never dismiss it as fanciful nonsense, trust your instincts, her father's voice, an expert on such matters, and then he was gone.

Ruth emerged in her habitual jeans and T-shirt, stowing her case in the boot she placed a cigarette between her lips and mimed the search for a light, then got in the car and reversed off the forecourt.

She continued to reverse back up the road until she came opposite the lay-by, then looking across at the other car she got out.

"Have you a light?" she called and gestured through the glass. He just stared, then removed the keys from the ignition and wound down the window. "A light," Ruth repeated, noting the microphone attached to the dashboard, she leaned into the flame, said thank you and re-crossed the road. It would soon be the rush hour, but for the moment there was no one else around except the two of them, the road was damp, the air still, Ruth cast a plume of smoke in her wake. Not bad, it was two years since her last cigarette. As soon as she had started the car and moved off, he picked up the microphone and began to relay his message.

Ruth spotted them a few miles out of Liverpool, still on the M62, a blue Ford three or sometimes more cars back, quietly following her down the motorway. Sometimes she speeded up to eighty and then gradually dropped back to fifty or sixty, the blue Ford appeared to do the same. She was alert now, otherwise their ability to always keep at least two cars away in the thickening traffic might have been enough to hide them, they were careful, dropping well back and only moving closer again when an exit appeared.

Each time she overtook another vehicle she returned religiously to the inside lane, hiding herself for a moment in front of the vehicle she'd just passed. Ruth knew a trick or two herself. First they must be lulled into the boring banality of her driving. She turned south at the M6 and held her speed at just under seventy, ahead lay some long slow road works, just after a junction she was very familiar with. The sun had emerged from its haze to shine upon her, and on the busy traffic around her.

She slowed, the timing had to be right, the repair works started soon after the exit was passed, they wouldn't have time or space to follow her. She moved out, checked their position, and squeezed into the slow lane again in front of a lorry toiling up the increasing slope, and as soon as she reached it she continued, swinging onto the empty hard shoulder.

Ruth hit the brakes, but not too hard, she didn't want to attract attention. She pushed down harder and the car came shuddering to a halt, a few yards from the concrete traffic barrier cutting into and sealing off the emergency lane. Up ahead the motorway narrowed from three lanes to two.

Now already opposite her, the tyres of the Ford screamed in anger as it too tried to slow down. The attempt was in vain, the car shot on past, trapped by the momentum of the surrounding traffic, trapped where there was no emergency lane.

Cursing, the driver tried to slow down enough to drop off his passenger, but the thundering lorries made it impossible. His passenger, the lighter of cigarettes from earlier, treated the effort with disdain, he felt no urge to share the slow lane on foot with a stream of thirty ton juggernauts. Instead he radioed their second car, which was due to take over in another ten miles, he'd hurried them up by the time his driver reached the far side of the road works and could stop.

The driver got out and stood by the car looking back and cursing, the passenger smiled, he'd told them what nonsense this was. In fact the back up car was too far away to get a sighting, and the whole thing was farcical anyway now they'd been so obviously rumbled.

Ruth reversed along the hard shoulder, laughing in relief and triumph, for four hundred yards back towards the junction she'd just passed. Then, after a quick U turn, at the bottom of the slip road, she drove slowly up against the flow, keeping as far over to the edge as she could. Only three cars happened to come down the other way, each in turn giving vent to affronted blasts of their horns, which she ignored.

The sun still shone as it had before, a blue sky had now broken through the last of the haze. The large red sun had gone, to be replaced by a bright yellow fireball, she laughed again, she was free of them, free to do as she wished, free to go where she pleased.

Freedom, Steven's voice again, not her father's - freedom, by which we mean, free from oppression. We do not mean free to do whatever we please, wherever we please and to whom we please. No, when we use the word freedom, we mean free from being dominated by others, not free narcissistic licence.

Long before the second car arrived Ruth had left the motorway behind, heading first west and then south, goodbye Gregory. She stayed off the M6, following country trunk roads until she reached the M5.

Ruth knew it wasn't that easy to say goodbye to everybody down in London, she would have to go there once she had seen Jim.

She had added another name to the list she must visit, Bruno Talad. He wasn't one of them, one of the friends of Steven Morris. He was one of us, a comrade, a drinking pal of Peter's, at least he still was two years ago, the last time she'd spoken to him.

She stopped the car and stared into space, Ruth knew how to find Bruno, just pick up the phone and ring, so easy, but who else would be listening at the other end, and who else might be there to meet her.

Was Bruno free these days, free from domination by others?

CHAPTER 15
Metaphysics

Peter was soaked to the skin, it was the afternoon of another long day, and nothing to show for it apart from one wild goose chase. Nobody had heard of Steven Morris, or anyone who even resembled him.

He sat in the car and quietly dripped onto the floor and the seats, everything was wet.

Outside the rain was increasing from a steady downpour to storm level. The car windows had misted up, hundreds of droplets were gathered on the outside of the glass, running to join each other at certain random places, and then for no apparent reason deciding to stream downwards together. His wet clothes were soaking the upholstery, he started the engine to get the heater going, and then began to struggle out of his coat.

He felt tired. He'd just done two miles on foot, following a wizened Welsh shepherd who'd led him right up the garden path. The old goat had grabbed Peter's battered photograph of Steven Morris, and waxed with enthusiasm that he knew this man, English, yes, on his own, older now, yes, he'd take Peter there in no time. Peter had had his doubts straightaway, something about it didn't seem right, he'd questioned six or seven people down in the village and no one knew anything.

Maybe he should stop mentioning a reward, these country yokels would be helpful enough without that, he could just say he was looking for an old friend, it was a matter of life and death, which it was. This one had needed nothing, had charged off, all to see some dirty old Englishman with white hair, sixty years old at least, and living in squalor in a cabin with no power or water. If he thought that looked like this photograph it was a wonder he could see the damn sheep, he could climb though, nothing wrong with his legs, or his lungs, just his eyes that were no bloody good. The speed they'd gone at, and still not beaten the rain. Peter knew he would ache tomorrow, a three mile round trip at a gallop on top of a long morning, all to get finished before the rain, and he hadn't done.

It was a damn nuisance, but he couldn't leave any stone unturned, he didn't want to backtrack. The name would be gone, he wouldn't be Steven Morris anymore, and who knows maybe his hair had gone white. So he must go slowly, covering the ground thoroughly, this was the second lone Englishman he'd been presented with in two days, it was amazing how many there were, but the consensus on yesterday's had been that he didn't look much like the photograph. His house was shut up, no one had seen him for almost a year, that was too long,

Peter's information was a lot more recent than that, he rubbed condensation off the window then opened it a little, but he still couldn't see. The view back to the coast had disappeared with the rain. This village really was the last outpost, there was a bleakness up here, as bleak as anything he'd ever seen anywhere, including Russia. It was the greyness; grey stone walls, grey skies, grey houses, bleak grey soaking rain falling onto dirty green grass and dirty grey sheep.

He looked around, the road he'd come up to the village on was the only way out as well. He was parked on the edge of what might laughably be described as the village green, the village grey more like, surrounded by an uneven tarmac road, the end of the line, with only a rough track to more mountains meandering away beyond.

What if Morris heard him coming, and literally took to the hills, Peter frowned, rain or no rain this area was too small to hide in. He would be baseless, people are weak on the run, making them easy to trap and destroy. The strong stand still, they don't change with the slightest wind. Peter nodded his head, agreeing with himself, an old Stalinist some of them called him, so what, he was proud to be steadfast, there are some things too sacred to question.

The damn sheep grazed everywhere, even on this excuse for a village green, not another living soul was in sight, just the sheep in the rain, brushing against the car as they passed, forever seeking that patch of greener grass, hidden maybe beneath this vehicle. He growled through the window, and sent one scurrying away, two others followed in case there was something to be afraid of, there was.

Peter sat there for awhile, lost in thought, and watched them begin again to chew their way along the roadside, anxious to carefully crop even that narrow verge. The rain and the clouds seemed to isolate each separate household, at least to the eyes of an outsider, its thin damp tendrils reaching even into the houses.

He felt tired, two weeks ago this had looked a lot simpler, it was a better place to hide than he'd thought, but someone had seen Steven Morris, plenty of them must have in fact. Morris was a Welsh name, Peter was learning a lot about Wales, he read books on the subject most nights, apart from anything else it endeared him to the owners of the small hotels he liked to stay in.

Recluses are almost better known than busy bodies, they engendered curiosity, the how and why of their existence, he would find him, not too long now, and Steven Morris would be his, and then we will see. We will see that some things are too sacred to question.

---oOo---

Dear Ruth,

As the human brain continues to increase in size it asks, HOW does the sun rise and set? WHY do the seasons change the way they do? Asks for the first time certain different kinds of questions, WHERE do our family and friends go when they die? Where will I go?

Will I join them there?

WHAT does my life MEAN?

Let's get back to that Inland Sea, the East Coast this time.

Social and Personal Wisdom

Limits of Bullying	MORALITY	**Metaphysics**

Responses to acts of immorality (Revenge)

Metaphysics is the seed of every human religion, the attempt to answer: What does my life mean? What will happen when I die? Are those who were so close to me but have now died gone forever? Or will I see them again?

The question of our place in Totality.

The question that only humans ponder, and that only METAPHYSICS can address, is thus first asked. Some way back we took a turn down a different road, a road called MORALITY, and now, as is the way with evolution, our still enlarging brain takes another turn off this road.

Metaphysics is the 'moment' of asking-about-MEANING. The moment that comes just before Metaphysics-Religion and the many varieties of Religions that follow. The many Religions that vary with our differing circumstances, influences, cultures and backgrounds, before this variety comes the 'moment' when ALL RELIGIONS ARE THE SAME.

Ra is the Sun God, but rainfall is the Male God fertilising the earth from which things grow, the Mother God. When do we feel good, in harmony, when are our bellies full and happy times, surely it is when we live lives that are in harmony with those-who-decree-all-this, the Gods.

This then is our PURPOSE this then is the MEANING of our lives.

To hold the Gods in reverence, to worship them in HARMONY.
They give us all we have, they give in times of plenty or they take away in times of famine.
This must be the RIGHT WAY to live.
To offend against this is surely Wrong.
Just as whoever is stealing from the seed store does Wrong?

By stealing what the Gods have given, he offends the code; he breaks the pact, worships the devil - HE DOES MORAL WRONG.

At the moment of the birth of questions about Meaning (questions about underlying reality, about METAPHYSICS) at this moment, the moment of THE BIRTH of Metaphysics-Religion upon the surface of this planet, instantaneously…
Morality becomes SUBSUMED WITHIN IT.

The roots of Morality are lost, they vanish from sight, and in a flash the child becomes the parent.
And the predecessor is henceforth unseen, hidden for thousands of years of unrecorded human history.

Hidden by the successor masquerading as the predecessor.

Metaphysics is good.

Every human HOPE, every youthful dream, of a life of adventure, exploration, a life of religious meditation, or of scientific discovery, are part of our personal metaphysical-religious system. All the ideas in our heads, along with the BELIEFS our parents and community have imparted to us, plus the ones we've gone out and found for ourselves, all these are metaphysics, all these are wonderful, marvellous life affirming metaphysics. The religion we choose (or none) to build for ourselves, from the materials to hand, is a PERSONAL view of our place, and the place of human life, within TOTALITY.
Every idea, before it becomes reality, every theory before it is proved by empirical observation in the real world, each hypothesis as yet unproven by science, all these are METAPHYSICS.

METAPHYSICS is the sixth great strand of human life.
Metaphysics is good because it is a source of HOPE.
Metaphysics is good because it is part of our INNER INSPIRATION.
Metaphysics is good because it is the way many of us relate to the vast empty Universe beyond ourselves.
Metaphysics is good because it keeps us going when all else fails.
Metaphysics is good because...

Metaphysics is good, but let me tell you of the illusion that the priest, the monk, the brahmin, the mullah, the imam, the shaman carries with him all of his life.
He thinks he is part of one single entity, a mass religion, a religion he shares with others. He is not.

Clearly there are COMMUNAL RELIGIONS. Religious frameworks common to members of a particular Society, but each one of us has behind this surface communality a PRIVATE RELIGION, a personal way of communicating with God, with the Totality beyond ourselves.

It is this unseen personal religion that is the basis of BELIEF, and it is this that provides the hidden foundation upon which all communal religions are built.
How could it be otherwise?
Religions are BUILT UPON BELIEF.
Or Faith is the other word often used, though you won't catch me using that, I dislike its sanctimonious overtones.

Where is this Belief?
It can exist nowhere other than inside the heads of the adherents of each religion, it is firstly a personal experience, and only secondly a shared experience. When you think about it, where else could it be?
Where else could BELIEF exist?
Except inside individual heads?

You don't believe me?
Show me the person with whom you agree about everything.

Show me the religious or social organisation of any kind that has not split and split, and split again, and again and again, into schism after schism, sect after sect.
Show me a MASS RELIGION, and I will show you a mass of rituals, rites, mores and laws by which human beings live, laws they use to produce certain modes of concerted action, but NONE of those million upon millions of individual beings actually believe in THE EXACT SAME WAY.

Raise up an issue, and you will see disagreement, debate and dispute, I will show you individual after individual, not cattle or sheep, ants or bees, but HUMAN INDIVIDUALITY.
Are you the same as the person next to you?

Do all your thoughts and opinions exactly coincide?
Do you agree with every word that your favourite priest, poet, pundit, pope, politician, guru, rabbi, writer or imam says?
Of course not.

Ideas and hypotheses, we humans live by them, we cannot BE without them, we cannot be sane, we cannot be happy INDIVIDUALS.
We need Metaphysics just as much as we need Justice and Morality.
Just as much as we need to 'do the right thing'.

Where did the world's Religions get the idea from that we can't pick and choose the parts we believe in and the parts we don't. Why would we put all our eggs in one basket? At their behest?
When there are some good things in one Religion but different good things in another. Every single one of them should be referred to the Monopolies Commission.

Let's be careful with words, they are important.
Precise DEFINITIONS are important.
Metaphysics is the Question/Answer routine that comes immediately before the Birth of a Religion, or before a new scientific hypothesis, and goes on as micro-metaphysics inside each of us FOR ALL OUR LIVES.

Atheism is Metaphysics, because it is a Belief System.
The real atheists are our cousins the chimpanzees, and the other animals - because they have no interest in, cognisance of, or questions about TOTALITY. Whereas our human so-called atheists are as fascinated by TOTALITY as the rest of us.

Agnosticism is Metaphysics - Buddhists are agnostics.
Islam is Metaphysics, Hinduism is, Christianity is, Judaism is, but these are just the famous ones on which the world's great Religions are built.
Unfortunately, crap like the 'Domino Principle' is Metaphysics too.
Remember that one?
A real beauty...
'If just one South or Central American country goes Communist then all the countries of Central and South America will follow, falling over like a stack of lined up dominoes'.
That was a crackpot Metaphysics of the CIA and others.
It was a belief system.
A part of the larger right wing US Metaphysics that said, 'no matter how oppressive the bullying dictatorship is, as long as it professes a hatred of Marxism, another Metaphysics, we'll support it'.

Doesn't that make you feel sick?

This is a Belief so strong that it produced a 'Foreign Policy' based upon Metaphysics, and NOT UPON MORALITY.

Which is insane, since it is Morality that lies at the heart of all human social relationships, domestic, national or international, whereas Metaphysics exists only in the heads of individuals, as an inspiration for their lives, AS INDIVIDUALS.

Let's keep it there, where it does so much good, let's not turn it loose to rule countries, societies, tribes, or even little families. It's not fit to rule Mum, Dad and a couple of kids, it's not fit to be let out on its own.

It's great inside our heads. We humans live by Metaphysics.

By our beliefs, our hopes, dreams, theories that make us willing to sally forth, and to try and try again, again, and again, in the face of incredible odds.

Belief, which includes the placebo effect, that makes us able to battle on with indefatigable fortitude, with never say die spirit, remaining positive when no reason to stay positive remains. Somehow staying positive even when we're in the grip of an illness as brutal as cancer.

HOPE - Metaphysics is the great guardian of hope, without which our lives become pale husks, transparent, weak, depressing nothings.

Without which we cease to strive, without which many of us give up.

Metaphysics-Religion: wonderful, inspirational, optimistic, positive life affirming Metaphysics - the thief, the usurper of Morality.

CHAPTER 16
Jim Kemp

Ruth eased the car onto a rough road that sloped sharply downwards as it left the weed strewn lane. It had taken some finding, and now it was late afternoon.

For a time it seemed to run back parallel to the way she had come in, but eventually it forked towards the river, and then down again to curve around a small lake, from the far end of which a stream disappeared into the undergrowth.

A mile or more away, vaguely visible through trees and shadows, Ruth caught a glimpse of an old rusting ship, it was slowly corroding, rotting away to one side of the estuary, being eaten alive by the salt laden air.

When she reached it, the farm and the farmer seemed rather odd, he didn't want to let her cross his land, he seemed reluctant even to speak to her, watching her closely, suspiciously. His appearance reminded her of pictures of Abraham Lincoln, without the hat. Home Farm, the place was strangely quiet, his dogs sniffed around her as suspiciously as their master, finally with some reluctance he pointed out the track she should follow.

Ruth got back in the car having closed the gate behind her, Abraham just watched, making no move to come across and help. It was a strange place, she shivered despite the hot sun, James Kemp was down here somewhere, drunken despairing Jimmy Kemp, the close friend of Steven Morris and the person who had actually introduced her to Steven.

Abandon hope all ye who enter here.

It is possible to know too much, to understand humanity too well.

She shivered again and started the engine, the air had become humid while the car had stood still, hot and damp and heavy, making it hard work even to breathe.

She drove bumpily along the side of an overgrown field, below her she could see how the water twisted between the trees and the folds of the sloping land, in places it opened into festering mud flats, she guessed what the beach would be like. Soon the edge of the field became a rough track and she was down on a level with the river. Water lapped around the car wheels as the track passed over a kind of ford on the edge of a salt marsh left stranded by the tide. Silence, then a dog barking a long way away, but no other signs of life.

She drove on, into another field, past the water and then through an open gate, as she'd been told it led out of the field and onto a narrow unmade lane, leading nowhere. The air was stagnant, stifling now as the hedgerows closed in, but when she wound the window down further the hedges squeezed into the car. From somewhere up ahead the air carried with it, drifting over the last few fields, the knowledge of something familiar: *hopelessness,* this was the place Jim Kemp had come to die.

Soon the hedges crowded in completely and she stopped the car. Thick undergrowth lay up ahead with only a footpath beyond continuing downwards. Ruth got out of the car and walked along the path, which soon opened out onto the 'beach'.

Lines of seaweed lay stranded on the shingle, further out the pebbles gave way to mud, which in turn gave way to water, which stretched, flat and placid over to the opposite bank.

On the far side there was no sign of life, not a house nor even a track, just a few empty fields and woodland rising to the top of a crest. While along the line of the river there was even less, before it twisted away to hide itself in the land. Flattened foundations close by were partly hidden by undergrowth, it was the sea, an estuary of many separated tentacles, but it seemed listless, having lost its way amongst land.

A figure that could only be James Frederick Kemp continued to paint a boat out on the mud flats without looking up, a dog sniffed at him and wandered away. Ruth kept her eyes on him as she crossed the shingle to reach the sandy mud, the dog, an old black Labrador, came to meet her. Further along the shoreline she noticed a terrace of two or three small houses, lonely and battered, one was clearly a ruin, but the other two still seemed intact, *Chez Jim* she assumed.

The whole length of the shore was a sun trap and the stench of salt and seaweed lay everywhere in the heat. Down here at the end of the twisting decaying track the afternoon was sticky and close, the heat beat back in a shimmering haze reflecting off smooth round pebbles. Flies rose with an irritated buzz as her angle of approach disturbed succeeding lines of seaweed.

Finally he turned, and as she grew closer Ruth could see how his face had aged, aged more than the time that had passed, more than the other faces she had seen. He had a full beard instead of the old Sundance moustache, and his black hair was wild and unkempt. Jim's face and torso were mahogany brown, and though his fat seemed solid from years of physical work, it made the whole shape of him appear as abandoned as the rest of this strange place.

He was wearing open toed sandals, Bermuda shorts, and a ridiculous grin, the boat lay behind him, and behind that lay the river, stagnant, hot and lifeless. He turned with a half hearted gesture back to the work in hand, and muttered something casually over his shoulder, almost as if he was talking to the boat.

But then he twisted back and shouted across to her.

The accent was thicker than she remembered, he sounded a lot more Devonshire than he had.

"Hello Ruth, come and sit down my lover. We're finally getting some heat. That's good - I need to sweat out yesterday's booze."

As she got close enough to reply he discarded his brush and dropped heavily on a ridge of mud. Indicating the spot next to him, he offered her his can of beer.

"I stopped for tea and scones not long ago, very Devon".

"Tea." He muttered scathingly, swallowing from the can and offering it to her again.

Thirty yards away the water lapped lazily as an unaccustomed swell broke its surface, as soon as it passed the dark salt water resumed its natural state, turgid, calm and listless.

"All that Navy action," he turned and looked east to the Tamar, "sends the odd ripple up here now and then". He lay back, closing his eyes against the glare and shading their lids with his forearms.

Ruth decided to accept his offer and drank.

"It smells as though you have been sweating for quite some time Jim," she drained the can, working on the theory that it would do her less harm than it would him. He grinned unashamedly, his mouth was all she could see, both forearms now hid his face. His torso and shoulders were wet with running moisture, lending a sheen to his skin and hanging as beads in the hairs of his chest. He was right it was hot, unnaturally hot down here for late afternoon.

"I'm a child of nature these days, before I gave up taking sightseers out in the bay I was forced to stand downwind of them. I have limited facilities here, but I get a special deal, my father did something for his father many years ago now."

"Yes, I've met him. Is it me or is he the spit of Abraham Lincoln?"

"Yes he does look like him. No relation though."

"A pretty weird guy."

"He is - but not so weird that he doesn't understand about loyalty. Loyalty that goes back a generation at that."

She sat down next to him.

"You know why I've come then Jimmy?"

"Of course I do," he looked at her as if she were treating him like an imbecile. "My brain's not gone that soft."

"I felt betrayed Jim." He sat up, and gazed absently at his half painted boat. "I'd thought he was the one who would never let me down."

Jim nodded and stared at her instead of the boat.

"I felt betrayed," she repeated, wondering if she was getting through to him.

"You weren't," he finally replied, and still looking at the boat shook his head.

"What do you mean?"

"This world is a bag of shit Ruth, but it's not so bad that Steve Morris would ever have touched a fifteen year old girl."

"Sixteen."

"Whatever."

"And?"

"What do you mean 'and', and what?"

"And that's it?"

"What else is there?"

"Everyone else has all kinds of things, Denise still thinks he had a sexual relationship with her,"

"No way," he interjected.

"Richard was involved but now seems to think he's been strung along and as for me, at first I was angry, about everything and at everybody, including myself. And Vardan, well, it's pretty clear he believes that her father was actually sexually abusing her, which he wasn't. Like you, he says Steven would never have touched her like that, forget about it."

"Ah Mr. Vardan, fancy he and I agreeing." Jim shrugged. "Where's he to now?"

"Nottingham."

"Ah, Karate country."

"So I gather."

"Oh he's not so bad you know, you never liked him, and neither did I that much. He's." Suddenly lost for a word he produced another can, as if by magic from a pool of cool muddy water, and opened it with a hiss. "You've caught me on a bad day, on a bit of a bender celebrating the start of summer."

"I've come back to find out why, I want to know why. Everyone has an opinion, they all have a position. Except Vardan who's above us all of course."

"Positions. Leave it all behind you is my pos-i-tion. It's all history. Steven Morris never loved anyone but you. That's his pos-i-tion. How long's it been? Two years?"

"Three."

"Really?"

"Really."

"Well if you say so, anyway he's not looked at anyone else in all that time, no one. For him there is no one else, never was, never could be, and as for why, who cares why? He had reasons, and whatever they were, I don't need to know them, they will have been good ones. He is Steve Morris and my good friend." He nodded to himself, took another long swig and tried to get up. "Steve never touched any fifteen year old girl."

"Sixteen."

Jim shrugged, then farted and got slowly to his feet, to face across the river.

"The king is dead," he yelled, *king is dead, ing is dead*, came echoing back from the empty fields on the opposite bank.

"I've not heard that in awhile," she smiled at him.

"The king is dead, long live the dead," he bellowed again raising his can and drinking to the echo, and then yet again "THE KING IS DEAD, LONG LIVE THE DEAD," his face set, waiting for a reply.

And then, it came *king is dead, long live the dead ... long live the dead, the dead*" the voice of Steven Morris came echoing back across the water from somewhere far away on the empty river bank.

"Spooky eh?" He grinned. "You remember that then do you?"

"Of course."

The king is dead, long live the dead. How can you right a wrong when you don't know what wrong is, don't know what right is?

"Do you remember the thugs Ruth?"

"What?"

"The thugs on the lonely street at night, about to beat an old drunk to death?"

"Oh yes, I remember that one too. Amongst others."

"Shall I tell you the answer to the riddle?" Jim grew close to her, like a conspirator in some crazy melodrama. "He's found the answer. Shall I tell you?"

"OK, yes, why not." He's lost it. The thought crossed her mind that he was completely mad. "Please do Jim."

And suddenly he seemed to sober up.

"You are walking alone down an almost deserted street. Up ahead, on the opposite side of the road, you notice four or five people grouped together. As you get closer you see it is four young yobs and one old drunk. Beneath the street lights, on the glistening pavements, an old derelict is about to be beaten to death. You are unobserved, there's no one else around.

"What is it right you should do? The drunk will probably die this winter anyway, out alone in the cold. The most he would do, even if you were to succeed in saving him, is to be sick over you or ask you for money for drink. You can hear him over there, as his pestering maudlin importuning for money turns into panicky pleas for them not to hurt him. He has realised the way the wind is blowing, but too late.

"If you were to cross the road to die with a ridiculous old drunk the decision would lack any logic whatsoever. If the thugs had not been there, and he had come weaving up to you repulsive and bellicose, you would probably have walked away with contempt. And now you are at the point of choosing to die with him.

"Notice I'm not asking which choice you believe you would make, that is for children - talk is cheap. You are my friends, I know you and I know you will do the 'right thing'. What we are interested in is why is it 'the right thing'? Why do we all feel that it is the right thing?

"If you were to slink quietly away hidden in the shadows, why would you feel that was WRONG?

"How can it be wrong - to do the 'sensible thing'?

"Why is doing the logical thing wrong?

"How can this be a Moral dilemma, when this drunken hopeless case is no cause worth dying for? Why are we open mouthed with horrified admiration over the person who won't desert the tramp no matter what?

"Steven used to say it was because the Moral thing is to never bully others, and so resisting the bully is the preferred choice, but now..."

"What? What? Hang on, hold it, that's new. Stop, stop Jim, that's not what he said. He asked us questions, the questions that he, he didn't give us answers, he didn't have any. He…"

"It's what Steven told us about the riddle - that Bullying is not one face of bad behaviour IT IS THE WHOLE OF BAD BEHAVIOUR. It is his … you remember how … how he."

"I remember everything, too much in fact so stop asking me, but he never said that. Those words, those weren't your words Jim, and they aren't Steven's old words, they're new words. They sound like him but I don't understand how you…"

"He's been here, he's told me these things."

"What? He comes here? He visits you here?"

"Yes, did you think only you could figure out where I'd be? He's been here many times."

"Many times? Many times?"

"He's my friend, my best friend, he's with me all the time. When I first came back from London, it was as if he was here already, as if he'd arrived before me."

"Yes but he must really have been here for you to…"

"This place is special Ruth, a place for Metaphysics, you can talk to *them* here. You can talk and they answer you."

"If you say so."

"Do you know who I saw Ruth, just last week, up there at the end of the beach?"

"Steven?"

"Walking with his little dog, dressed in his long coat and beard."

"Go on then, who?"

"Charlie Darwin."

"Oh God, so you're seeing them now too? The same as Steven?"

"The very same."

"And what did he say to you? I've a feeling he said something?"

"The following proposition seems to me in a high degree probable … namely, that any animal whatever, endowed with well-marked social instincts, would inevitably acquire a moral sense or conscience, as soon as its intellectual powers had become as well developed, or NEARLY AS WELL DEVELOPED, as in man."

"I remember that quote too, so don't ask. How come you're suddenly sober, I think I preferred it when you were pissed."

"Hush now, I want to get this last bit right."

"Another day we might run, or try to ignore it, on another day maybe we would have done THE WRONG THING, and looked the other way, but somehow today, however crazy, this is where the buck stops. To hell with it, I choose involvement, and if it comes to it I choose death.

"And if it's such a dumb thing to do why do we admire that choice so much?"

"When was he here, when was Steven here Jim?"

"Do you see Ruth? Do you see? Bully and Anti-bully are the basis of all Morality."

"Yes Jim, I see. I understand."

"Wherever you see immorality, the bully…"

"I said I understand, I see, I can hear him too, but when was he here?"

"I see Steve all the time Ruth, every night now, every night."

"How come you're spouting shit one minute and the next can't answer a simple question?"

"This is a holy river Ruth, a place where…"

"Sweet Jesus! When has he actually been here?" She shouted at him.

Ruth looked around … half expecting.

"He's always here Ruth, he's always with me lately."

"Yes," she tried patience again, "when, when was the last time Jim?"

"A month ago, I think…"

"You think! Are you that far gone?"

"Maybe longer, maybe less. He said you might be coming, and here you are my good friend." He smiled clumsily putting his arm around her, and seeming for a moment far happier than before. "As large as life and twice as ugly," he whispered, with his unkempt beard against her ear.

And with that he turned and was off, back in the direction of the half broken down terrace of cottages, he'd talked too much, he was dry, he was tired, and he'd run out of beer. Ruth sat and waited, how had Jim retained all that, she supposed he had always been more erudite drunk than sober, but even so how many times would Steven have had to have been here for Jim to trot that out so clearly.

Many times, many, many times.

She carried on waiting, letting what he'd said sink in. *Bully versus Anti-bully, there it was revealed - a revelation.* Nothing happened, the sky didn't turn red. The old black Labrador stood up, came quietly over for a patting, and wandered off again. Ruth lay back on Jim's narrow strip of sand, surrounded on all sides by mud, and covered her eyes with her arms as he had done.

After a while she stood, and walked towards the edge of the listless water, time seemed to stand still, three years hadn't passed, everything slowed down. Morality was Bully/Anti-bully, his question answered, everything was here, here on this strange shore, there was no need to go anywhere else. It was all here, wherever she went it would always be the same as here, becalmed on this excuse for a beach. The trees across the water stirred slightly for a moment, then stopped, the sun was sinking, up river, to the west, it glinted off the surface of the water.

Everything still looked the same, but everything was different. Ruth sat down by the water to think. The king is dead, long live the dead, nothing stirred, silence, timeless silence. A stupid thing Steven used to say, often as a toast, it sent shivers through her, he was here now, she looked around again. *Don't you know that nothing is too sacred to question? Nothing, nothing, nothing. Don't you know that knowledge, no matter how painful, is always better than ignorance?*

This place had something to do with him for sure, the way that echo had come bouncing back, he must love that, the silence, but not just silence, the stillness now that Jim had gone. There weren't even any birds, no gulls, why was that, nothing, nothing stirring in the fields opposite. Ruth looked around again, still half expecting, but there was no one, not even Jim's dog.

It took James Kemp quite a while to reappear, but eventually he came, stumbling over the shingle, a four pack in one hand and a half empty whiskey bottle in the other, the black dog in tow once again. It looked like a long evening ahead. She walked back to meet him, and they met as he dumped himself down on a prominent mound of mud a little way short of the boat. She took a can from his hand, and noticed he was a lot more drunk than he had been before.

"You drink way too much Jimmy," she said looking down at him. He leaned forward, peering against the sun, his bloodshot brown eyes were screwed into slits.

"Been the whiskey," he muttered, "but it don't matter soon Steven," Then he threw back his head and gave a barking laugh.

"What?" Ruth asked, sitting down next to him as she opened the can she was holding.

"He knows, all used up Ruth. You knew, that's how found me."

"Don't go stupid on me now we've still got some talking to do."

"No we haven't. Time for you to go find Steven, time for bring him here."

"Can't you get in touch with him?"

"Vardan knows, he knows, not crawling to hi," but his head dropped down, and it was lost in a mumble.

Jim slumped back on one elbow, sinking into a patch of dirty sand.

"Vardan knows,"

"Knock it off. Get a grip Jim."

He looked up.

"Vardan knows, fine, rather have him than … at least Jeff's honest. When he doesn't tell you something it's cos he thinks you should work it out for self. Not cos he might want use it against you in't future."

Ruth nodded, and watched as he seemed to gather his wits, and liven up again. Jim was right, it had to be Jeffrey. She'd always known she'd be going back, back to see Jeffrey Vardan, but first, she sighed to herself she'd have to see Bruno.

She needed to know whatever Peter knew, needed to know how close he might be. She would have to risk running into Gregory, or his private army, or something worse.

The beast, the something that takes fathers from their children, and then it ... one head of the many-headed beast.

"Ah Jimmy," she shook her head in wonder, "I don't like drunks, I don't like weakness. Didn't I ever tell you that?"

"Like me better than some, I'm not so bad," he stopped, sat up and managed briefly to focus on her.

"No?"

"No," he gathered himself. "Despair's a clean wound. It's the lies that fester and puss, lies that ooze, lies infect round you, and those around them, until bring down a plague on all heads."

"OK…"

"Despair isn't pretty look at, but not contagious, it's clean and out in open. When you lie you force others to lie, you force lie upon them. You force them to, to…"

"Yes?"

"Have ten babies when two would have done. And you," he stopped, looking almost embarrassed.

"Carry on you're doing fine. A brilliant recovery in fact."

"You force lie down throats … then they spew it back onto someone else, or pass it in milk from their breasts. Give me despair and truth, to hell with lies. No, not so low in your esteem as…"

Finally he trailed off.

Then he looked up at her defiantly, "not so low some," sweat dropped off his chin. She stared at him and he stared back, then he went suddenly blank again. That seemed to be it, end of speech.

"OK Jimmy. You got me, you're right." She squatted down next to him, face to face, eye to eye. "I give in."

There was no reply, only silence, not the call of a bird, not a breath of air, not a ripple disturbed, only silence.

CHAPTER 17
Bruno Talad

Ruth had been late starting off, she'd hung around to try and talk to Jim when he was sober, but he had been slow waking up, and even slower coming out of it. She'd got nothing for her trouble, and now it was evening again, but still warm, the sun was breaking through the clouds as she reached the edge of London.

Ruth got out of the car on a busy tree lined road, the house was an end terrace, small and square like its occupant, who was just over forty, with a brown square face and a worn brown suit to match. His alert and inquisitive brown eyes surveyed her carefully as he embraced her, then he led the way in.

"Comment ca va?" she asked.

"Comme ci comme ca, come on in, you look tired," came the slightly accented reply.

The two downstairs rooms had been knocked into one, and there was an old fashioned French window at the back which opened out from the lounge onto a sloping lawn to the rear, Harrow sits on a hill, and the flat plain of London lay spread out in the distance.

"It's been a while Ruth, we should have kept in touch."

"No we shouldn't. And that's why we didn't. You were Peter's friend not mine, and you couldn't be both." She seated herself in an armchair at the front of the house. "And I make friends easily Bruno."

"Well maybe," he conceded as he flopped down into the armchair opposite and studied her for a moment. "Tired, and hungry I hope?"

"Starving, I seem to remember my last meal was lunch, yesterday."

"Good. Come and sit at the table, I worked through and got a load of food on the way back. I'll have it ready in ten minutes, I'm hungry too."

Ruth moved to the table, overlooking the patio, while Bruno busied himself in the kitchen. At the back of the house, beyond the garden where the land fell away, elevated above the houses, silver trains passed along a brick viaduct outlined against the sky.

"Quite a view, eh Ruth?" He deposited the first hot dishes on the table. "When night falls, and the trains are lit up they travel as if they're suspended, all against a background of darkness."

"It reminds you of home, right?"

"Their home maybe, not mine." He smiled and returned to the kitchen to bring more plates. It was quite a spread: rice, fried onions, curry, with all the trimmings.

"It'll do for two meals. My little friend and I live off the stuff," he explained depositing a bottle of wine of about twice normal size on the table. By using both hands while Ruth steadied the glasses he succeeded in pouring a large glass for each of them.

"What's this? A wife?"

"No, a live-in friend. That's life for us international news hounds you know."

Ruth laughed.

"What's so funny?"

"You, you wouldn't know a scoop if it came up and bit you in the leg."

"Don't be so sure. My sources aren't what they used to be I have to work at it now. International political analyst maybe suits me better." He poked a finger at her, and started to eat "same office - smaller staff."

"What's your friend like?"

"Don't embarrass me - she's young. She'll be along later, she's gone to a family gathering, you'll see. I'm something funny and foreign with a dark hidden past, she is something spoiled, with money, as foreign to me as I am to her. Oh God I'm ashamed," but he was laughing, "sitting here with you, and I've got a rich toy-girl in tow."

Eating and watching the trains in the distance they talked about history, the future could wait. Bruno had opened the French window and a breeze drifted in, bringing the last of the day, while their talk of the last years of comradeship drifted out as so much hot air.

When their glasses were empty and their stomachs full Ruth explained about her recent visits, and in particular the details of Gregory Allen's appearance.

"What's he after?" Bruno mused aloud.

"I don't know. Tell me about Peter, what's he doing? Where's he gone?"

"He's gone to Wales, North Wales after some tip off, to find and dispense with this Steven Morris. He's been told Morris is 'in West Snowdonia', he's on the coast, with a view of the sea."

"And?" She prompted him.

"And nothing, that's it."

"That's it? That's all he's got? Nothing else?"

"Nothing else. Well he may have more, but if so he hasn't confided in me."

"Maybe he doesn't anymore?"

"Well there is that, but I don't think he's got much. He was setting off on a search, not paying a call at a definite address."

They sat in silence, mulling over their exchange of information. In a little while Bruno got up to fill their glasses.

"North Wales, Richard's there, the girl was there, Hope. Steven's half

Welsh ... I once went there with him, it was a trip he took me on to sort of show me the north, the places he ... there was a place, I think I know where..."

"Stop! Don't tell me. For Christ sake have you forgotten everything?" He looked around, as if someone who shouldn't hear was in the room with them.

"Sorry. He showed me this place, a place that was special to him."

"Fine, but don't tell me anymore for God's sake."

"It's not a house or a village or anything, it's just a place he might visit, somewhere he might be close to."

"OK, but keep it to yourself," he insisted.

"Someone's bothering you then?"

"Yes, I'll tell you shortly. Ask me about something else."

"So Peter's as serious about this as ever, setting off with so little?"

"Oh it's serious alright, he wants this - badly. He must consider the information reliable, the phrases used are quotes from Steven Morris to an unnamed third party. To someone Morris thought he could trust," Bruno twisted around in his chair to look out at the last of the evening. "It's not much," he said, twisting back, "but maybe enough, so Peter thinks anyway. Come on I'll put the coffee on, and we can sit out there on the steps, take your wine with you."

The garden plunged away into ornamental bushes, and then a tangle of brambles covering a plot of open land beyond. It was quiet, the momentary lull that comes at twilight, a brightly lit silver train rumbled over the viaduct.

"I love it out here," he said as he came back, handing her one of the cups.

"It does remind you of home then?"

He sat down next to her.

"You keep saying that" he said with a sigh. "I don't know where home is anymore. I'd grown tired of their hypocrisy, their expediency, their ends that justify means, long before I arrived over here, but not Mr. Barrow. Even now, when everyone know it's all over, Peter carries on as if nothing has changed. With our so-called ideals in pathetic tatters it sits there, just sits there for all to see, you know this..." his voice tailed away.

"What sits there?"

"His enjoyment of causing suffering to others sits there, as naked as the day it was born ... with all its camouflage removed." For a moment longer they avoided looking at each other. "But you've always known this?" He looked at Ruth questioningly, and put his free arm on her shoulder, pulling on it a little to look at her.

"Not at first, but yes, for a long time," she answered him.

"We started out as Muslims."

"Who became Communists."

"Maybe we should have stuck to being Muslims?"

"In a pig's eye."

"Yes I know, anyway you can blame your parents." They sat together in silence for a moment. "All this effort," Bruno murmured, "over something that's none of his damn business anyway. It was his brother's life and his brother's business, meanwhile the KGB have got their noses up his arse."

"That's whose bothering you?"

"They're all over us, KGB, or FSB as we're supposed to call them now. Or maybe ex-KGB, or even ex-Stasi, God knows, you can never be sure nowadays. These are FSB though, the main man is a Russian and I think the other three are too, but they speak German all the time. I don't know what that means - if anything. I think it's unofficial. I'd say they are doing a favour for someone, protecting someone's new life, someone's new business life."

"I don't understand."

"Neither do I really. They watch me, and I listen to them. I'm still pretty good at that, my equipment is not much out of date - yet."

"I understand that, I meant what are they doing, why are they on you?"

"Oh, well there are plenty of them who've left this business, the various services of the various regimes. They've been made redundant, downsized out of existence, and now they are 'security consultants', private policemen, arms dealers, drug dealers, bodyguards, God knows what. Others have gone legitimate, have got their money into proper businesses, and these are the ones who are vulnerable - to a blast from the past."

"Yes, yes, I'm with all that for Christ's sake!"

"Sorry, sorry, I meant this must be some German thing. In Russia it doesn't matter what they are, the place is wide open, but in East Germany, Poland, or anywhere south of there rumours of your past can ruin you overnight. They have to be more circumspect, or they'll end up with a career cleaning toilets. Yes?"

"It's private then."

He looked at her again, without looking away this time.

"Ruth they … these people, they can't afford loose ends. They are those you and I wake up in a cold sweat dreaming about, and will for the rest of our lives, it just happens that for awhile they were on the same side as us."

"In theory. On paper."

"Yes, exactly, in theory. Anyway, now they want to cover their tracks, these are people who don't want any scandals breaking out in the future, people who want to be sure."

"Our secret army."

"Our ex-comrades, and in particular Peter's close ex-colleagues. You know these people as well as I do, you know what they're like, they were our masters, they were always … what do you want me to..."

"I know, I know, OK I see, but you and Peter, you never worked together did you?"

"No, but we have certain … acquaintances in common. Someone feels threatened, I don't know who, you know what Peter is like, who wouldn't feel threatened? Let's be frank, he's a fucking mad man, no one can predict what he... They're all over us, we who have a history with them, who have had the stupidity to help them, or even worse, the arrogance to defy them. What a fool I've been Ruth - I've done both. I, we, we don't fit anymore, we're a nuisance, we're a problem."

"Or you might be."

"Yes, we might be." Silence, the rumble of another train, the thought occurred to her; *he's afraid. The indestructible Bruno Talad is afraid.* "Peter especially might be, I know how to keep my mouth shut."

"At least Peter has only helped them?"

"Yeah, but it won't save him. What they're after now is anyone who doesn't fit anymore, those of us who the changing times have left behind, anybody they think, in their thick headed Russian way, might be dangerous *Dummkopfs!*" He snapped in disgust. "God in heaven - we were always so much better than them, streets ahead," he tailed off and stopped.

"I hadn't realised, I suppose I should have."

"Why should you? You don't have the mentality, you never did, you come from a different branch of the family, but you know them, you know what they're like. You understand what I mean?"

"We're being watched now then?"

"Ja naturlich," he stopped. "As I said they speak German, I've been listening a lot, but I'd rather speak Spanish, *naturalmente* I mean. There's a van in the street whenever I'm here. They don't seem to be watching the back, and there aren't any bugs, I still have the necessary to check for those, and I have my ears of course. I can listen to them from here, so I'm getting to know them, strengths, weaknesses, soon they will be my friends, and then … I can take advantage of them. Maybe, unfortunately they're not stupid at what they do, just at thinking beyond it."

"Will they follow me when I leave?"

"I think they might." He hesitated...

"So they're looking for Peter?"

"Yes he gave them the slip, he's not taken them to Wales with him. They've called to see me once about that, they'll be back again as soon as you've gone."

"Maybe I should take them to Wales? Would they stop Peter from killing Steven?"

"I wouldn't bank on it," he was quiet for a moment. "I don't know, they probably don't know themselves. To tell you the truth there's a wonderful irony here, I don't actually know for sure which one of us they're after, Peter or me.

"I'm pretty sure they're doing a favour for someone, it could even be some Serb gangster, in which case it's Peter they're after, on behalf of someone who thinks he's a danger to them, or might be. Who knows? They'll watch us for awhile and then suddenly..."

A silver train glided through the air in front of them.

"What have you told them about Peter?"

"Nothing, I told them about Steven Morris, about Peter's vendetta, that he'd been tipped some clue as to this persons whereabouts, I said I didn't know where, I told them history, only history. They'll have been asking others as well, same reply, from people who really don't know. But they'll be back, now they've seen you." He looked at his watch. "They'll just about have you identified."

"That fast?"

"Yeah, they have all the gear, they're not that unofficial. You'll have been photographed when you landed, they never forget a face, that is their machines don't."

"So I've put you in danger?"

He gave a Gallic shrug and a sound like blowing out air in reply.

"I could have told you not to come, although the phone's tapped actually. I could have called you back but I thought you might do me a favour."

"How?"

"They haven't the manpower they used to have. If they follow you I'll know that I may be in the clear, that it's Peter they want, they could be just toying with me, stringing me along. I think they'll follow you to get to Peter. That could give me a breather, maybe even a chance to disappear before they disappear me, why wait and find out they were after us both. Though God knows how, and God knows where ... I don't really feel as brave as I talk. I'll have to tell them what I know, especially since Gregory Allen seems to know something. I'll say I got it out of you."

"Where is Peter now, this minute?"

"I don't know - he's not been keeping in touch. Someone rang him, and off he went."

"What kind of someone was that, I wonder?"

"I've no idea. Someone like me - a traitor." Bruno shrugged again. "Who knows? Anonymous was what I was told, but he must know. Otherwise why place such reliance on it?"

"And how did Gregory get in on this?" Ruth wondered aloud.

"I don't know, maybe he just noticed Peter was missing?"

"No. He knew about Steven. That's why he came to me. He knew a lot, I could tell, there was a confidence about him, he knew enough to know he wasn't going to find Steven Morris without me, even with all his money."

"He's that hard to find?"

Ruth hesitated for a moment.

"Steven's his real name, but Morris isn't. I've no idea what it is, nothing criminal he changed it a few years before any of us met him. He explained it as a Hindu thing, the taking of a new name when you consciously turn away from the life you've lived and turn towards the religious or philosophical life."

"So neither of you know each others real names?"

"That's right, how'd you like that, the great lovers don't know each others names. Peter never believed it of course, but I do. He never called the police, thought he could sort it out. Thought he could find her and Steven himself. Then when he couldn't... Could get no further than a false name, and a person who worked for cash in hand on construction sites, he saw something sinister."

"He would, I would."

"No, it was nothing like that. The trail was short and cold because Steven Morris is an oddball, not because he's a spy."

"Hmmm"

"Peter saw a plot. Something put together by enemies of the brothers Barrow."

"Yes, that bit I do know."

The long grey twilight grew darker. Bruno put down his cup.

"Come on inside Ruth, I have to make a phone call."

They went inside, he left the lights off. She stood next to him and watched him dial in the gloom.

"Who are you calling?" Ruth asked.

Bruno briefly turned quizzical brown eyes on her, not losing the sequence of numbers. Then he covered the mouthpiece with his hand.

"Come a bit closer and listen," he whispered.

The phone he had dialled was still ringing, and carried on doing so for a while. Finally it was picked up, but still no one spoke.

"Hello?" Bruno said. "I recognise your voice."

More silence.

"Do you recognise mine?"

Then, just as you thought no one was ever going to speak a laconic voice finally replied. It had a trace of a foreign accent, but she couldn't place where.

"Perhaps, I could if I worked at it."

"I've just been told that Mr. Gregory Allen has information regarding the whereabouts of Peter Barrow."

"Indeed."

"Worse, if he were being discreet, I would know nothing about it." A momentary silence...

"Now that sounds true," came the leisurely reply.

"I can say nothing further now, my informant is still here."

"I see, and his motives for not informing me?"

"I defer to you on that of course," Bruno replied. Ruth noticed that perspiration had gathered on his upper lip.

"Indeed," the voice lingered tantalisingly "indeed" repeating it again.

"I must go," Bruno broke the connection and then immediately started to pace about the room.

"What a voice," Ruth said.

"Yeah, the most laid back Russian you'll ever meet - though I hope you don't."

"That was no Russian."

"Come on Ruth," Bruno smiled sadly. "You know who that was, what that was, Christ you even know where that was. His name is Striganev, Comrade Colonel Striganev if he still has a rank, his friends call him Strigo, if he has any. I'm certainly not one of them. We were supposedly on the same side, back when there were so many sides you just couldn't keep count. My side doesn't exist anymore." Ruth nodded. "And later tonight, probably while you and I are asleep, he will shatter an old man's illusions, the fantasy he has friends in high places."

"Those who have illusions at his age deserve all they get."

"Very well. Now let's be careful, no one is safe from them. I'll have to call him again tomorrow, though he'll probably call me - God what a mess. When I think of how long I've kept one step ahead of them." He was looking straight through her, his eyes vacant.

"Not you Bruno. Surely you're safe?"

"*Non. C'est moi aussi maintenant.* They'll be coming for me soon, the trick is knowing when."

"Surely they can't..." He focussed on her and that something was in his face again, the same as earlier. That something she'd never ever seen there, before tonight - *fear.*

"Yes they can, I'm no longer immune, not anymore Ruth." He looked at her. "They're going to take me to a little dark room in Kensington

Gardens or wherever they do it nowadays, it'll be night - it's always night. They'll get me in there, and just for fun, just to get started they'll kick me around for awhile. Until they're bored you understand, or tired, or consider it's time to start the damn questions. Then they'll ask me all kinds of things, to which we all know there are no answers, otherwise they wouldn't ask them. And we know what comes with the questions, the fun part, the little extra pressure, just to help keep you … on track."

She raised her hand to his cheek, and for a moment his voice tailed away.

"I'll cry, I'll probably scream, I'll cry a lot actually, I'm that type, I know the types. I've watched them, often, too often, through secret panels, one way mirrors, at those who I've…"

"Stop."

"Those who I've fingered, those who… They'll call me a traitor. A traitor to this, a traitor to that, there are different kinds. Over and over again they'll call me a traitor. They do that to everyone, but in my case they'll really mean it."

"Stop, that's enough."

He was looking into a past a long way away from the room and the trains outside. His gaze focused back on her.

"Sorry," he said.

"Run," she whispered in his ear.

"Where to? My side doesn't exist anymore remember? I'm out on a limb, the people who protected me, who slipped me into this country, all gone. I'm alone. No, no let's get this right I'm surrounded by my 'allies', the friends I originally changed sides to work for."

"Run anyway. Always run when you get the chance, and think about where to later."

"What's that, the Chilean way?"

"*Si, naturalmente.* My father's way."

"All the friends who could help me have 'retired'. I'm alone."

"Come to me, run to me. As soon as I sort out this little mess I'll help you."

"Thank you, maybe I will at that."

"And Peter's to get the same treatment?"

"No," Bruno shook his head. "He's classed as English, and he has the passport to prove it. He's in his own country, they don't own him the way they think they own me. An accident would be their style with Peter, a drug overdose, some reasonable pretext, but me, they're going to do to me Ruth, what I've helped them do to so many."

"Not while I've known you."

"I sent them hundreds Ruth, hundreds. I gave them a small country. I chose to betray my country, I…"

"Stop it, there were others besides you. Stop it."

"OK, OK I'll shut up," he stopped, and stared out at the long slow dusk.

"You betrayed your country for your ideals, your people rather than your principles." She came round to his other side and whispered in his ear, "that makes you my kind of man - run to me the moment you get the chance." He smiled, at their reflections in the French window, and nodded his ascent.

"Peter can't even see it. Jesus Christ, they're out there watching us now, and it was the same at his place, but he won't have it, he says they've always watched him - his allies. I sweep this place once a week for bugs, but not him he thinks they're 'just nosey', he thinks he can't be touched, he..." Bruno stopped at the noise of the front door.

"Your friend?"

"Yes, that'll be Chris, we won't talk about this anymore, she's really very young. She thinks such things don't happen, she thinks..." he stopped and smiled. "She thinks this is England, *asseyez vous*."

CHAPTER 18
In its Entirety

Dear Ruth,
We must be precise, some definitions before we continue.

GOOD/BAD and RIGHT/WRONG: by defining happiness as the surfeit of PLEASURE over PAIN that every last one of us seeks - this in turn defines the difference between the words GOOD and RIGHT.
PLEASURES in general are felt as being GOOD, whereas our MORAL pleasures are felt as being RIGHT.

We perhaps say casually that a particular event, a change of career, felt 'right', but what we mean, and should say strictly speaking, is that the change felt 'good'. Right should really be reserved for Moral issues but instead the word Right spills over from the Moral to the general sphere, or conversely we place Good as opposite to Evil, and befuddle the issues and ourselves in this way also.

Since Evil is ultimate bullying, Ultra-Wrong, its opposite should strictly be Ultra-Right, not Good - which is a far more general observation on our many varied pleasures.

To have sex with our life partner, or to see a film and go to a restaurant, or go on holiday feels good, because sexual (or other sensual) pleasure is non-moral. It is pleasure compared to pain. Yet afterwards we might say (mistakenly), 'that holiday felt right' - how easily are words, and thereby important meanings, jumbled up.

Right (non-bullying) is the opposite to Wrong (bullying), and therefore it would be more accurate to say this is a Right person, and that a Wrong person, than this is a Good person and that a Bad person. When sex feels good, the sun on our backs or the food we eat feels good, there is no moral element, only a comment upon the most ancient driving force of all, PLEASURE as opposed to PAIN.

When we say this person is a good tennis player or that one is good looking, we are also being specific about non-moral attributes, therefore the use of good is correct, but when we say Gandhi was Good we confuse things.
We know what we mean when we say it; Gandhi was a Morally Good person. But it would be clearer to say that Gandhi was a Right person, Gandhi was RIGHT (but not in the sense of being correct, rather than incorrect - a further linguistic complication).

CORRECT/INCORRECT: things are made worse by this use of the word right (and wrong) in the sense of correct and incorrect. Which is of course the reason why saying this is a Right person and that a Wrong person sounds strange to us. I think it's too late to change and re-train ourselves but, as we sit here together for philosophical purposes, we must use our words with care and be sure of what we speak.

GOOD is derived from the PLEASURE/PAIN mechanism, whereas the word RIGHT is derived from MORALITY.

DEMOCRACY: despite all the rhetoric, despite all the complicated and erudite books about politics, there are only two forms of government; there is democratic government, and there is totalitarian government. It's hardly likely that you of all people don't know the difference, but I like this couplet I've made up, so let me remind you anyway.

In a democracy when you don't like the government, you get rid of it.
In a dictatorship when you don't like the government, it gets rid of you.

It's really very simple.

Bully versus Anti-bully in governmental form.

Except that all too easily democratic institutions and intentions can turn into dictatorships.

I see a thief - or do I?

Is this stealing from the seed store a venal act of greed, or are the Council and their wives keeping all the best and most food for themselves? In which case that which has the surface appearance of theft is in fact an act of liberation against a ruling elite. And that which appears to be democracy is really aristocracy - a dictatorship of certain wealthy families.

Is he stealing from or for the people?

Is this act that of a thief or a liberator?

An act of political hegemony in a struggle between rivals for power, or a blow against tyranny?

Is he a terrorist, or a freedom fighter?

Bully or Anti-bully?

Al Capone or Robin Hood?

Democracy is a word, just a word, a word that gets bandied about by all kinds of people, for all kinds of propaganda purposes, so we must give it its true definition. Democracy is the means by which we attempt to control the most dangerous bully of all, the STATE.

The means by which we try to control THE GOVERNMENT, who in turn control the police, the army, and in many countries the lawyers, the press, the secret police and the death squads as well. *And we know, who is worst even amongst the death squads. It is those who torture before they kill, those who torture right up to the point at which they kill. Bullying fortissimo, bullying taken as far as it can go.*

Democracy is a word, a concept designed to control the Bully of bullies, it is not a sacrosanct end in itself. A word that so many are busy chip, chip, chipping away at, and can often devalue, it is 'in name only' if it fails to control the Mega-Bully it is designed for. All too often we see democracy degenerate into the maintenance of a wealthy ruling clique, a corrupt Bullying minority, a privileged upper caste.

I see our thief, he leaves the grain store, but I still cannot tell from this brief glimpse, which he is, thief or liberator? Criminal or Robin Hood? We need more facts on which to base our judgement, we sit upon a never-ending jury all our lives, and we gather facts, information,

GOSSIP, more information, our thirst seemingly insatiable. Who is the bully here and who the victim, then I'll cast my vote.

A vote we never ever change, we ALWAYS VOTE THE SAME. Never changing parties, we vote the bully is immoral, in this court oppression's always wrong. All that changes out there are the circumstances of who it is we think is bullying whom.

The factory junior bullied all day long goes home, and once there rules his wife and children with his fists, his boot, his belt upon their backs. All that changes is our view of who the bully is, and who's the victim now.

Some people look for a pattern in history, well this is the pattern, the bully and the bullied, the tyrant and the freedom fighter, the upstanding citizen and the thief. The king and his barons, the feudal lord and his subjects, the landowner and his tenants, the capitalist and the proletariat, the husband and his wife, the business man and his workers, the army and the people, the Party and the peasants, the father and his children, the masters and the slaves.

I give you human history and its pattern.
I give you Bully/Anti-bully.
I give you FREEDOM from repression - the only Moral law.

Morality, the single principle of THOU SHALT NOT BULLY, as we have seen is not just the backbone of society, is not just the sole driving force of each and every human society there has ever been or ever will be, but is in fact the whole of Society, is the very stuff of which it is made.

This one principle is the bottom, top, middle and furthest flung corner of the mechanism by which we co-operate one with the other, this one single principle - IS SOCIETY. Is the sole basis of every relationship between each person on this planet and the person next to them, the whole of it, the whole world of human relationships, in its entirety - period.

CHAPTER 19
Chinatown

The clouds had rolled in early, after two days of clear afternoons the rain was back. Back with a vengeance, torrential once more, Peter drove upwards, towards the farthest end of the valley. The grey world closed in on him again as he passed by a row of five silent houses, small, with tiny blank windows and dirty grey pebble dashed fronts, staring out beneath stark hoods of slate. They looked upon a dour misty world hidden from the coast by the clouds, he cursed and drove on as the deluge increased.

The wipers lashed at the windscreen, never quite clearing it of rain. Morris was up here somewhere and somewhere up here he would die, those who hide from the world are easy to hunt down and kill, their safety is all illusion. One fights for what one believes in, or one sacrifices it to those who are willing to do so.

Fools, there is no escape from the Peter Barrows of this world. He laughed, a hard bitter laugh, but not today it would be night soon - he would have to turn back.

---oOo---

It was night time in Chinatown, outside the restaurant window the street was bathed in the long bright blues, yellows, reds and greens of flaring neon lights, Ruth stared out through a reflection of herself, maybe it was all a dream. She was in Hong Kong on an art trip with Paul, or at some conference, soon she'd wake up and find that Steven Morris was dead, as he almost was three years ago.

Only he wasn't, Ruth smiled at her reflection, he was alive, she'd seen the message in the eyes of his two closest friends.

"Me too, I won't be changing sides. Not this time around baby ... till death do us part." A waiter materialised alongside her, casually dressed, white open necked shirt and black trousers, inscrutable and westernised. She explained that she was talking to herself and would order later, Ruth was back in Liverpool, Mr. Jeffrey Vardan was staying over, and they'd arranged to meet here, any moment now he would walk through the door, any moment now somebody would, maybe even Steven himself.

It was Jeffrey who eventually sat himself down opposite her, picked up the menu, and insisted that he would be paying the bill.

"You're just an old fashioned boy Jeffrey."

"Yes that's me, two and a half thousand years behind the times."

"No, more games Jeffrey, time's running out."

There was a great crackle of frying from the next table. "Good idea Ruth," he leaned forward as he spoke. The muscular torso strained at the short sleeved shirt, muscular but not over developed. "This place I mean, it has about it the smell of my childhood, strange how a smell can evoke so many memories."

"Jeffrey..."

"What have you been up to Ruth? You're looking good."

She told him. He listened carefully, nodded attentively, and ordered their food. When she'd finished talking he sipped his tea, studied the restaurant, smelled the air coming in through the open window, and still had nothing to tell her.

"Jim thinks you're as thick as thieves with Steven."

"Ah Jimmy, he sounds pretty down, I'm sorry to hear that. We're all as thick as thieves, you me, Jim, maybe even Ricardo. All except Denise, and Iain Black, you didn't see her hubby if I heard you rightly?"

"No, he's not worth it."

"Too busy making money, and her spending it I'll bet. There's a man who might betray Steve to Peter."

"I just told you. I think it was Steven himself, to get the whole thing over with."

"Maybe. Wouldn't Peter know his voice?"

"I doubt it."

"Still, not a thing worth risking. At least not if one were laying bait of some kind."

"OK what would you do Jeffrey?"

"I'd spook someone like Iain. Someone who's loyalty is skin deep if that, and then he'd go bleating to Peter, or someone who knows Peter."

"Do you know something?"

"No," he said, picking up the teapot again, with an exaggerated air of innocence.

Ruth shrugged, it was immaterial.

Jeffrey was pouring more tea, holding the pot a little too high so it gurgled into the cups, but didn't quite spill. "The tea ceremony," he winked, the food arrived as he finished. "No alcohol tonight."

"Why? What are you in training for? Fighting Peter Barrow?"

But he only smiled inscrutably, and then began to eat.

"Iain Black," he said again

"What?"

"You didn't notice Ruth how suspect he always was, you didn't notice because he always professed," he pulled a face, "the correct political line. Window dressing, he was suspect from day one. You can guarantee what Iain would do if you asked him for a favour - make an excuse. He'd betray Steve, without pausing for breath."

"What does it matter, it's going over old ground, I've already seen Denise."

"That's what we do though isn't it, us real-philosophers? *Go over and over old ground, just in case something's been missed or not taken into account, and it's waiting around the next corner, ready to pounce, ready to give us a nasty surprise.* Remember that one?" But he continued on, without waiting for an answer. "That Iain Black was never really one of us, he was a materialist sitting in our midst, us idealists, we should never trust materialists, because basically they're selfish."

"What does it matter now?"

Sensei Vardan continued to eat, in his ruminative methodical manner.

"Maybe nothing. But if you went over there tomorrow, early, before they're out of bed. Iain would be there, as well as Denise, and we might find out exactly how Peter Barrow knows what he knows."

"We?"

"We idealists," he nodded, hesitating in the face of another mouthful, dangling dangerously on his chopsticks.

"When did we become we?" Ruth asked.

"When your karma improved," he grinned, and began chewing again. Ruth snorted in reply.

"Why do we want to know how Peter knows what he knows?"

"We don't."

"We don't?" Ruth queried, smiling sweetly through her exasperation.

"No."

"What's this? The Zen pupil must approach the master many times before he gives them a straight answer?"

"Oh yes," his face creased with real laughter, "bravo Ruth you have been swotting up."

"One tries," she waited, and copying Jeffrey carried on eating.

"Anyway no, we don't."

"Give me a break Jeffrey."

"We don't. You want to know." He prodded chopsticks in her general direction.

"Do I?"

"Yes. I'm content to sit here, eat the food, smell the air, shoot the breeze, pass the time, drink the tea and wait."

"For what?"

"For others."

"And I'm not?"

"No." Jeffrey shook his head emphatically.

"Why not?"

"I don't know. Maybe it's because you want to change the world, whereas I only want to change myself."

"And that's all you've got for me?"

"Almost all," he smiled across at her before continuing to eat.

"Jeffrey?"

"Mmm."

"Peter probably won't have a gun, he likes other weapons, blades, weapons that cut. He doesn't usually carry firearms in this country."

He looked up, suddenly serious.

"That's good."

"Up to a point. On the other hand, if you'll forgive the pun, he once cut three fingers off the left hand of an acquaintance of mine using garden secateurs."

"Jesus Christ!" Jeffrey winced, "that's not so good."

"No. There was a lot of blood, it took two men to hold the guy down, and he was tied to a chair as well."

"That's bad. You saw this?"

"No I wasn't there, I was told, and saw the result."

"So this person lived?"

"Oh yes, he knows how to keep them alive. It was a disciplinary measure, a reminder, to the man himself and to all those who would see the state of his hand."

"Jesus, that is bad."

"So when Steven calls you, and says, pop over and kill Peter Barrow for me, I'm assuming you will go?"

No answer, just a kind of guttural sound from low down in his throat as he carried on chewing.

"You're going to have to kill a human being. There'll be no other way do you understand?" There was a moment's silence. "Or will you shrug, sit back, and let fate take its course. Isn't that what you Buddhists do, go with the flow?"

Finally Jeffrey was serious.

"No, that's not how it works actually." He made that strange guttural noise again low down in his throat, "I'm a special kind of Buddhist, I'm a Zen Buddhist, and know even then that I am a special kind of Zen Buddhist. Know without any doubt in your mind, that any resemblance between the Dalai Lama and me is a fantasy.

"Is an illusion born of ignorance, OK?"

"OK."

"Good."

"Good?"

"What do you think is going to happen Ruth? Do you think I am going to stand by and do nothing, while some animal does whatever he wants to the greatest human being I've ever met? Do you think I have trained my whole life for that? Do you think that is what any kind of Buddhism is about?"

Say that again, again, say it again you arrogant beautiful pig headed phenomenon. That's what you are, you're a force of fucking nature backed by a Religious aberration. Jesus Christ you're a Samurai, you really are a fucking Samurai, and your Lord is in danger.

You will not, you cannot betray a TRUST. Oh you cunning bastard, you cunning, cunning bastard, you hid it, you hid it, you were my kind of man all the time.

"I don't know, you tell me."

"It's not going to be like that Ruth. Not even the pacifist branch of this Religion of mine lie down and let you walk all over them, they resist. So try and imagine how those of us on the other wing behave when faced with evil."

"And you'll be OK with the killing that has to be done? As I've tried to tell you this isn't some game."

"If it has to be done. What do you spics say, *que sera sera*, you got that bit right about us Buddhists. But that's an if..."

"If...?"

"Steve is in touch with me Ruth. I'm to wait here in town for further instructions, I'll give you the address of my Hotel before I go."

Finally, hallelujah brothers...

"And what does he have to say for himself?"

"He says you will bring with you people who want to find Peter Barrow. And these people will do whatever has to be done with Peter. I'm just a bit of insurance."

"What people?"

"He said to tell you it was he who stirred up the pursuit."

She felt for a moment as she had with Denise, gloating that Ruth had been used, and then she'd felt it again on that so-called beach, when Jim had said he had been there, often. She felt Steven's presence, could feel his breath on her shoulder, so close, so close to her now, she turned round. For a moment she almost expected to see him, sitting at the table behind her, with that smile, and those eyes.

She turned back and leaned across the table towards him.

"Well maybe I will, but it won't be who he expects. If I bring anyone it will be Russians, sent by long time friends of Peter's who think he's betrayed them, or that he might do so in the future. They aren't exactly my idea of the cavalry coming to the rescue."

"Just the same, they..."

"Oh they might, they might do anything, they live by their own code, of who stuck by who, and who didn't. But Peter is still loyal to those he considers 'deserving' of his twisted loyalty - so they might help him -

not you. Why should they help you and Steven? Tell Mr. Morris that from me, and tell him I gave Gregory Allen the slip long ago, and this is a whole other ball game."

"You can tell him yourself Ruth, he knows this is no game. We're not fools we both know how much we need you. Your phone number please, Steven will be calling you soon." Ruth looked at him, but barely heard what he was saying anymore.

How can you right a wrong when you don't know what right is, don't know what wrong is? Oh I know you, I know what right is, I know what wrong is, I've always known, you are right, you are the only right I know, you are right for me.

She strained her ears again to listen, his voice was calling, calling her, calling Jim, calling Jeff, and finally calling Peter, calling them all.

---oOo---

Strigo was lost in thought.

A professional beating can be a worse liability than death, afterwards there is a feeling of nakedness, a loneliness, an exposure to hurt. There is a timidity, a defencelessness and nervousness in most people, there can be a reduction in confidence even in trained personnel, in all but the very hardiest - and a lack of confidence is always a liability.

He mustn't let either of his younger charges get caught alone with Barrow, and as for the older one, he was an old dog, a tough old dog, but not one who could or would learn any new tricks.

Strigo tore himself away from his thoughts, and looked out on the long grey dusk, it was time to go back to his hotel and have dinner, to stay here would be to cramp the boys' style. It was also time to have Hansi bring Talad up from London, they might be hanging around here a few days and he had a reputation as a slippery customer.

Strigo didn't like to leave things to chance. He sat where he was a moment longer. He had a hunch about Ruth Carrim, a few hunches actually, he'd seen the file, he liked her, she'd had teeth. She was going to lead them where they wanted to go, she was a good omen, he looked around him and then squeezed out of the back of the car and stood up, stretching lazily bathed in neon light, on the edge of Liverpool's tiny Chinatown.

"Keep me in the picture. Call me if she starts to head out of town."

"Yes sir."

Strigo led from the front. Leaving even routine action to others allowed one to become too detached, he would be up late tonight, he liked to be awake when the world was asleep, it gave him a sense of being one step ahead, he was thinking while they were in bed. And if it

106   **BULLY GLARES AT ANTI-BULLY**   Book-1

sometimes proved an illusion that was OK, he wasn't worried, he still enjoyed the feeling, and was well able to separate illusion from reality.

Strigo was a pragmatist, a realist, a professional, an exporter of fear, and a master of the art of *realpolitik.*

Many have died at his hands, some very slowly. He was no longer a full time Colonel in the KGB, nowadays he had outside interests, he was an international businessman*, ein Geschaftsmann,* a security expert, and a womaniser, *mit zwei Frau aus Russland und eins aus Berlin.*

CHAPTER 20
A Telephone Call

*H**e was speaking now, whispering things, whispering things in her ear. Coming closer, closer, he was here.*

What does the realisation of the Bully/Anti-bully principle mean for us in our everyday lives? Next we must tackle the northern shore of that Inland Sea and clear up certain realities that lurk hidden behind some other words.

Social and Personal Wisdom

Limits of Bullying   MORALITY   Metaphysics

Responses to acts of immorality (Revenge)

SKILFULNESS
We will start as most youngsters do, with masturbation.
Obviously there is neither a bully nor a bullied so it cannot be immoral.
What then is it?
Rather than call it natural (which I'm sure it is) and thereby dismiss the attitude of old time religion out of hand, let's look at it for a moment. Someone masturbating cannot possibly be behaving immorally, because no one else is involved.

Is someone snorting cocaine behaving immorally?
Not if they are only hurting themselves alone. But yes if they hurt their friends, or spouse, parents or children. The moment their habit hurts someone else, including someone they steal money from, or should be turning up to work with or for, they are behaving immorally.

It is for the hurt TO OTHERS that we call such habits Morally Wrong, and of course for what the drug pusher does as he manipulates, bullies, gets others hooked, but not for what addicts do solely to themselves.

That is something else - behaving stupidly maybe.

When someone falls victim to a debilitating drug habit or masturbates to the exclusion of an adult sexual relationship, there is surely something unwise in their conduct, yet it cannot be immoral.

The Buddha calls such actions UNSKILFUL.
They exhibit a lack of personal wisdom, and no matter what the underlying psychological reasons these habits can often lead NEXT to immoral behaviour. The drug addict begins to increasingly 'put upon' his friends, spouse and other relations, and hence we counsel against 'being unskilful', we counsel that such things are unwise.

SIN
This is a concept by no means exclusive to Buddhism, the seven deadly sins of Christianity, indeed the whole Christian concept of sin, deals in the same coin - the POTENTIAL to behave immorally. Many of us though, including many Christians, often miss out the word potential in our condemnation.

Anger, lust, avarice, gluttony, sloth, pride, envy, none of these human attitudes are immoral in the way that torture, theft or murder is, but they can, when we are in the grip of them, lead to immorality.
Lord knows there are times when it is right to be angry, as Jesus was in the Temple. Right to be briefly proud, and natural to lust, a time (when totally exhausted) that it is right to rest to the point of slothfulness, even a time when envy can spur us forward into making a greater effort with our own lives.
But when these attitudes take us over, we have been UNSKILFUL, we have taken a step towards an immoral act.
An act that hurts others, an act that BULLIES OTHERS.

'SINNING' BY THOUGHT.
In Matthew 5.27 Jesus says that sinning by thought is as bad as sinning by deed, "I say to you that every one who looks at a woman lustfully has already committed adultery with her in his heart".

Well I say to you, that this sinning by thought being as bad as by deeds, is an enormous mistake, a mistake that lies at the heart of the difference between skilfulness and morality.
It is a council of perfection that we must call time on.
'Sinning' by deed is to hurt someone, bully someone, oppress someone, and is therefore IMMORAL. 'Sinning' by thought is to be UNSKILFUL

and is to demean only oneself, and though unwise, can never be immoral, as long as one never carries out one's fantasies.

Religions offer advice about skilfulness and the best routes to happiness, as do psychologists, psychiatrists, self help books and the like, but when a religious teacher offers it, there is a tendency for it to be seen as Moral advice.
But Skilfulness is NOT Morality, it sits on the other side of a boundary.
It is POTENTIAL immorality.

I prefer the Buddha's terminology on this issue - the concept of sin is a Christian disaster zone.

SERIAL MONOGAMY

Could there be anything immoral in having a long series of consecutive sexual partners, as long as each previous relationship has been properly and sympathetically ended before the next one begins? We may advise someone that it is wiser, or more skilful (by which we mean that it will make them happier), to aim at fewer good quality relationships, rather than rushing on to the next all the while notching up one's score.

However as long as no one has been used, manipulated or otherwise bullied, then although personally we may think a vast succession of sexual partners is overdoing it, and is not a 'healthy sign', is in fact UNSKILFUL, nonetheless there has been no immoral behaviour, since no one has been bullied. And … no bully, no crime.

Steven pushed himself back from the table, and sat staring at the descending drizzle.
That's what Hope's father had been like, unskilful, pushing, pushing, wanting for her, wanting her, wanting her to fulfil his ambitions, not hers, wanting her to play a role for him. People are so blind.
He'd spotted it the first time he'd managed to get close to them, after only half an hour of Hope and Daddy in the same room together, where she was being paraded, in lieu of a loyal little wife. He couldn't believe his eyes, couldn't believe his luck, couldn't believe no one else could see it. Couldn't see the weakness, the chink in the armour.
Couldn't see her unhappiness. Steven looked back at the memory. All he'd had to do was reach out, and wait, and listen, and be there, just be there. They all had eyes, but they hadn't admitted what they saw. See it, know it, admit it, to do otherwise is to be an ostrich, one who sees one thing, but pretends it's another. One who lies first to self, and then to the whole world, rather than admit that some part of the Metaphysical

framework by which they comprehend the world is wrong, wrong because it won't take, it can't take the fact they've just observed - and so denies it.

Steven's thoughts stopped for a moment, he sat there ... blank ... staring away into space.

The idiot, loving a child that way is not so disastrous, and fifteen is hardly a child any more. Although in Hope's case no one seemed to have noticed. If the phenomenon is occurring why deny it?

It is the denial buried so deep it's not even acknowledged that causes the pain and the guilt. All you had to do was admit it to yourself, fool, there are no perfect parents, and once you admit it you can stop it. Stop it before anything happens, stop it from happening out in the real world, and stop it without guilt.

What was there to be guilty about? You were less of an ideal father than you thought, more human, more driven by sex than you thought?

Fool, none of this matters, none of us is perfect all of us are human. When you deny the fact though. When you tuck it away deep in your unconscious, where your actions still betray it, but your mind won't acknowledge it. When you deny the fact because it doesn't accord with the theory you have of yourself, your ego, doesn't agree with your self-image. Now you are in trouble.

Now you are weak.

Now Michael Barrow you are mine.

Now you think you are strong Michael the Egotist, Michael the Self-deluded, but really you are weak. Now if I choose, and I did choose, you are my prey, now you are my plaything, to do with as I will.

What did you think?

Perhaps it would magically go away of its own accord?

But it didn't did it?

How could it?

To change things you have to do something for God's sake.

It haunted you instead. What was so bad about it? I could tell from Hope's whole demeanour that you were innocent of incest, even though I made use of it. I lied. I made use of the doubt by airing the subject, by allowing people to admit to themselves what they'd seen hints of before.

And low and behold - it worked!

And how it worked - with what speed!

Oh you were guilty all right, guilty of plenty, bribery, blackmail, aiding and abetting murder, but we can leave incest off the list.

Although ... given time, who knows... Far from seducing her, as they thought, I may have saved her from seduction, and she knew it. It's why she came with me, why she trusted me, although I admit she didn't know what I had in store for you - daddy dearest.

As for the waiting world?
Well...
You have the crime before you - but was it ever committed?
Do you trust me?
Did I take from that child or did I give to her? Did I use her or did I deliberately let her use me? Did she leave as she came - a lovely young virgin, a wonderful young butterfly about to spread her wings? Maybe her wings even a touch more open for having got to know me?
Or did she leave sullied and dirtied by knowing me?
You know me, what do you think?
Do you trust me?

SOCIAL SKILFULNESS
Which brings us to questions of group or social skilfulness.

Prohibition in the United States was Social Skilfulness, for much bad behaviour, pain, poverty and suffering is caused by our over indulgence in alcohol. The personal over indulgence is UNSKILFUL, the resultant bad behaviour, pain and suffering OF OTHERS is IMMORAL.

It seems highly likely that the first Group Councils do not just deliberate about Moral matters, they will have wrestled also with other decisions concerning the welfare of the tribe.
'The winter is barely over, but the camp is partly flooded, we could strike camp now and head for the highland, the damp has already killed one baby. By leaving now we would arrive early in the upper pasture and get the best pickings, but it will probably be cold there still another month, one or two of the old ones might die on the journey.'

Questions that weigh alternatives: how many might die down here now compared to striking camp early, may be decided on a Utilitarian basis - by weighing THE GREATEST GOOD (greatest Pleasure as opposed to Pain), OF THE GREATEST NUMBER.
Notice that the Moral system called Utilitarianism, though it considers other people, is still nonetheless about Pleasure/Pain, as we shall see in the next example, it is therefore a secondary Moral system.

'Or should we stay and harvest the spring fruits down here this year, as we sometimes have, but if we do who will stay to dry and store them in the heat of summer. How many should be left to do the work, and should we leave warriors to protect them, or do we need them all for the upland hunt? Will it be dangerous to split our forces, there is still bad blood between us and our neighbours across the river?'

Humans face many questions, imponderable and difficult concerning the welfare of the tribe, but though they lie along Morality's boundary, they are not primarily Moral questions.

Some questions are almost scientific matters.

Applying the KNOWLEDGE from previous experience as to whether an early flood means a good year for the spring fruits, or whether a harsh winter and sudden thaw usually precedes good grazing in the mountain pastures.

And these can lead to Moral issues.

Let us suppose that a method of manipulating plants is discovered and this will enhance food production but with environmental risks. Let's say that its proponents state; "it would be immoral not to develop this science, because with it we can feed the hungry of the world".

When faced with these difficult questions, I go back to first principles, I seat myself quietly down and project myself back as best I can, back to those early days, those days when Morality had not long been with us. Back to an idealised time of my imagination, back to the first Group, formalised by the First Resolutions of the first Council, back to when things were a little less confusing.

Suppose one of the group discovered a new source of food, a fungi or a vegetable, or maybe a way of cooking to make something previously inedible, now edible.

DUTY

It is not his or her cleverness or the time spent developing the idea that is the ethical element here, surely it is how willingly he or she shares it with the Group?

For without the Group, without the support of our fellows, each of us is alone, alone against the elements, alone against the big cats that hunt this land, alone without speed, without big teeth, alone without the pack as our support. Surely therefore this clever member of our Group has A DUTY TO SHARE.

The great new invention sounds like a good cause but the Moral element here is about one thing and one thing only, the corollary of not bullying, TRUST, unselfishness, sharing what you have with others, sharing what the extended family Group has with all its members.

The Moral element is sharing all the food in the world now.

Or if you are going to come up with a new way of producing extra food, for the claim that it is a Moral act to be true it has to be given FREE OF CHARGE to the starving.

If the people urging this development do not intend to give anything away free of charge.
If in fact they intend to make farmers and governments pay through their respective noses for it, we can see that **the Moral claim is false**, it is a smoke screen. We see now why it was that that claim always seemed a little off key, always seemed a bit thin. The claim of Morality, which happens to be conveniently allied to profit, always is - a lie, a big fat convenient commercial lie.

On a Utilitarian basis the profits made by a few might be considered to be offset by the extra hungry mouths fed by the new invention. However most of us would hardly want to claim such a computation as the basis of all Morality.
For the hungry, if they really see any extra food as a result of it, then it's better than a kick in the teeth I suppose, but it isn't Morality.

This or that business venture may well do some 'Good' in the world, but it is only Moral if it is done FREE OF CHARGE, which means the cost to the receiver should be sufficient only to cover the production costs of the inventor. Moral acts are those services that are given freely, done free of charge for one Group member by another - not services offered at a price. And especially not at a high price.

Imagine trying to claim that ripping off a poverty stricken farmer, is a moral act. It is the opposite - it is theft.

The phone was ringing...
    She surfaced from a chasm of sleep in which the ringing first formed part of a forgotten memory, then an intrusion as yet unrecognised, and finally wakefulness and the realisation that the telephone was ringing through the top floor flat. She sat up, tipped herself from the couch onto the carpet, and grabbed it, scattering the papers she had been reading everywhere. Goodness knows how long it had been calling her.
    "Hello?"
    "You've been bothering my friends."
    All traces of sleep disappeared. Telephones distort human voices, but after three years she still recognised this one.
    "You have no friends," she replied settling herself down on the floor.
    "How easy it would be if that were true. I could stop this foolishness

tomorrow." The voice continued, warming to its theme. "You see my friends, even after all this time, still expect things of me. I promised that my philosophy ... that ... that I would split the world apart and then re-make it. I made a promise and I'm expected to fulfil it. Oh I know they don't say so openly, these are sophisticated people, they would earnestly deny such immaturity, such foolishness, but I know, I know them, I know that's what they want."

Silence... *no they don't you crazy bastard, there's only you and me even remember.* Silence, the sound of two friends breathing. Breathing and listening to breathing, down a telephone line.

"OK, you have a few friends, I'll grant you that."

"And don't they expect...?"

"OK yes they do, you're right Steven, they do."

"We made a pact? And they're going to keep their side?"

"Yes they are, of course they are."

"So I must keep mine. A deal's a deal?"

"It is."

"How could I do otherwise Ruth?"

"You couldn't."

"You're a friend of mine aren't you?"

"Yes," she said, scarcely breathing.

"Before I met you I thought I'd chosen the life I had because I wanted to be some kind of saint." He hesitated, "isn't that ridiculous?"

"No."

"Now I know it was for one reason only. Not for sainthood at all, but like so many other males, so that I could present my life to a woman I wanted more than life itself, and say here, here is the life I have lived and the things I have done. They have all been done to impress you, to impress you into thinking I'm something worth looking at twice."

"I'm listening. And I'm looking - twice."

"Good, good. I have a message, I have a message and I'm going to make the world listen to it. For you, I'm doing it for you because isn't that what any man who wants to be your man has to do?"

It used to be, but you don't have to do anything else to impress me, you can stop right now.

"Yes it is. That's what I'm wanting, you're right, that's what I always want."

"Good, good I got it right then."

"You did."

"Good, and what is it you want from me now, at this moment?"

"Where are you?" she asked.

"Here with you."

"Peter's coming. I'm wanting to know, want to know where you are."

"Why?"

"So that you aren't hurt."

"Try again."

"Because I love you."

"And I love you."

"When can we meet?"

"Soon."

"Peter will be soon."

"Peter will be dead."

"You're crazy, he's hard to kill you know, you don't..."

"I know I will never fall victim to a mindless thug, an angry thug with only blind vengeance, stupid blind vengeance on his so called mind."

His intensity silenced her as it came crackling down the line, *his utter and wonderful complete madness.*

"Listen,"

"That would be too much ... that the Gods know, would be going too far."

"Talk sense Steven, he's dangerous."

"And what am I, Ruth? Am I not dangerous? You don't have to take my word for it, ask around. Ask anyone, ask, ask ... ask Michael Barrow if I'm dangerous or not. Oh sorry I forgot. He's dead isn't he?"

"Yes - dead and gone."

"Don't you believe in the Gods, don't you believe in me?"

The question lingered on the air - she started to answer, but then just sat there listening to the steady rhythm of his crazy breathing.

"I believe, I believe in you Steven, I ... believe in angels. I believe in anything you want me to believe in angel."

"Good, good. We'll meet at that mausoleum to my grandfather, you remember I took you there once. There are a lot of abandoned quarries round there, you'll know it when you see it, but you'll need some directions. Have you got a pen? I'll tell you where and when to find me."

"Go ahead," Ruth pulled one of the envelopes he'd sent closer to her.

She wrote, blanking out the dreams, the nightmares, the other lovers, all of them, holding onto the phone and that voice, no need to touch, just the voice, no need to touch at all, light, blinding light down a telephone line.

"Hey Ruth?"

"What?"

"Don't forget to bring Jeff with you."

Oh God that laugh, to hear his voice, that felt good, but the laugh... She could see his eyes - the laugh was a message, it was the laugh that had first made her wonder *maybe there is a God, maybe there is a God after all.*

They were back together again, *light, blinding light down a telephone line.*

CHAPTER 21
The Docks

Nowadays mile upon mile of Liverpool's docks stand empty. The eighth wonder of the world, the longest waterfront in history now disowned and deserted, quay upon quay, berth after berth, all without ships or men. The oldest docks are silted up, locks rusted, tidal gates jammed, useless for shipping. Small inner city industries steal quietly in, paying knock down rents for falling down buildings.

The nineteenth century docks to the south have already disappeared, their great empty jaws filled in and paved over, or turned into yachting marinas. Little pleasure boats bob and tinkle where slavers used to tie up and lay over. Some of the warehouses to the north of the city are still in use, and these docks stand waiting, the quays empty, as if ready to accept an influx of ships at any moment.

Although in practise they are no longer working docks, there was one entrance that was always open, day or night for the Irish Ferry.

It was night, always night when they came. Turning left through the gate for Belfast, instead they always headed straight on, following old signs for freight only, on along the wide dark alley set between the warehouses and sheds, on toward the river wall, ignoring all the left turns for the enclosed dock. On across the rumbling cobbles and the last swing bridge, finally turning left beyond the main Dock when all that's left is the wind and the darkness.

Here they switched off their car lights - and walked.

Back beyond the shadows across the other side of the dock, somewhere back there is a brightly lit city of half a million people, but out here none of it reflects off the dark still water. Out here is the wind, the dark, the cold and the memories, of how things used to be.

Bruno had passed a car, and knew he'd be there, waiting.

Why did these bogeymen always insist on meeting somewhere like this? To spook you he supposed, this was the kind of place where, on a cold grey morning, someone spots a body floating or beached on the ebbing tide, a bloated unrecognisable ten day old body. The last few hundred yards were on foot, Hansi had stayed behind indicating where he should go, back across the side of the branch dock and over the footbridge along the sea gates.

The stench overpowered him as he pushed against the huge warehouse door, it slid noisily open and he stepped inside - cattle food, piled as high as the roof beams. Sickly, nauseating mountains of the stuff, imported from God knows where, or exported for all he knew, and wallowing and nesting in it hundred of pigeons. The sound of his entry disturbed them, fluttering and foolish in the night.

Eventually most of them settled back down on their rafters, or into the meal, and Strigo broke the silence as soon as he'd eased the huge door back almost closed.

"I am pleased you have come so quickly."

Very funny, despite himself, Bruno felt nervous. Avoiding being alone in a place like this with one of the Strigos of this world was a thing his whole career had been built on. Bruno tried to look around in the darkness, a thin shaft of pale light came in from outside through the narrow gap at the door. He was slowly getting used to the smell, and to the occasional pigeon still flapping about.

He felt calmer now they were talking.

"We used to use this place for drops at one time." Strigo reached past him and found something there, which he placed in an outer coat pocket, it was heavy but Bruno couldn't see what it was, "you can leave something here a long time before it gets found".

"Isn't this all a bit dramatic? I'm an unknown journalist not a military defector."

Strigo suddenly stepped close in the darkness.

"Indeed. Is that what you are? Have you forgotten who you're talking to? We both know very well what you are. Don't we? How would you like to come home with me tonight, Mr. Journalist?"

Bruno, though loath to, took a step back.

"Try it, Colonel, and see where it gets you," he replied.

"I might just do that. I don't like traitors they make me itchy, I don't like traitors of any kind."

"I can be trusted. As a young man I was loyal to my country. And then when I came to work for you, I was loyal to you. And I've remained so."

"Indeed. Well maybe, maybe... Yes I remember now, yes you were loyal to your country. Right up until the day you turned traitor." Strigo came closer, "well let's get something straight, neither you, nor your psycho comrade, are going to get the chance to betray me and mine. *Verstehen sie?*"

Bruno took another reluctant step back.

"*Ja. Ich verstehe.*" This was foolishness, there was no point at all in antagonising them. "Perhaps we'd better stick to the matter in hand?"

"Very well," Strigo's teeth gleamed briefly as he moved past the door to glance outside.

"What will you do now?" Bruno asked.

"Wait. Ruth Carrim's car is wired up, so we wait and we follow her to Wales."

"You saw Allen, of course."

"I most certainly did, he is out of it now, though the details are not for you."

"Good. And how can I help?" Keep it pleasant, he thought.

"For the moment all we can do is wait. Wait for him to surface. After that we'll have a little talk, he's behaving very carelessly these days. You just tag along with us, and we'll see what happens. I know you want to do your duty, I know you have always done your duty. Here..." he abruptly finished, clapping Bruno on the back and producing first one bottle and then a second, one from each coat pocket. He pulled off the tops with an opener, "Our beer. You can buy it in London these days."

"I know," Bruno took the offered bottle.

"I was in Berlin you know, before Belgrade?"

Bruno halted with the bottle at his lips.

"And?"

"And here's to us, and them that's like us," he raised his bottle.

"Old times," Bruno followed suit.

"Duty."

"Yes, here's to doing ones duty."

"Prost."

The sweet strong beer doused out the taste of the animal feed.

CHAPTER 22
Forgiveness

R uth stared into space. Without looking at what she was doing, she absentmindedly still held the phone in her hand. Then she put it back to her ear, they were together now, it was only space that separated them, the voice, that laugh, those eyes, here in this room.

Listen to me Ruth.

There is only one important thing in all this, only one. I freed that child, that teenager, freed her from parental expectation. When they thought I was seducing a minor, I was crossing the road to help a stranger. When they thought I was preying on the innocent, I was preying on the guilty instead. When they thought I was being a hypocrite, I was practising every single word I'd ever preached.

She was sitting cross legged on the floor, surrounded by what he'd sent her. There was no one on the other end, and yet, she could still hear his voice. She picked up the last of the envelopes in front of her and read, or was it listened now, to what she already knew, to what she had known all along.

The final southern shore…

Social and Personal Wisdom

Limits of Bullying   MORALITY   Metaphysics

Responses to acts of immorality (Revenge or Forgiveness)

FORGIVENESS: at what point between revenge that is so bloody that it is a murderous over-reaction on the one hand, and the never ending turning of the other cheek recommended by Jesus on the other, does the tide stop on Morality's southern shore? Not where do you or I in an angry or a quieter personal moment draw it, although that is a factor when aggregated across us all, but where is it that Morality actually ends, and something else takes over?

Does Morality stretch from the Justice of reciprocity, an eye for an eye, all the way to the unlimited forgiveness JC and the Buddha advocate. Or does it stop being Morality somewhere before this extreme?
After all neither Confucius nor Moses nor Mohammed would agree with this idea of endless forgiveness.

The early humans suffer under Dictatorships of bullying Alpha males, but they crave another kind of social arrangement. Not a bully but a leader who is strong, understanding, sympathetic, firm but FAIR. A few hundred thousand years earlier they'd have had no chance, but now he is something more, he has to be something more for his voice to hold sway, to keep the respect of his clan.

He no longer relies upon bullying, oh sometimes he still lashes out, but now at his discretion he also FORGIVES. In order to BE FAIR, to meet the new demand these creatures place upon each other, he must, forgive sometimes. And he must cajole others into forgiving also. Group unity, forgiving one another, group coherence and harmony are forever on his mind. This is his job, and also in his interests, a strong well ordered group equals survival, of the group, of his wives, his children, himself and his genes.

I'm concentrating on the Alpha Male, and this won't impress you, but there is a reason Ruth. Later on I'll explain, and we will see how this Alpha Male is knocked off his ancient lofty perch. You'll like that, and you'll also like that it is the second greatest turning point in the whole history of Morality amongst us. They crave another social arrangement, but how do they get it? We will see, indulge me please, for in order to bring him down and for us to see how important this is, we must first set him up. The Alpha Male who no longer stands alone is called the 'Big Man', so let's call him that, and leave until later how he actually comes to be demoted to Big Man, and how important an historical 'moment' this is.

The Big Man is more prone to stand back from a carcass, especially in cold hungry times, taking a little less for himself he pushes forward the younger weaker pack members instead. This Big Man is no longer feared, though certainly his strength is respected, this leader is respected but also trusted, trusted more than any other member of the co-operative.

Here is a different kind of leader, no longer the wolf pack's bully of bullies. Much preferred when compared to the old domineering leader. Despite his demotion, in some ways because of it, he now has to judge others, someone has to, even in these early days, someone has to run, the Department of Justice.

He has to watch by secret glances, because he needs to know who the liars, vindictive and work shy are. He finds he partly knows by instinct, can almost tell, as we all do, the way they act, look and speak, but he needs to be surer than that, JUSTICE, FAIRNESS, FORGIVENESS prey upon his mind, as it preys too on the harmony of the group. There is a glue that binds society together, this GLUE is TRUST - and when it is betrayed, the OIL, the soothing balm is JUSTICE.

There are always four choices before the Department of Justice:
1. Bloody retribution (overkill - the barbaric response).
2. An eye for an eye (reciprocity - the Old Testament response).
3. Forgiveness, one, two, three or more times, with a warning, don't do that again (the 'new' response).

This last is LIMITED FORGIVENESS, giving others a chance, part of the 'new' phenomenon appearing in Group life - occasional, sometimes even frequent acts-of-selflessness-towards-other-group-members.

Actually there are only three choices at this time, because the other one came later:
4. UNLIMITED Forgiveness - put forward in different ways by Jesus, Buddha and certain aspects of modern psychology.

The backdrop to these responses is that we all wish to sift out those who on the surface appear trustworthy members of a sharing society, but in reality are grasping selfish individuals out for all they can get. They take advantage by pretending fair dealing, while siphoning off all that they can for themselves - the selfish. And the step beyond the mere selfish, those who are siphoning off all they can for themselves by bullying others - the immoral.

They think it's clever, have you noticed? They think the rest of us are fools, think the rest of us are somehow thick, not to see that this taking what you want, when you want it, is what life's 'really' about. Well that's fine, you carry on - only don't cross my path baby, because I believe that there are plenty of circumstances in which Mohammed is right, and Jesus wrong, Confucius right and the Buddha wrong, there are circumstances in which one can forgive too much.

So my question is - does Morality stop at Limited Forgiveness? Or does it extend to UNLIMITED FORGIVENESS or Unconditional Love as the psychologists call it?
Unconditional Love is vague terminology so let's straighten that out first, because it should really be called Unconditional Trust.
And trust and loyalty are the cornerstones of human Morality, not 'love' a word we use for many other things, too many other things.

TRUST
Here take this food, take this water, come closer to the fire.

Let me help you with that, sit here, there's a storm coming, there's a herd of wild beasts coming, there's a famine coming, sit here by me, let me protect you, for it is my PLEASURE so to do.

No don't thank me, don't thank me, it is MY PLEASURE. It pleases me to help you, and especially to do so without any hope of gain.

My generosity makes me feel GOOD about myself.

It thrills and pleases me more than mere words can say to offer this, my stronger helping hand to you, a weaker member of our pack.

And it thrills me too to see that look of friendship I see shining in your eyes.

Here give me your hand.

I have seen those looks before.

Oh yes, I know how long they last - sometimes forever.

So don't thank me, I thank you. I thank you for giving me this chance to be the best a human can.

For it matters not to me how weak you seem this winter.

One day, years from now, one day when neither of us expect it, you'll guard my back without me ever asking, maybe even without me knowing that you've done it.

And you...

You will feel best about yourself if you guard and save me without my knowing it - because this proves you do it ALTRUISTICALLY, without the hope of gain.

And this is just the way we are, we humans.

And this is what we call TRUST.

It is Unconditional Trust the psychologists really mean, and it is this that allows us to use the mechanism of Unlimited Forgiveness. We humans are actually capable of giving to others WITHOUT ASKING FOR IMMEDIATE or even ANY RETURN at all.

This is just the way we are, SOMETIMES. And those that are not, those that are so selfish as to be disloyal, and so disloyal as to bully other members of the troop, these we do SOMETIMES FORGIVE, but other times we have to take action against - to make them stop.

Ruth, as humans evolve it is Trustworthiness that begins to compete with strength and beauty as the most desirable of human characteristics, in one's friends, one's colleagues, one's children, one's parents and one's mate.
TRUSTWORTHINESS, for amongst all the other qualities we desire in a lover, we desire that our chosen partner should be FAIR. We desire that they should treat us, their closest ally in our joint venture through this life, fairly and thus MORALLY, openly with forgiveness but also to chastise us a little when we behave badly.
In addition to love, we desire above all things, fairness and justice.
We expect the world to BULLY us from time to time. But from our closest ally we expect NEVER TO BE BULLIED, never to be treated IMMORALLY.

It would be unrealistic of me not to admit that many of us are sadly disappointed in this regard.

CHAPTER 23
Waiting

Waiting, waiting and more waiting.

Waiting, waiting and then … action, the waiting is over.

It is 6.15am and there are signs of movement, they wait again, alert and watching their machine, and at 6.22 Strigo receives a call. He stretches across the woman, waking her as he picks up the phone.

"Boss?"

"Yes, it's me."

"We haven't had a visual, but she's moving. Not towards the tunnel though."

"OK. I'll be ready shortly. Tell Hansi to tail her first, make sure it's her and then drop back, you can come round and pick me up. Oh, he's to take Talad, I don't want to ride in the same car as him."

He put the phone down and remained sprawled contemplatively across the body beneath him. Was everything just as it seemed? Was there anything he might have forgotten?

She watched him, he was foreign, his voice gave that away, but there was something else about him too, another factor, something mixed in with his being a foreigner. His body, his face, but most of all something in his mannerisms, and his smell, even his smell seemed - what was the word? Dangerous, that was the word that sprang to mind, scary, cruel, merciless, she shuddered. A puckered scar ran along the outside of his right thigh.

"Is it time to say good-bye already?"

Strigo looked down, bringing her slowly into focus, he was careful, knowing the women most likely to enjoy his generosity. The ones he could bribe, the ones for sale a cynic would have said, but Strigo ate cynics for breakfast, biting their legs off first so they couldn't run away.

"Almost time," he said as he lowered his mouth onto hers.

Outside, a fine sea mist still hung in the air, the sun would soon send it on its way, but for now as he walked it drifted in changing patterns between the trees along the street. Out of habit he scanned the quiet early morning road, eyes left, eyes right, quick casual glance behind. A horn blast sounded up ahead and Strigo waved, then waited for the car to draw up alongside him.

"Did you see her?" He asked, as he settled himself in the front seat.

"Yes," came the answer, "Hansi is following her down, the Karate Kid is with her, she's been to pick him up."

"Yes." Strigo nodded as he checked the log - everything was entered, they knew him too well to forget that, Ruth Carrim and Karate Kid, blue Vauxhall, registration number, time, everything was there.

They took over from Hansi after Conway. Nothing much was happening, Strigo dozed and then began to think of the woman again, love was easy he'd always found, they had to be ugly and bitchy for him not to like them - both, neither was enough on its own.

He'd first seen her the day before yesterday, serving lunch in the Hotel wearing a little black and white uniform. Not so tight that she looked silly as such things sometimes did, just enough so you could see what was moving under there, he'd called her over, once, twice, three, or more times to refill his coffee cup - he'd never drunk so much of the stuff.

"Damn it," Strigo cursed. They must have missed a turning, she was somewhere behind them, high up and to the right. "We've missed her, turn round."

"There's been no road off," replied the driver. Strigo turned towards him in his seat.

"No? Then she's switched to a Chieftain Tank, because she's going up the side of that bloody mountain somehow. Turn this heap round and find that road." The driver cast a glance at the boss. Without another word he did the seemingly impossible, an eight point turn on a narrow rural road between high stone walls, and a moment later they were roaring back the way they had come.

The road was there, on the left, a narrow opening in a dry stone wall looking like the entrance to a farm, tucked in the corner of a bend next to a bridge. It began climbing upwards immediately, twisting back and forth through the undergrowth, then out into woodlands and fields, but still steeply upwards.

It narrowed still further, passing the occasional farm where they left dogs barking noisily in their wake, the main road and valley were becoming visible now, a long way back down below. The boss was getting restless, up ahead the fields were almost at an end, beyond that there was only the wild and boulder strewn mountainside.

"Go carefully, she's stopped," he said. They rattled across a cattle grid and were out on the open mountain. The sky overhead was blue, but the sea was still dark green, far away to their right.

A mile or more up the road a small grey village lay partly in the light, but also partly in the shade of a massive mound of slate. A towering heap piled a hundred feet or more in the air, it brooded over the houses below.

It threatened them, with … with something, maybe retribution, who knows, *yea though I walk in death's dark vale*, ran through Strigo's head.

"Stop. Pull off at the next bend, keep us facing the mountain," he was studying the map and the terrain in turns. Finally he got out.

"The scan's moving again … slowly."

Strigo surveyed the slopes up ahead, raising the binoculars and then lowering them again as he looked around by turns.

"What does the monitor say now?"

"Up the hill, to the left and behind the village. Stopped again now."

Strigo looked above the village.

It seemed as though half the mountain had been eaten away by some hungry beast, by something greedy, insatiable, *by something human*.

Let's admit what we are he thought.

CHAPTER 24
Meeting

Steven lowered the glasses to his lap and stared at the land and then at the sky above, had he ever seen it look quite so blue? Then he smiled, the car was still stopped and the someone who had got out was scanning the slopes with binoculars. He raised his own glasses again, but whoever it was had already got back in the car, seemingly just sitting tight. He looked over into the main pit of the quarry, then he got up and started to scree run down the steeply sloping broken rock and slate waste, at several of the bends in the path loose stones and slate cascaded away from him.

Ruth turned to look as the first clatter of rock announced that he was on his way, and followed his descent by sound alone until finally she saw him. A few minutes later and there he was, after three years of being apart, a figure emerging from a shadow, slithering down further, lost for a moment, then out on the quarry bottom, still running from his rapid descent. His short leather jacket was open, as he picked his way between pools of dark water, still black despite the blue overhead. The binoculars hung on a strap round his neck.

"You brought company Ruth," he shouted as he jumped from the last pile of slate.

She looked at him, getting very close now. This was sealed from the moment he'd walked across that room, was introduced by Jim and had pretended he'd met her before, somewhere else, from some other time. He'd done it to separate her from the party of men she was with, it had worked, and incredibly she'd gone along with it. She had called him darling, a word she never used, until pretty quickly he'd asked her to dance, and they'd been alone together, for the first time ever in their lives, on that long ago first night. It was soon obvious he was no dancer, but that wasn't important.

She'd known the moment she'd seen him, the moment he arrived at her table - this was something different. Known just from the way he'd spoken to her, ignoring almost with disdain the whole party around her, this was something not encountered before. Had noticed his eyes and how they looked at her, his eyes were looking at her the same way now, dark, friendly, alive.

She grinned.

Steven stuck out his hand, she clasped it, touching his skin again after three strange years in limbo.

"Till death do us part," she said.

"Yes, till death do us part," he tightened his grip momentarily.

"It's good to see you - darling," she said very quietly.

"And me you," he replied almost whispering, keeping hold of her hand as he leaned forward to kiss her cheek.

"Have I brought someone with me?"

"Looks like it. Any idea who it might be?"

"Probably ex-KGB, or current FSB after Peter."

"Good, let's head on home and try not to loose them."

"They'll have me bugged, I saw no one on the way down. There was no one close enough to follow by sight."

"Bugged? This gets better and better."

"Maybe. Who were you expecting? Gregory Allen?"

"Maybe, who's he?" he grinned at her.

"I shook him off."

"I wanted you to bring someone, anyone, some enemy of Peter's, to save Jeff from this - so that he would be a last line of defence not a first."

Words, what are words?

They stood there and looked at each other, nothing much seemed to have changed. He looked paler, tired maybe, but the eyes were the same, *eyes that see everything,* she shook her head to clear his voice from inside it. No need for that now, it was here next to her. He let go of her, they were together after three lost years. They should have been married with a squalling brat in tow, or at least one on the way.

"Shall we go now?" She asked, breaking their trance.

"Yes let's go."

He came back to earth and they walked over to Jeffrey, a handshake, a slight bow from Jeff, and Ruth could feel the warmth between them, a glance at each other and now a slight nod from Steven. Then one hand lifted and placed over the clasped hands, and ... released, they turned back towards Ruth.

A Samurai and his Feudal Lord, a *Samurai who would never betray a trust, never, no matter what the price, the higher the price the greater the pleasure in not giving ground, the higher the price the greater the honour. I must, I absolutely must not let you down. I will lay down my life for you Lord, I will do whatever you ask of me.*

Jeff would follow them in Steven's car.

Just as in the Dojo, Ruth had a moment in which to watch him.

He seemed bigger, as he walked ahead of them towards the cars his movements were different, cat like, commanding, a kind of deliberate certainty about every footfall, exactly like that night in Nottingham.

Lord I am with you, fear nothing Lord, I am thy staff and comforter.

Silent, watchful, aware of everything, every sound every change in the light, he seemed to loom over them both, for the moment eclipsing even Steven as a presence, eclipsing even the vast empty chasm of the quarry itself.

Yea, though I walk in death's dark vale, yet will I fear none ill.
For thou art with me, and thy rod and staff me comfort still

"How far is it?" She asked as they drove out of the quarry.

"It's only the other side of those hills," he indicated to their left. On either side now the slate widened out as they left the gloomy chasm, shaking along on the bumpy haul road. "Just follow your nose downhill," he murmured, as they careered past other bumpy tracks off to each side. He leaned close to her, smelling her hair, there were a thousand things to talk about, and all he wanted was to bury his face in her neck, into that 'transport you back in time' aroma, part breath part body smell. How could something be so familiar yet so impossible to conjure up in memory?

"Can't you sit back and relax?" She asked. "I found my way in, I can find my way out."

"Sorry, I was smelling you". He leaned back, "making sure you were real". She smiled, but kept her eyes on the track.

"Turn left when you get back to the cross roads, it'll take us up around the back of the quarry."

After passing through a small village they entered a second, Steven asked her to stop the car on the far side of it and got out his mobile, "last bit of decent signal before home". He got out of the car, and Ruth joined him.

"Hello, it's me, Steven."

Silence. Ruth couldn't hear the reply.

"Yes we're on. Go to him in about three hours from now, take it easy. OK, OK - to suit yourself."

Silence, and a squawk from the phone.

"Take the photograph of us and … be careful."

Another squawk of electrical noise.

"OK I know, call me as soon as it's done." He replaced the phone in his shirt pocket. "Setting the bait," he said, shrugging out of his jacket and throwing it onto the back seat.

"Who was that?" she asked, as they got back in the car.

"A farmer I sometimes work for, Peter's close now, we might as well get it over with."

"I see. You're still on the lump, eh?"

"It's the only way to live darling, why pay taxes? With taxes come records, with records comes retribution, and as you heard I'm still Steven Morris too."

"Isn't that a bit risky?"

"Maybe, but the name means something, and I don't use the surname much. My father died two years ago, so that's both of them gone, and it was a name he liked, his mother's maiden name. He was quite happy when I took it and left home, or maybe it was just the leaving home part he liked. Anyway I couldn't throw away the name you knew me by. For awhile there it was all I had of you."

"Where's Peter now?"

"Pretty close, south of here, less than an hour's drive. There are a few farmers I've worked for down there, I told them to expect him."

"Did you call Peter yourself and tell him where you were?"

"More or less." Steven nodded. "It's time to finish this thing, I can't hide forever, I'm running out of money, my Dad didn't leave me much, I've eked it out doing odd jobs, but I'm no farm labourer. And besides I had to find you. I got Hope to tell her Uncle that I'd waylaid her full of apologies for whatever it is he imagined I'd done."

"You're still in touch with her then?"

"Yes, we're best mates, she forgave me for her father's death."

"And she's still in touch with Peter?"

"Not really. She speaks to him on the phone. They're supposed to get together sometime."

"Sorry about your Dad."

"Thanks - she told Peter that nothing sexual ever happened between us, but it made no difference. Even if true, he told her the family honour was at stake. The way I'd stuck my nose in where I didn't ought to, you know the kind of thing."

"Only too well."

"So next we tried a different tack. I told Hope the words to use to her Uncle, I was praying he would do nothing. But as we will soon see, he came running."

"I see."

She twisted round to look at him. He winked in reply, she'd forgotten about that, the turn of the head, some people are naturals at it and some aren't.

"And Gregory?"

"I don't even know who Gregory is, or who anyone is, but I knew Iain

Black would still be in touch with people, he always knew who was who amongst your lot didn't he?"

"He sure did."

"I figured he was the type who don't change their politics even when they get rich, which I'd admire actually if he wasn't such a self centred bastard. Anyway I called him, just Iain, deliberately not Denise, and gave away no clue to my whereabouts. It was interesting to do it that way, I spooked him by asking for help, a job, a place to live, I told him Peter was after me, he'd somehow found out where I was, I thought he'd go bleating to someone, and that someone might come to you."

"To one of Peter's enemies?"

"That's what I guessed. From the little I knew."

"And if that hadn't worked? And no one had come to see me?"

"I'd have called for your help more directly through Jeff. I needed you on so many levels, but I didn't want to be presumptuous.

·   "What right did I have to assume you still wanted me, I had to see how you responded. If you came looking for me, then maybe … maybe we could pick up were we left off. I hoped the time was right."

Jeffrey, who'd stopped behind them, had walked up and now stuck his head in the open window by Steven. "We've got four hours, maybe five at most."

"So you told him," Ruth nodded at Jeff, "about Iain, that's why he suggested I pay him a visit?"

"Did he? Course I did, inscrutable my arse," Steven grinned.

Jeffrey merely nodded in reply, no smile his face impassive, focused, impenetrable. He'd hardly said a word all morning, the strong silent type that's how she liked him best.

They drove on and turned left, moving up towards more deserted buildings, the landscape here was even more gaunt and barren than before. They were behind the first row of hills, hidden from the worst of the slag heaps, instead to their right, loomed a massive mountain of boulder strewn heath. Below it was a bog, scattered with small lakes or large pools, two narrow roads entered different parts of it to reach two separate houses.

"That's the house to the north," he pointed, "the one with the pile of slate behind it."

They drove on, meandering to the rear of the same waste strewn hills they had previously passed at the front. Slowly they began to move towards the distant house, as they drew closer, closer, the mountain loomed larger, and the track changed from a metalled surface to old broken stone.

Ruth was hanging onto the shaking wheel, hardly able to reply to his comments on the land and the one lonely farm they had passed. She finally pulled off the worn track into the space at the front of the house.

The mountain seemed claustrophobically close now, overwhelming the whole scrubby plateau, overwhelming its two lone houses. Even overwhelming the heap of slate brooding over the house itself, while in the distance to the west she could make out a narrow strip of blue - the sea. The yard was sweltering in the late morning heat, it bounced off the cobbles and the stones of the walls. She looked around again as he moved off to open the door, not too bad in the sun, she thought, but in the rain?

As soon as they got inside Steven began to make sandwiches, he felt more nervous than ever now that the phone call was made.

"Ruth, you and I are going for a walk, let's have a couple of hours to ourselves, this is serious, God knows what's going to happen. There's half decent phone reception round the south of the mountain, we'll get a call there as soon as it's on, Jeff can keep an eye on things here."

"Yes. OK."

Before they left Ruth watched Jeffrey settle himself down, in the only shade of the yard, in case anyone arrived earlier than expected. There was an air about him, it wasn't just those cat like movements, it was difficult to say what it was, not nervousness. Almost the opposite, more like anticipation, he was at peace. *One day you will guard me, one day when you least expect it you will guard me.* He was ... fulfilling his destiny came to mind. *I will do whatever you ask of me. It is my pleasure so to do, it is my calling, my purpose, and my fate.*

As soon as the sandwiches were made Steven led the way out of the house. "Come on we'll walk part way up the mountain first, to a place where we should have a view of our new friends, and make sure we haven't lost them. We'll go up here," he said pointing as he closed the door and looped the glasses across one shoulder. The sky was as blue as a postcard even far out to sea now, and the air felt hot away from the shade of the house.

On their right the land dropped down to the worst of the bog before sweeping briefly back up again. Running along the side of the slope was a deeply rutted path just wide enough to take a tractor, it led them away from the house and towards the mountain. They walked together until it started to head down again where Steven followed a narrower path that began to rise to their left, forcing them to walk in single file.

"Once we get up this stretch," he said, "we'll be onto the lower face, that's when it gets a bit steep." Ruth grimaced behind him. It was steep enough for her now. "We'll be climbing about five hundred feet altogether," he said.

"You said a walk, not a climb."

"This is a walk," he laughed, stopping to let her pass. "Five hundred feet isn't much around here."

They strode on towards the shallow sweeping crest that formed the immediate horizon, beyond lay mountain after mountain. Before long Steven crouched down on a small grassy plateau and scanned the valley with his binoculars. Ruth knelt on one knee beside him, trying to avoid the sheep droppings. "Usually you can only see the first of those," he nodded at the panoramic view over his left shoulder.

"It's a hell of a view Steven."

Ruth could see what must be their route, climbing a little further but then soon levelling out to cross the next sweeping field that covered the hillside. A single stone wall appeared to extend all the way to the cliffs below the summit itself, but they weren't going up there, no need.

"Let's go, we'll stop about half way along that stretch." The path had levelled off and it wasn't so bad, just like walking up a steep city street, except here the air smelled clean, and the silence lay unbroken over everything. They were alone apart from the sheep, who scattered before them whenever their paths happened to cross.

Soon Steven stopped again, crawled forward, then threw himself flat down and slithered out to some gorse at the edge of a ridge. Using the glasses, he quietly studied the land spread out far below.

"There they are," he said, as Ruth wriggled up beside him. "Here, take the glasses, look down there in the old quarry buildings." Ruth struggled with the focus but then it came suddenly clear. The grey stone and slate roof seemed so close she could touch them, a jumble of sheds set around a turning area which was actually part of the track they had taken from the village to Steven's, she remembered passing through them. At first she could see no one, then as she was about to give up she spotted him, a solitary figure sitting in the shade. A figure dressed in city clothes, *a figure left over from the Cold War.*

"I thought they'd wait there - they could stop him there, he has only one reason to be coming past them."

"They could, let's hope they do," though she doubted it.

"They can watch the road from the village without being seen and still command the way into here." They slid back down again below the ridge. "Let's eat, it's a long time since you've had one of these," and he broke the giant sandwich in half.

"Now this I haven't missed." Ruth took half of "the Steven Morris sandwich."

"Not for the faint hearted."

She smiled at him.

"I was watching you make them. Very quick - you've not lost your touch."

"Down there", he waved his half of the sandwich downhill, "amongst those old quarry buildings, sitting waiting. Sitting down there are the last ~~warriors of a~~ great battle in its death throes on this earth, the battle between Capitalism and Marxism. You are one of those warriors too."

"Was."

"Purely by coincidence you understand, this was also at the same time a battle between Democracy and Dictatorship." He raised his sandwich then it drifted down again. "Remember?" He asked raising his sandwich again and this time taking a bite.

"Don't you start, Jim kept asking that. I'm here because I remember, I remember everything. Especially an insult."

"Sorry, of course you do, for which I'm thankful."

Ruth looked around with the glasses, she could see it all stretched out before her in the late morning sun.

"You can carry on."

"Thanks, Capitalism versus Marxism us intellectuals saw as a battle between two rival economic theories, actually it's a dispute between two different Metaphysical hypotheses." He bit into his sandwich again and watched her as he chewed.

"Theories that became Metaphysical-Religious Beliefs for some?"

"Yes exactly," he nodded still chewing.

"Keep going, I like it".

"But Democracy versus Dictatorship, that was always and has always been a Moral battle. It can never be anything else, and now we see why, the Dictator is the Alpha Male writ large, and Democracy the attempt to control him."

"Bully/Anti-bully?"

"Oh how nice to hear you say it like that," he was still chewing, "I don't get much feedback."

She put the binoculars down.

"I remember everything, except one thing."

"What's that?"

"I didn't remember you were an intellectual."

He looked at her.

"I'm an intellectual without an intellect, you understand?"

She reached out to touch his face. Then bit into the thickest quickest sandwich ever made. They watched each other, he gave one of those long lost winks, that turn of the head.

They soon finished, neither of them had much appetite, which was just as well, because he hadn't brought much to eat.

"Ruth when one human tortures another unto death, philosophically speaking, can you not with justice dispense upon them a response that is one category down from their original offence? In the case of those who torture-unto-death other humans, this would be a quick and pain free death."

"Now I don't have to remember – you're here."

"Would this not be a form of forgiveness? Comparative mercy, and a response that Mohammed, and Moses, and Confucius would all sign up to? Because it is a category of response below, something less than the original act?"

"Well..."

"In return for a terrible crime, they receive a speedy pain free delivery from this world."

She put down what was left of the sandwich.

"If Jeffrey kills Peter today it will be self-defence."

"And self-defence is something separate to my four categories?"

"Yes."

"Akin to an eye for an eye - but forced upon us by our attacker?"

"Yes."

"And that forcing a hurried decision onto us by the attacker? I think that makes it part of Limited Forgiveness?"

"You mean an eye for an eye is forced on us, otherwise we may have reacted with what you are calling limited forgiveness?"

"Yes."

"By which I understand you to mean that one forgives a number of times in an effort to improve the other party's behaviour, which is more forgiving than responding instantly with an eye for an eye."

"Yes, that's it, payback after a warning and a let off, is better than lashing out instantly, but we have no choice with self defence and so should be given the benefit of the doubt that we are forgiving."

"So Steven, you have four categories of moral response: overkill, an eye for an eye, limited and then unlimited forgiveness."

"Those are the four 'cold responses', with self-defence as something in between Reciprocity and Limited Forgiveness."

"And what are you going to do with your categories, my intellectual-without-an-intellect?"

"I'm going to propose to you that Limited Forgiveness is the system that built the Moral world, and thus that it is JUSTICE. And that the Unlimited Forgiveness that Jesus and the Buddha ask us to try to live by takes us somewhere else."

"Yes, I read that. Or did you say it on the phone?"

"Soon we will be getting together with Peter Barrow. Soon I will be bringing him to his final judgement. Obviously in the situation before us, I and those who help me can claim self-defence, and rightly so.

"A man is coming here to kill me, and no doubt given the chance, from what I know of him, he'll torture me before he does so. I want to kill him yes, I want him dead and this thing over with yes, but I don't want this to be 'only' self-defence, I want this to be something else. I want this to be JUSTICE, I want this to be Justice for us all, for the sake of the whole of humanity."

"And because you lured him here?"

"Yes I did."

"Well then," said I, "as heir to this argument, tell me, what is this saying of Simonides that you think tells us the truth about doing right?"

"That it is right to give every man his due," he replied...

She waited for him to carry on.

"To kill quickly one who has tortured-unto-death many times is merciful compared to what he has done to others. It is can therefore be considered an act of clemency, in terms of Limited Forgiveness. Surely Peter should really be tortured just a little before he is killed?"

"You don't mean that."

"You won't let me torture him? You want to be merciful?"

"Yes I do, and I know you do too."

"We'll forgive him then and kill him quickly. Something he himself has rarely granted to others? What do you think?"

"Well if you..."

"And remember before you answer me that we have agreed that there is such an entity as "a fate worse than death", and that this entity is continuous and unremitting torture-unto-death. And we have also agreed that we are sometimes called upon to kill as a favour, as an act of mercy, and thus to kill is not always an act of bullying."

"I can't get a word in, will you..."

"Therefore I put it to you that there are certain cases, where to kill quickly is an act of mercy, when enacted upon those cruel, cruel few who torture-unto-death their fellow humans."

"Shut up and let me speak. Don't piss about, this is not one of your theoretical pie-in-the-sky examples for discussion. You know I'm not the forgiving type. Your timing was perfect as always, you appeared just as I'd seen enough, too much of him up close."

"Stop there, that's answer enough for now, we need to get up to the lake, the sun is moving and we mustn't be late."

They asked Caesar, that great dealer in death; what is the sweetest kind of death? To which the great man replied, 'the kind that comes without warning'.

God grant me, and you also, the unexpected death. Amen.

CHAPTER 25
The Lake

Around one last corner and there it was, the face of the mountain towered above them, craggy, sheer, impossible to climb, it took her breathe away, while before them lay the lake, cold, calm and glacial, filled by 10,000 years of water. The arms of the great rock face swung out towards them, enclosing the sides of the lake, stretching along half the length of each side, a three-sided hollow, the rock scraped clean and removed by the ice. It had taken two bites on its greedy way downwards, leaving a thin strip of land in the middle, almost dividing the lake into two.

He turned to Ruth before they descended into the bowl and pointed out the waves breaking white, far away to the west at the end of the Straits, with Anglesey beyond. On the highest of the hills opposite them to the south there was a huge telecommunications mast, no wonder the signal was good up here.

"Just wait a moment now and the sun will come around that promontory, look there at the far end. Soon the whole surface of the lake will light up. Come on, it doesn't last long."

They walked down the grassy slope towards the edge of the water, and here he stopped at a small stone hut he used as a store and occasional camp. At the door he took hold of the padlock and then stopped and turned to her again.

"What do you think?"

"Be at peace Steven, it's Justice. Even though you lured him here, it's Justice."

"He enjoys inflicting pain on others of his species then?"

"Yes, I've seen him up close, he is a torturer, and he has tortured many. He has tortured some unto death, I wouldn't like to say how many, he was a soldier on my side, but by accident of birth, in fact he could have been on any side. He enjoys inflicting pain. He has done it many times, more times than I want to talk about, he has been a soldier in a cruel civil war. You know yourself that he has cleansed ethnically, and he has tortured them first, he has tortured-to-extinction, and so your criteria hold good. He is the worst kind of bully and only death will stop him. I certainly couldn't."

"And most men tremble at your touch."

"No, that's just you darling."

"It's Justice then?"

"It is, be at peace."

"Good."

"Provided we can bring it off..."

"Good, and then if it is Justice, I want to know why it is?"

"Why? Why? Don't you ever stop? Because it is right to give every man his due, that's why, that's what Justice is. You've said it."

"But would others agree, would we get a consensus from society's members? Our own society? And would other human societies agree?"

"Some will some won't, who cares. Who cares what Society thinks, they don't know what we know of this world. They don't know our world at all."

"Oh yes, our? Our! I'm admitted then?"

She laughed, and touched his face again. They still hadn't kissed, best to save it for later, no point in tasting something you can't have.

"You were admitted the first time I set eyes on you. No, no the first time you spoke to me, no let's be precise, a few moments after that first conversation. But now you have been hunted, an outcast in fear of your life, so now yes, you are fully admitted."

"I need do nothing further to impress you?"

"Nothing at all. Just kill him, let's get it over with and let Justice be done. Or will I do it for you? I'm armed, there's a hand gun in the car."

"Thanks but no, I don't want you to do it. I'm armed in my own way too."

"I mean it. You need do nothing further to gain entry to my world."

"No, it must be me, or Jeff, or those thugs down there. Not you Ruth, that wouldn't be right. That's not the way, that's not in my plan. It will be OK, you'll see. Come on, I have one last thing to do."

He turned back to the padlock, unlocked it and hurriedly opened the door. The roof was removed by releasing a chain from inside so that he could sometimes sleep up here under the summer stars. Once this was off Ruth could see a round shape covered by a tarpaulin on top of an inflatable mattress, he pulled this off to reveal a drum.

Steven carefully manoeuvred the drum out through the doorway and hoisted it over his shoulder by a strap, there wasn't far to walk, they soon reached the narrow spit of land dividing the lake. Once there he took it off and settled it carefully into place, with its lower rim jammed securely between two rocks. In this position it was flat and at about waist height, he then turned to the wall of rock stretching up to the summit above, and hit the drum.

As he hit it, instantly it seemed to her the first beat hit the rock face and came back across the water. Followed by another and another, again and again. Until, with the echo around them on every side, he shouted.

"Never was I not ... I am the beginning the middle and the end of all that lives."

...the beginning the middle and the end, came echoing back to them. Then with the drum struck now in a steady beat, even louder at the top of his voice.

OF WORDS I AM OM THE WORD OF ETERNITY.

OF PRAYERS I AM THE PRAYER OF SILENCE; AND OF THINGS THAT MOVE NOT I AM THE HIMALAYAS...

Back, back it came, every word of it.

AMONG MEN I AM KING OF MEN...

AND OF ALL THINGS THAT MEASURE I AM TIME. I AM TIME NEVER ENDING TIME."

He moved to one side to free himself of all encumbrances. "Come over here Ruth and hit this drum for me, I can't do everything for God's sake."

I AM THE CREATOR WHO SEES ALL, I AM DEATH WHICH CARRIES OFF ALL THINGS, AND I AM THE SOURCE OF ALL THINGS TO COME.

...I am death which carries off all things, and I am the source of all things to come.

I am the goodness of those who are good.

I am the knowledge of those who know.

And know Arjuna that I am the seed of all things that are; and that no being that moves or moves not can ever be without me...

CAN EVER BE WITHOUT ME.

It seemed now to come back louder than the original.

But of what help is it to thee to know of this diversity?

What I have spoken here to thee shows only a small fraction of my infinity.

Know that with one single fraction of my Being I pervade and support the Universe, and know that I AM.

KNOW THAT I AM, KNOW THAT I AM, KNOW THAT I AM...

Steven took a breather, but the echoes kept on - the mountain was talking to them.

"Evil is coming here to see me, Satan is coming to have a little chat, the angel of death is coming, for a *tête-à-tête*. What shall I do? When this angel of - this angel of pain-inflicted-for-pleasure-on-others arrives for his little visit? When the angel of slow-agonising-torture pops round for a few quiet words?"

He looked now to the summit, towering above the rock face and spread both arms wide. *What shall I do? Lord help me, WHAT SHALL I DO? And where shall I find the strength to do it?*

Lord help me. LORD HELP ME, SHOW ME, LORD SHOW ME HOW I SHOULD ACT, LORD SHOW ME WHAT I SHOULD DO AND GIVE ME THE STRENGTH TO DO IT.

Who was asking and who was answering, as Ruth hit the drum, the questions and answers tumbled over each other.

He who works for me, who loves me, whose End Supreme I am, free from attachment to all things, and with love for all creation ... HE IN TRUTH COMES UNTO ME.

Those who set their hearts on me and ever in love worship me, and who have UNSHAKEABLE FAITH these I hold - these I hold DEAR TO ME.

But they for whom I am the END SUPREME, who surrender all their works to me, and who with pure love meditate on me and adore me these I very soon deliver from the ocean of death and life in death BECAUSE THEY HAVE REACHED IN TRUTH MY VERY SELF.

... THEY HAVE REACHED IN TRUTH MY VERY SELF.

...REACHED IN TRUTH MY VERY SELF.

...IN TRUTH MY VERY SELF.

Ruth could hear…

These know that I am the knower in all the fields of my creation. And that I AM ... ABSENCE OF THE THOUGHT OF I, ABSENCE OF THE THOUGHT OF I, I AM ABSENCE OF THE THOUGHT OF I...

Ruth realised that Steven's phone was ringing.

Peter Barrow is coming, driving fast down sunlit roads, Peter Barrow is coming, the rain now gone, Peter Barrow's coming, coming here now.

Time was up.

He stopped to answer it, and gradually the echoes quieted down.

"OK I'm ready, as ready as I'll ever be," he said and closed it. In the background the voices seemed to be still there, somehow gathered around them. Ringing in her head.

He put the phone in his pocket, "we're on."

"There's no other way to stop him," she said again "kill him and be done".

"You know him well."

"I know him as no other."

"Let's go."

A lot quicker than going up they were soon well on their way down.

Along sunlit roads, beneath a bright cloudless sky, winding at speed between high stone walls, Peter Barrow is coming, face set, greying hair cut en brosse, the Bully is here, driving fast down a quiet country lane.

No trace left of the rain now, the blight of his search is gone, he pulls the sun visor down and opens the window as he accelerates, faster and faster, the torturer is coming, coming here now.

Coming for revenge, coming here now.

When they got back Jeff was sitting much as they'd left him, wearing the same loose white T-shirt but now with tracksuit trousers, *you can't lift your leg high enough to crush a man's windpipe with the ball of your foot if your clothes are too restrictive.* He'd moved his position and the remains of his sandwich lay forgotten on a plate beside him. Steven tidied it up as he went inside, while Jeff, now pacing slowly backwards and forwards in the increasing shade continued to concentrate on every single step. Practising what the Buddhists call walking meditation, he stayed outside to greet their 'guest'.

Ruth joined Steven inside.

"OK Ruth when Peter comes in, sit there where I sat to make the sandwiches, stay seated in his way so he can't sit down, I'll be here. Peter will have to sit by the door, then you move around past me to the window, so that Jeff gets your empty seat. He needs space. I moved the table there yesterday, Peter will be stuck by the door, across the other end of the table opposite me, with you in by the window and Jeff with his back to the room."

"He gave you an answer then, up there?" Ruth asked.

"Who?"

"Your God."

"*Mi Dios?*"

"*Si, muy bueno, bravo!*" Ruth clapped her hands.

"You're laughing at me, you dirty atheist."

"No, no I'm not, I just wondered, if maybe?"

"No, no answer, just courage … and inspiration. You could face Peter Barrow alone, with no help from anyone. I know you could, but I can't. I've called him to me, I've said come hither, come hither to me my dear, come hither to me, but now I'm scared."

"I'll say it again, I have a weapon. Neither you nor Jeffrey has killed before. Let me do it."

"No I'm OK, I have courage for the moment, and as it happens all my work has been for this moment. The moment when, for the first time in my life I would ask a woman to marry me."

"Bloody hell."

"I know, like I said on the phone. All so that while I was rendering to her the account of my life, I would never, not once, have to look down at my feet and mumble with shame."

"You've nothing to be ashamed of, nothing, but this is a hell of a time for a proposal."

"I know, I pray it's not my last chance. Ruth will you marry me?"

She leaned forward, put her hand on his face and finally kissed him.

CHAPTER 26
Peter Barrow

*T*he face behind the wheel was impassive, perhaps a faint sneer, perhaps just concentration, the face of experience, a big middle aged man. The heavy lorry battered aside the rear corner of a vehicle that was in its path, caught another instead and continued to lunge forward, to engulf the red sports car, it drove the car back, back into the side wall of the underpass, crushing it mercilessly, crushing it to pulp between the front of the truck and the unyielding concrete beyond. The face of experience smiled, a job well done, Marc Walosh wouldn't be troubling Michael Barrow again, if you want something doing, do it yourself.

"You did it yourself Peter, I'll bet you did it yourself. After all this was your brother that Marc Walosh was a threat to, the start of his new career, his much hyped arrival on the political scene, oh he was going to take the world by storm your brother wasn't he? What things he was going to do, your brother, when he made his big move, his big move from representative of his people to representative of the people. What cages he was going to rattle, what worlds he was going to change." There was no reply. Steven had started off in conciliatory mode, but it had got him nowhere, it was pretty clear Peter hadn't come to talk. "You remember Marc's death, you remember the 'accident' Ruth?"

"Of course, who could forget it."

"And?"

"And that's why ... now it makes sense ... of course." She turned her head towards Peter. "You murdering bastard, Marc was a good man."

"There were too many of you in London weren't there?" Steven continued. "You were tripping over comrades, ex-comrades and those in between, who had been comrades once and had then changed sides, even some who had changed sides back again. You were forced to reconcile yourselves to an influx of people from your mother's home, people who you thought you'd never see again in your lives, people with memories, people who were a damn nuisance. Marc Walosh was one like that, he was a nuisance on two counts wasn't he? He knew things about 'the brothers Grimm' - and had the evidence to prove them - that would be best left unsaid if Michael was to have the public life he craved. And at the same time he was a rival candidate for the same constituency as Michael."

"You didn't know Marc Walosh, he wouldn't spend five minutes on a cream puff like you," Peter growled.

"Oh really? Marc liked to talk about the first time he met you Peter, though he didn't like talking so much about some of the later stuff...
There were several of us in a burned out building, on the edge of a burned out town, four nervous men, all with their hands in their pockets. In Peter's case it was his inside breast pocket, he must have been wearing a shoulder holster, and it was he who, smiling his wolf smile asked all present the pertinent question.

"Doesn't anyone have any fingers?" and took his hand empty from his pocket, there was a collective relaxation and other empty hands began to appear. He brought us together, all sharing the same tension and its release, three warring factions sharing a moment of peace, a brief moment of mutual trust. Soldiers, knowing what each of the others had been through. Not Moslems and Christians, Orthodox, Catholics, or Communists, not soldiers from Bosnia, Serbia or Croatia, just soldiers, just human beings weary from months of fighting' satisfied? Enough?"

Peter just stared at him, with no acknowledgement of anything.

"I knew Marc Walosh well enough for him to trust me in a crisis, trust me because I was outside his usual circle trust me because his judgement told him he could."

More silence.

"That meeting was a good moment for Marc, he spoke of it often, a moment of comradeship, he said. This was a long time before the predicament that later brought him to me, feeling the humiliation of imminent betrayal - no matter how loyal he'd been, watching things he could barely stomach ... watching himself, watching... All that counted for nothing now, because he was in Michael's way. Isn't that right Mr. Barrow?"

"Yes," Ruth replied, "that's pretty much it Steven."

"Marc Walosh is dead, he's dead for sure, it's over, his life is over."

Steven looked slowly around the table.

"Or so his enemy thinks, but this one put a deposit in a bank that never closes, the safest bank of all, the bank of banks, better than any safety deposit box, better than any paid assassin, the bank that made the loan that built the Moral world. A living human being, but not just any human being, a friend, a comrade, a brother who can be TRUSTED."

Peter continued to stare straight at Steven, almost through him.

"Yes he's dead, crushed against a wall by one of his own tribe. But I hear his voice still clear today. Remember this one, remember what he was? Remember how you murdered a man full of ideals Peter Barrow? And admit how well I knew him."

'When you are born, you cry and the world rejoices, try to live so that when you die the world cries and you rejoice'.

His favourite proverb ... and ... his favoured funeral...

"They will carry my coffin out into the sunlight, there will be people lining the roads, they have come because they know, that to be there is to have a part of me live inside them forever. For all you need do is keep talking to someone, and that someone never dies.

"They will carry me towards the hearse and then carry me through the town where I was born, and the banner on the top of the hearse will proudly proclaim my epitaph. HERE LIES ONE WHO HACKED AT THE ROOTS OF EVIL, WHILE THOUSANDS HACKED AT IT'S BRANCHES."

"This was the man you murdered, these were his dreams, dreams of a life spent giving to others, not a life of betrayal and ethnic cleansing, not crushed against a wall."

"Psychopath," Ruth muttered half to herself.

"This is who you murdered. Now tell me again murderer, tell me again that I did not know Marc Walosh."

"You knew him Steven." Ruth replied to and on behalf of her former lover.

"Marc knew his life was in danger, so he passed a copy of all he had on you Peter over to me. Didn't you realise he was bound to give it to someone for safe keeping? Or maybe you thought whoever it was would be too scared to publish?"

Still no reply was forthcoming. Peter had not said much even at first, the sight of witnesses Ruth supposed, but he was saying even less now, a dangerous time.

"That Marc Walosh was a nuisance wasn't he, edging ahead of your brother in the stakes to get the seat Michael wanted, but knowing too much about your history to be brushed aside in the usual manner. You didn't have much choice did you, the way you creatures think it was a bargain, two for the price of one? Wasn't it?"

Silence.

"Wasn't it? Of course it was."

More silence

And then...

"You're a dead man talking. That's what you are sonny."

"Oh it talks! It talks, the murderer speaks."

Peter just nodded, again and again, almost to himself.

"There were a few things in Marc's collection of photos and papers, and a lot more still that he could only tell me about, with no proof to back it up, but as you found out I had enough to release to the waiting world. Released into all those places where Michael's reputation was riding high, and oh my how it crashed, whew, how it all came tumbling down. Isn't that why you're really here? Because of guilt? It was you and your advice as to how to 'handle things' that ruined your brother's dream."

"A dead man talking."

"I used the things he did, and the things he didn't do as well. Maybe that's why you're here, maybe it's the irony, the 'Injustice' of what I did. Because what I did 'wasn't fair'? Maybe that's what diddled with your brother's head so much, maybe that's why he hit the ground so hard? I confess I enjoyed that, it gave me PLEASURE murderer, bringing him down with accusations of incest, that was rather a nice touch. It's what we humans call Justice, and if you end up paying for a crime you didn't commit and getting away with ones you did, well, we humans call that Rough Justice - but we still call it Justice."

Peter carried on with his strange nodding gesture.

"It was so quick though wasn't it? That was the impressive thing, total meltdown, amazing how quickly fair weather friends can disappear. Well it certainly made an impression on Michael, eh Peter? Amazed him into an early grave."

Peter stopped nodding and settled back in his chair, suddenly at ease. Relaxed, assured, the angel of death, the angel of endless-torture, was ready to do business as soon as the moment was right.

"Keep going, just keep going. Talk away, talk away, if that's how you want to spend the short time that remains, before you die."

A cloud, from somewhere a shadow hit the yard, and came in through the window, casting its cool gloomy seal on Peter's words.

"You don't scare me, you nothing. You're just another big mouth, same as your brother, you're all mouth and you're going the same way."

"Talk away, I'll just sit here and listen. And watch you, such things interest me."

Steven revved himself up again.

"I suppose those who knew you would believe anything of you two, after all you believed it yourselves. All I did was give Hope friendship and support, then off she went with a friend of mine, for more friendship and support."

"Whatever you say liar, whatever you say. And whatever you want to say, how people spend their last moments is always fascinating."

"All the rest you did for yourselves, with your 'worldliness', with your 'knowledge' of human motives. Your brother's ruin was all for nothing, his daughter was still a virgin, he was ruined by the rottenness inside himself and you couldn't fix it, I like that. You could fix anything, well you didn't fix me uncle, you didn't fix me."

"There's time for that yet."

"No, you're out of time, you never saw me coming and you'll never see me leave."

"There's time."

"You idiot, do you still not understand? It was I who called you here. Called you here to die. It was me, I deliberately told Hope what to say about where I lived '*in a house with a view of the sea, but only just*'.

"Sound familiar? You fool. I dropped down from the league above, I came down to give you a beating, because I'm more devious and more ruthless..." He stopped and leaned across the table, "sucker, there are no rules in the big league."

Peter continued to stare at him. And then...

"Keep talking dead man, time's nearly up."

"OK - I will. The whole thing was a put up job, she wanted to escape from Daddy, and from you, to get away anywhere. But she couldn't say it, oh she tried, but no one was listening. This way the act was done with the appearance of it being out of her control, and she was able to get on with her life, she's at drama school now - right? Right?"

Peter started the nodding again. It was as if it started whenever he was losing the initiative.

"I helped her to escape, and we're still good friends. How would I know these things if we weren't good friends? I've spent three years in hiding partly on her behalf, of course we're good friends, she thinks I'm bloody marvellous - I gave her her life, *I gave her her life*. And you, you have come here for vengeance, have come here to avenge something that never actually happened."

They stared at each other across the length of the table, just ten feet and the whole of human history between them.

Bully glares at Anti-bully, and Anti-bully glares back.

"I'm bored with this," and with that Peter Barrow the angel of death-preceded-by-endless-torture began to get to his feet.

"Kill him, kill him for me Jeff, finish it before he kills me. There's no other way, no other way out of it now."

Vardan kicked the chair to one side and stepped quickly back, into the space of the whole room behind him. Karateka like space. Sharp and alert his gaze never left Peter Barrow, who stood now in the more confined area by the front door. Vardan's stance was similar to a boxer's, except his hands were lower, and there was a greater springiness in the use of the legs. He moved into space, surveying the room, dominating it as he had the Dojo that night an age ago.

The big man with the grey hair stared across the table, its length still stood between him and Steven. He turned to the Samurai, there was no way through, except through Jeffrey.

"Stand aside. Do you want to die for that? A seducer of children? Die for a mass of weakness and lies, talk and excuses? I was killing men when you were barely off the breast. Have you ever killed a man?" His hate seemed re-concentrated now onto Jeffrey Vardan, "have you?" He leered at Jeffrey, "have you?"

No reply, just watchfulness, no fear just a terrible certainty, something hard, like stone in the eyes.

"You're a civilised chap who plays rough games. You're no killer. Do you know what I am?" Peter calmly fished out a cut throat razor. "I'll cut your throat first, then hers because she's betrayed me, and after that I'll cut him - slowly, very slowly." Still no one spoke. The Karateka remained silent, alert and watchful. The ploy was an old one, and was about to backfire.

"No. But I know you're go..." He was still in mid sentence as he launched his attack. It's least expected during speech. Unconsciously one listens for the end of the sentence. The inflection must be kept perfect, sudden in-drawn breath is a fatal give away. Everything kept deadpan, that is the secret. The feet are always in motion, shuffling, feigning and balancing. Keeping the opponent disconcerted, making it difficult to take aim.

The weight is rarely evenly distributed, concentrating first on the front and then on the rear leg. With the body weight to the rear it leaves the front leg free for those short snap kicks which, by keeping the opponent at bay, reduce the need for the boxer's high guard. While the weight at the front frees the rear leg to cover maximum distance and deliver thrust kicks followed by full body weight. Kicks that land with a force which will break a bone or burst a vital organ.

The kick came in mid-sentence, but it was like no kick you've ever seen. The weight had shifted backwards and so the front leg came up off the floor in a feint. Thus the jump was launched off the back leg while he still spoke, and with the whole of his body moving forward. His rear leg flashed through the air at speed as the front foot stamped back down on the floor again to solidly root the attack. It was then Ruth registered he was not wearing shoes, as the hardened ball of his foot thrust out to a focus at throat height.

Peter Barrow knew many ways to cause pain to others. Most of them he'd learned by experience and experiment, but none of us ever win the fight with time, and Peter was now forty six. Whereas Jeffrey Vardan was thirty five years old. Peter still worked out once a week in a local gym. Sensei Jeffrey Vardan trained at least three hours a day, about three hundred days a year.

Barrow was surprised and off balance, but he moved fast enough to save his throat and take the kick on the shoulder. Vardan's thigh was still swinging upwards through and beyond the horizontal as the whiplash action of the lower leg, hinged at the knee, drove the kick home. For that split second of contact the whole of the leg focused stiff and straight like an iron bar.

The recoil of explosive shock was transmitted down the rigid second leg and into the floor, no energy was dissipated the way it is with a swinging roundhouse punch or kick. Not a single kilowatt of power was lost, all of it went into Peter. His collar bone splintered beneath it, or rather above it, for the focus was aimed above and beyond the shoulder. That's where this kick thought it was going and if it had to smash through a collar bone en route, too bad.

He was spun around and crashed against the door to the stairs as two hundred pounds of raw energy exploded on the top of his chest. He tried to move back as he slashed out once, slicing through trouser leg and skin, but he was stopped by the wall behind him. There was no escape, he was a standing sitting target, with no room to get out of range, even for a second. As he stumbled upright the attacking foot was stamping down to become the springboard of the next attack.

Peter was still moving quickly, unaware of his pain. He parried the second kick, delivered by what a moment ago had been Vardan's back foot, it was aimed low down at his groin. He stopped it with forearms crossed, blocking the shin between both his wrists. It was the only way, anything less would have been swept aside by the force of the onslaught. The shock jarred them both, but Jeffrey Vardan had all the momentum, and Peter Barrow lost his grip on the razor.

They were close now and the head was the obvious target for the oncoming Karateka. One never gives second chances and though the punch is not a killing blow it can open the way. Straight right, straight left, straight right a flurry too fast for the eye, always two knuckles explode on the target, no nice big cushion called a boxing glove, then step back to deliver the finish. The first had split a cheekbone, blood oozed from the nose flattened by the third. There was a pause, the head hung forward a little, slightly dazed and over to one side, a defenceless target. *Finish it*, this time there was nothing to stop the savage front snap kick.

The human thigh is far more powerful that anything the arm can muster, and with regular practise is no less accurate. The ball of Jeffrey's foot with the toes turned back, struck home beneath the chin. The head whipped backwards as the foot continued to a focus aimed somewhere above the skull. A scream filled the room, but not from Peter, it was every last gasp of air leaving Jeffrey's lungs, it was total rigid focus, total release of body energy. It was death calling Peter home, finally calling home one of its earthly emissaries.

The neck cracked and the body became a corpse. It hit the table and rolled from there to the floor, half propped up by his discarded chair and the wall by the door. Jeffrey crouched instinctively over the body, left knee bent and right fist pulled back on right hip. Nothing more was needed. Peter Barrow was as dead as Marc Walosh, as dead as if he'd been crushed against an underpass. *Give every man his due...*

It had taken three punches, three kicks and ten seconds, it had been quick, the way it should be for us all, and brutal the way it had to be for Peter. At least he was still going forward, or thought he was, right up to the end. If only the rest of us could say the same, with the assurance, bordering on arrogance that Peter had shown for the whole of his final scene.

Jeffrey stepped back.

A hissing sigh escaped from him, a release of tension. Ruth moved forward to check Peter's pulse, there was none. The way he had fallen it was pale confirmation of the obvious. Steven dragged the body clear of the table, and quickly searched through the dead creature's pockets, a coil of wire, a knuckle duster, a heavy cosh, no gun, torturers weapons.

Ruth noticed blood from the smashed face now seeping into the carpet. They covered the body with a rug from the back of the room, Jeffrey slumped into one of the armchairs, staring blankly at the empty fireplace and nursing his leg.

"That's the end of the past," Steven looked over at Sensei Vardan, "thank you Mr. Vardan, for my life," and then looked at Ruth in turn. Jeffrey said nothing, Ruth nodded. Then she bent picked up her shoulder bag and quickly slipped something into it that was lying there on the floor, almost under it.

Something that looked like a 9mm Automatic, what did you think, that I'd stand by and let an animal loose on the greatest human being I've ever met. She looked over at Jeffrey.

"Come on Steven, let's get him fixed up, make him some tea while I bind his leg, he's as white as a sheet. Then I'll go down the road and tell them what's happened, let's get that over with before we call the police."

"OK, I'll stay here but be careful, I'll be with you as you drive down that bumpy track. Thank you, for everything, for what I just saw."

Strigo was first through the door with Hansi behind him. He took in the heap on the floor and also that there were no weapons in evidence, in one quick sweep of the room. Steven was seated again at his place at the table. Jeffrey was still sitting in front of the empty fireplace, sipping tea with his leg bandaged up and staring at nothing. Without turning his back on either of them Strigo reached the body and threw back the rug. His hand felt the neck as he knelt on one knee, then he replaced the rug back as it had been before.

"He was out to kill me, as you know. Mr Vardan here is a friend for my protection, he had no choice but to kill him. Nothing else would stop him."

Strigo looked around the room again, more slowly this time.

"You were expecting him." It was a statement not a question.

"Yes. It's been a long business."

"You have good friends. Self defence can be a tricky plea."

"We have a witness."

"Indeed," Strigo murmured almost to himself, as his eyes rested on Ruth. He looked around again more carefully, his eyes halting briefly everywhere, slowly taking in all there was to take in.

He smiled, "Good-bye then, and good luck".

At the door, he turned with Hansi at his shoulder.

"You've done well, but don't get too excited, he was marked for an early death, you mavericks are always marked for early deaths."

"We may surprise you," Ruth replied.

"Indeed," he smiled at her again, the smile of a wolf.

Hansi smiled his agreement. Understanding nothing he followed his master out.

CHAPTER 27
Aftermath

It was the early hours of morning before the police left, taking Jeff with them for now. It was over, they were alone, the clouds were drifting in. The wind was rising as, sheltered by the house, they watched the cars disappear down the road, leaving emptiness, the vast silent sweep of the edge of the mountains, the lowland, the sea, the future, the past. He turned to her.

"It was self-defence in the end wasn't it?"

"It was self-defence yes Steven, but, though I would not have advised sparing him, there was a moment when we could have done."

"Before that final kick you mean?"

"That's right, he was no threat then."

"And Jeff looked at me?"

"He did."

"And I?"

"Gave that … little nod."

"Imperceptible nod. You don't miss much do you Ruth Carrim?"

"I don't miss anything. Otherwise I'd be long gone from this world by now."

"Of course, stupid of me to say that."

"It's OK, I'll let you off."

"I judged him then, I did have the courage of my convictions. I see so many things now that I didn't see when I started all this."

"Tell me."

"Marc came to me saying his life might be in danger. We knew each other slightly and then got to know each other well in a short space of time, I was honoured, for some reason he trusted me, thought I was someone he could turn to, knew that I wouldn't just laugh it off, or blab about it to others. Knew that I would act if need be, that I could be relied upon to do something, would keep the agreement sealed by a handshake, and if it all came to nothing and he realised successfully the public life he hoped for, his failure of nerve would go with me to the grave. I made a promise Ruth."

"Yes I see that."

"Marc was... You know what Mahatma means right?"

"Great Soul."

"That was Marc."

"I can see that too. I liked him Steven, what little I saw of him"

"I always wanted to be a Great Soul. Just imagine if after your death that's what they called you, like Gandhi - Great Soul. Just imagine that, that would be ... everything. I'd give my right arm to be called Great Soul, no my left, let's not get too carried away, I'm right handed."

"You are a Great Soul."

"No, not like Marc, I don't have his courage, or yours. But I had to do something, I took Marc's evidence to the police but it wasn't enough. They weren't interested, but I got people's attention, incest always does that - and then told them instead. I took Hope away from them. I wrote my letters." he stopped and grimaced at her.

"Go on."

"I did what I could with the weapons I had, I didn't know what would happen, but I had to respond. I didn't expect Michael to implode like that. I thought he'd just hit the bottle, that was his bag."

"That's true, he was a drinker."

"It was you who told me that."

"I know Steven, I know."

"Of course you do, sorry."

"Don't worry about it. You didn't pull your punches, you didn't leave anything to chance."

"No."

"That makes you my kind of man."

"Thanks, that's good to know. I was just giving it my best shot, responding the only way I knew how. I didn't expect Peter Barrow to be so persistent either, but it was fine when he did. It meant I'd made a sacrifice for my beliefs, I'd done something, something..."

"I understand all that, I understand everything. Look at me, look at me. You did well."

"Even when I found myself in love with you, I had to go on..."

"I understand that too, I do, I really do."

"And then later I had to get you back. I'd fallen in love. Even more incredibly, now I could finally approach you. Not as an equal, I've not suffered like you, or fought evil like you have. What I've done here is peanuts compared to the sacrifices, the pain, the living in constant fear, that you, your father and mother, and all the people who fight repressive regimes make, with..."

"Hush Steven, I understand."

"With only courage and honesty against razor wire, electrodes, terror and lies. But at least now I could look you in the eye, at least now I could approach you. At least now I'd done something... "

"Stop, stop a moment. I understand. I understand everything. OK?"

"OK."

"But next time we have a row or something comes between us, and you want to kiss and make up, just apologise, OK?"

He stopped

"Just say sorry?"

"Yes."

"And you'll forgive me?"

"That's it. I'll forgive you."

He looked at her, close enough to be visible in the darkness and the first spot of rain.

"Sorry for all the subterfuge, but I couldn't blithely sail back into your life and assume we could take up where we left off. Sorry for all the pain I caused you last time. Sorry for now, sorry for then. My apologies for all of it, I should have handled it better than I did, I should have included you more in all I was doing. I should have trusted you from the start I should have... "

"I forgive you."

"You forgive me?"

"Yes. *De nada. Estoy bien.* You are forgiven."

It began, very gently, to rain.

"Thank you."

"I'll marry you Steven, anytime, any place you say."

"Once I'd met you there was only one reason I did all this." *Hush up, wouldn't even the threat of marriage shut him up.* "I knew what I had to do, I knew that Ruth Carrim wouldn't be impressed by anything less. I saw there was only one way to deserve your love, I had to show you that I would sacrifice everything for a TRUST.

"Because that kind of sacrifice that kind of selfless act is the principle that lies behind all human Morality, the sacrifice of everything..."

"Hush, I'm impressed, very impressed, now be quiet."

"One last, just one last thing please... I wanted to be able to look you in the eye. I wanted to deserve the love and RESPECT of the greatest human being I'd ever met. I won't let you down, I promise you, I'll do whatever has to be done to deserve you, to deserve your TRUST."

"I know you will Steven, you couldn't betray a trust, you're just not made that way." *You're just not made that way, not made that way, not made that way...*

Book 2

What it is, What it is not and … Where it has been

"What is all this nonsense, Socrates? Why do you go on in this childish way being so polite about each other's opinions? If you really want to learn what justice is, stop asking questions and then playing to the gallery by refuting anyone who answers you. You know that it's easier to ask questions than to answer them. Give us an answer yourself, and tell us what you think justice is."

Thrasymachus interrupts Socrates in Book One of THE REPUBLIC

Introduction

I had two good friends when I was in my teens, one was called Tom Foster and the other Steven Morris, well we'll call him that. We used to talk as teenagers do, about the world and everything that's in it, only the talks we had were a bit different to the talk of our other friends. And those others tended to drift away when our talk turned, as it often did, to philosophy, turned to which of us believed in God or ghosts, or Buddhism, or Communism or a whole host of allied subjects.

They say that to be a philosopher you must have a philosophical problem to solve, well we had one. Nothing special, it was the one we all have. Except, as you'll see, we never found anything else in life more important, or more fun, than solving it. Yes we were odd I suppose, but you'll have heard the saying "there's a pleasure sure in being mad, that only madmen know".

Physicists such as Stephen Hawking talk about 'a theory of everything'. By which they mean a theory encompassing all the physical phenomena of the Universe, but all you and I are interested in, because we rub up against it and the problems caused by it every day and sometimes even every hour of our lives, is a theory of Right and Wrong. We need this, somehow from somewhere, just to function alongside others of our type, that is the only 'everything' that applies to our daily lives. And it was this need, the solution to that peculiar human conundrum that drew Steven, Tom and myself together.

The need to know the truth about Morality.

Well the years passed and as often happens we kept in only tenuous touch with each other. I always seemed to have an address for Tom, but he gravitated down to London whereas I stayed "up north", and we didn't see anything of Steven, he just disappeared, to Australia rumour had it.

Then Tom fell ill, a brain tumour, and out of the blue, as if he'd been keeping an eye on us for all that time, Steven got in touch again. A bit spooky really, if you're that way inclined, because I remember as an eighteen year old that my grandmother, who took a fancy to Steven, once said of him, "he'll be able to tell when you're dying, if you're a friend of his he'll know". She was Irish, and dying at the time herself, slowly and gently in the back bedroom of our big old end terraced house, so that's what I put it down to, but I always remembered it.

Anyway he reappeared again in our lives, and he brought with him a disjointed story, his story, the story of his life since last we were together, and more importantly the philosophy he'd worked out while living it. A mess of notes describing a moral system, a manuscript of a kind, repetitive and disjointed, but there it was, he'd never given up on our youthful quest. All Tom and I had to do was listen, and read, and then produce a book from his piles of notes. A big task, and his only condition for giving his copyright away? He insisted we weren't to die while we were doing it, no matter how long it took.

It turns out he'd actually spent far more time in North Wales than New South Wales, he was over in Australia for awhile though, lying low and visiting relatives. Book 1 is the story of what happened after we lost sight of him, and we'll get back to the rest of it again in Book 3, the next part of his intellectual adventure though is what follows here.

*We'll take up his philosophical quest where we left off, he was asking Ruth "is it Justice". I should note here, in case you aren't aware of it as I wasn't, that when you translate the Greek of **The Republic** into English there are two meanings to its central question, either 'what is justice' or 'what is doing right', so we are still considering both.*

He was asking her, since torture-unto-death is worse than murder, whether or not it can ever be considered Justice to grant such a torturer-unto-death the moral response of a quick death-without-torture. And she agreed it was, but she was too involved to be neutral, so the question now is what should us neutrals answer?

To consider his question more properly, surprise, surprise, we must first go into his proposition more deeply, the proposition that the whole of what we humans call Morality consists of Bully glaring at Anti-bully, and Anti-bully glaring back.

We must take another turn around the shores of that Inland Sea, and pick up on some things there that didn't quite fit into Book 1.

We'll start at a place Steven didn't start at funnily enough, with a definition of Bullying. Tom and I have teased it out from amongst his notes along with a review of the three great traditional philosophical explanations of Morality, so that we can see which one of them Steven's proposition resembles most closely. As he once said to Tom and myself - try this for a theory of the whole of Human Morality; beat this if you can.

1. What it is

1.1 The Concept of Bullying

In a way definitions of bullying are barely needed. We all know what bullying is, we all know because this knowledge is built into us at birth. However for the pedantic, the Codified Morality, the lawyers who administer it, for the letter of the law, and for completeness:

- Bullying is the UNPROVOKED hurting, intimidation or persecution of a weaker or smaller person, or section of society.

- Bullying can be the torture and murder of thousands or millions by a brutal Dictator, or it can be minor manipulative behaviour between close members of some tight knit community.

- Bullying is always selfish and is the opposite of Sainthood, which is always selfless. *Obviously by Saints we don't mean the very many persons the Catholic Church chooses to grant sainthood to. We use the word Saint here in its generic form, to mean those of any religion or none, who devote themselves and their lives TO OTHERS - Gandhi was not a Catholic but he was a Saint.*

- Any RESPONSE to an act of AGGRESSION, an act of Bullying, is itself Bullying only if it is disproportionate to the provoking act, hence the need for RESTRAINT and the concept of 'reasonable force'. *'He deserved it', encapsulates the above - 'it' is the retribution visited upon someone. Appropriate and not disproportionate, it may even be some natural disaster unconnected with any attempt at human justice. Whatever 'it' is, it has happened to a bully, and those who feel they have been bullied find it to be fair, to be Justice.*

- Human Rights - all human rights are actually part of one single right only, the-Right-not-to-be-bullied.

THE CONCEPT of RIGHTS
Let's digress for a moment onto the subject of animals, because it highlights the fact that all rights are actually sub-rights of one over arching all-consuming Right. We earn these rights by doing our Duty towards others, by not bullying them, by playing fair with them, by

pulling our weight as opposed to being a slacker and a drain on those around us.

We have already established that animals can have only a proto-right to a life free of human inflicted torture, because they are not able to perform the Duties expected of members of the human team.

To kill an animal quickly and then eat it, having not tortured it in any way first, is not immoral by the tenets of B/A-b Morality.
Hunting, Fishing and Shooting for sport rather than for food are all bound to be Bullying, because as soon as you use the word sport you introduce the concept of 'enjoyment'. These sports are immoral because Bullies take PLEASURE in the exercise of UNOPPOSED POWER.

Sport is without doubt about Pleasure – and is 'for the fun of it'.
Nothing Wrong with Pleasure nothing Wrong with fun, but in this context it is what makes the act into a bullying act, and it is therefore immoral - I can't see how it can be anything else.

One hears protests by those who like to hunt with hounds, that banning hunting infringes their Human Rights. But ALL RIGHTS are granted as a protection from bullying - one cannot have a RIGHT to BULLY (even animals).
That would be a complete negation of the concept of Rights.

There can be no 'Right to Bully', the phrase is a contradiction in terms. It is THE BULLY who destroys the Rights of others by Bullying in the first place.
All human rights are granted in the face of Bullying.

All Human Rights are Anti-bully.
Human Rights can never be pro-bully, as those who enjoy this activity in effect claim.
Rights are granted in opposition to bullying.
Rights are not granted to Bullies.
Bullies take what they want by force, in the teeth, in the face of the Rights of the rest of us. (Or the proto-right in this particular example.)
All Rights are Anti-bully, Anti-bully, Anti-bully.

Hunting for sport (rather than for food) is bullying and therefore immoral, but I'm picking on hunting here only to illustrate that ALL RIGHTS ARE ANTI-BULLY and that this is in fact the one and only Right there is. Such sports as hunting are not as bad as the torture-unto-death for every single second of their lives of battery hens and pigs reared and confined in factory conditions, because hunting grants, in theory, a reasonably quick death to a wild and free animal, rather than a whole life of stunted, tortured deformity.

Despite the many human rights we talk about, there is only one Right, the Right-not-to-be-bullied by others.

So we can see that in that great document pushed through the United Nations in 1948 in response to the Second World War, and in particular to the Holocaust, every single clause is Anti-bully, Anti-bully, Anti-bully.

The Universal Declaration of Human Rights

1. All human beings are born free and equal in dignity and rights.
2. Everyone is entitled to all the rights and freedoms set forth in this Declaration, without distinction of any kind.
3. Everyone has the right to life, liberty and security of person.
4. No one shall be held in SLAVERY or SERVITUDE.
5. No one shall be subjected to TORTURE or to cruel, inhuman or degrading treatment or punishment.
6. Everyone has the right to recognition everywhere as a person before the law.
7. All are equal before the law and are entitled without any discrimination to equal protection of the law.
8. Everyone has the right to an effective remedy by the competent national tribunals for acts violating the fundamental rights granted him by the constitution or by law.
9. No one shall be subjected to arbitrary arrest, detention or exile.
10. Everyone is entitled in full equality to a fair and public hearing by an independent and impartial tribunal.
11. Everyone charged with a penal offence has the right to be presumed innocent until proved guilty.
12. No one shall be subjected to arbitrary interference with his privacy, family, home or correspondence, nor to attacks upon his honour and reputation.
13. Everyone has the right to freedom of movement.
14. Everyone has the right to seek and to enjoy in other countries asylum from persecution.
15. Everyone has the right to a nationality.
16. Men and women … have the right to marry and to found a family.
17. Everyone has the right to own property.

18. Everyone has the right to FREEDOM of THOUGHT, CONSCIENCE and RELIGION.
19. Everyone has the right to freedom of opinion and expression.
20. Everyone has the right to the freedom of peaceful assembly and association.
21. Everyone has the right to take part in the government of his country.
22. Everyone, as a member of society, has the right to social security and is entitled to realisation ... of ... economic, social and cultural rights.
23. Everyone has the right to work ... everyone has the right to form and join trade unions.
24. Everyone has the right to rest and leisure.
25. Everyone has the right to a standard of living adequate for ... health and well being.
26. Everyone has the right to education.

If certain members of society don't receive an education or similar rights, they remain permanently in the underclass, the lowest caste of society, all condemned to clean up after the rest of us. To forever undertake the dirtiest, foulest, meanest and most back breaking jobs, when they have work at all that is. How subtle are the ways of the bullies, especially in large modern mega-societies, and notice too how easily we slip into being bullies.

'Human Rights' are intended to stand against the various social, political, economic and educational ways we can be victimised and bullied into Society's underclass. These are all manifestations of the one single all encompassing Right, the Right behind all rights, the Right not to be Bullied by others in the human team.

27. Everyone has the right freely to participate in the cultural life of the community.
28. Everyone is entitled to a social and international order in which the rights and freedoms set forth in this Declaration can be fully realised.
29. Everyone has **DUTIES** to the community.

In return for the human rights of Free Speech, Thought, Conscience and Religion, the RIGHT not to be Tortured, and not to be kept in Slavery or Servitude, in summary the **Right-not-to-be-bullied**, one has DUTIES to the Group one lives amongst.

30. Nothing in this Declaration may be interpreted as implying ... any right to engage in any activity ... aimed at the destruction of any of the rights and freedoms set forth.

- DUTY: the concept of Duty is part of the definition of Bullying and we must look at this more closely now because there is an omission here that occurs when we use the term 'Human Rights' too loosely.

We must clarify also because Duty has become an unfashionable word.

Which of us three teenage boys was most hung up about duty I wonder. Hung up is incorrect, duty was important, and its call impinged upon us in all our families. By what I've always assumed was a coincidence, we were all sons of older than average parents, Steven's in particular, his father was 53 the day before he was born. So our parents were all of the generation who fought in the Second World War, Steven's father was actually too old to fight, he was born in 1899, what a fascinating year I always thought to be born in.

Steven and his father didn't get on, and because Steven wasn't around I suppose you could say he died in my arms, certainly in my presence. He was on his own by then and I felt I owed him something, for past times sake. That is the kind of duty I mean, the kind you owe to kith and kin, and to close friends, I took it on for Steven's sake. I wonder now as I write this, was it just a coincidence, that we each had old fashioned parents and that sense of duty.

Me the most I reckon and Steven the least I think now, he was the most on fire of the three of us, the most relaxed around adults, and girls of course, though it wasn't hard to beat me at that. Duty, I've been beset by duty all my life, I'm re-writing this because of duty, not because I expect anyone to ever read it.

I've not been the kind of doormat that some erstwhile 'saints' can be, nuns and the like who devote their lives to the sick, I've never lived my life at the behest of others. I don't devote myself to others, but I'm aware of certain responsibilities to others, my relations, colleagues, certain old people I've known since youth around this parochial backwater. Like Steven's father, an interesting old boy actually, an Architect, and almost a monk at one time, a white father whatever the hell that is, they were Catholics I was C of E - and about a quarter of me still is incidentally.

No I don't mean the old 'sacrifice your life for your Country' stuff, or for your ungrateful children either, or ungrateful husband, or by becoming a drudge to others for the sake of the Lord. No, not that old style let's take advantage of the poor schmucks who gave themselves up to become doormats with no life of their own, left wondering why they were so put upon and unhappy. That's not the duty that bound the first human groups together.

Without a sense of Duty there is no trust - without trust there is no Moral Order, it's that important. The real meaning of Duty is doing the opposite of bullying.

No wait - Duty is a bigger thing than that.

What about an example?

When someone persists in taking a petty case all the way to the Court of Human Rights, by appealing and appealing, and won't take no for an answer, essentially to get their own way, why does it seem so revolting? And why does it undermine our faith in the Court and its processes?

Is it not because our rights come to us from the Group, only as a result of the active part played by each of us, the contribution each of us makes to the Group? Our Group grants us our rights as long as we fulfil our duties. *Or more accurately the Group assumes we will do our duty until events prove otherwise, our single duty-to-be-fair-to-others (to not bully them and to sometimes put ourselves out to help them).* Whereas the Court of Human Rights automatically assumes we have done our duty, because it has no way of checking to ascertain otherwise.

Thus we are revolted by the sight of someone taking their pathetic little case as far as they are allowed, when we suspect that they are not the kind of person we would be able to rely on to do their duty. And it is this 'as far as they are allowed' that can undermine the court, that can render us contemptuous of its well intentioned but never ending granting-of-rights to those who are failing to do their Duty.

The Right-not-to-be-bullied doesn't grow on trees. No, to speak in correct philosophical terms, everyone doesn't have rights, there are no Rights floating round in the air. They must be EARNED by pulling your weight, by BEING FAIR to others.

Many claimants of their precious rights ignore this and we despise such claimants when we think they are all about claiming all they can, and not one jot about fulfilling their obligations, their one obligation.

We grant the same rights to all to be fair, we have to in practise, it's an administrative necessity because of the size of our massive societies. But we mustn't forget that we do this on the assumption that they have done, are doing and will continue to do THEIR DUTY, even though in massive modern societies we can't check up on them the way we could in the small groups of our beginnings.

And then, when we see this type of person whingeing about their Rights, that is when some of us lose respect for a Court that not only can't check up on duties performed, but is also too stupid to realise it should.

This is a problem of large societies, but what it illustrates is that the Right not-to-be-bullied is earned by us fulfilling our DUTY to take an active part in Group life, to sometimes-put-ourselves-out for others.

- ENDLESS TORTURE is the ultimate act of Bullying.
  We've discussed this, everything Steven says is really about this.

So just a word or two about the torture, pain and suffering brought about by a slow lingering illness. Strictly speaking of course a disease cannot 'bully' - because other species, in this case micro-organisms, legitimately attack us in evolutionary terms.

All the same the image of the illness as a bully serves to clarify matters. We are coming under attack as if from a wild animal, and we grapple with it using sufficient force to defend ourselves, including fighting it unto-death.

If we think it is reasonable to apply the principle thou-shalt-not-bully to animals, and thereby seek to minimise their suffering at our hands, then the concept can cross the species barrier to micro-organisms as well. In the one case we seek to reduce the suffering of other species and thereby be FAIR in the use of our POWER over them, in the other we seek to outwit the little bastards that carry disease.

Normally the doctor is engaged upon a fight with this almost invisible bully. But, when the bully has so much of the upper hand that the conclusion is inevitable, and the waiting for the inevitable is so long drawn out and painful, then death is a release from pain, and an end to suffering.

A few doctors don't seem to understand this, and become fixated instead on 'keeping people alive as long as possible by whatever means possible' as being their duty.

Ironically when they do this they can sometimes be assisting in torturing-someone-unto-death, the ultimate act of immorality.

1.2 Designer Babies and Abortion

L *ast but not least, Steven's final criteria, in his search along the western shore for the limits of the definition of the concept, 'TO BULLY'.*

- If endless-torture is the extreme limit of the Bully/Anti-bully principle, and thus is the full stop that defines it, where is its gentle hidden start point?

One place is the smallest unprovoked impoliteness or snubbing of another, because such petty minded spiteful insults are the subtlest form of bullying. Sometimes of course we use such slights as a means of letting others know we are displeased with them, and if they have ill-used us or hurt us in some way, they are then a justified RESPONSE to bullying. But when unprovoked, being impolite is bullying, and is often the start of more and worse to follow.

DESIGNER BABIES, SAVIOUR SIBLINGS AND MANIPULATION
Next, take the case of a couple with a very sick child. They want to have another child, so as to produce a baby who would be a supply of the necessary bone marrow to help save the first sick child. But they can only do so by in vitro fertilisation, so as to precisely manipulate the fertilised egg.
The manipulation of one by another is the gentlest of immoralities, but it is still immorality, manipulating someone TO SUIT OUR OWN ENDS is immoral, even when nothing is stolen, nor any blood spilt.

To produce a child for the purpose of saving another, understandable as the parents' feelings are, is nonetheless a manipulation of the proposed baby, and those who manipulate others are bullies.

When we say, 'I feel used' it is said as if this feeling is a 'bad' thing, as if those who use others are doing a bad (Wrong) thing, and this is because to use others is an act at the gentler end of the Bullying Scale. And even though in this case the users are caring parents who will no doubt love and support their new child for the whole of their lives, the Moral issue is the MANIPULATION of ANOTHER.

Maybe the new baby will grow up to love big brother, or maybe these siblings won't get on at all, but either way, this new person, now a human with the same Moral Rights as every other member of the group has been

USED. And not just used, has been born, no matter how much also loved, so as to specifically be USED, indeed for the primary purpose of being USED, albeit to save another.

And that is why this act of DESIGNER BIRTH is immoral.

Of course it is all done in a good cause, the cause of saving a life - the parents do not want to loose their first born, they are being caring about an ill child. Hence the difficulty faced by our medical ethics committees, but the act itself is unethical, because it is Bullying, it is the most gentle, the most subtle, the least brutal bullying any of us are ever likely to encounter, but it is a subtle form of bullying nonetheless.

It may be that the Manipulated, when he or she grows up, will be the big hearted type who will think the whole business of their birth is wonderful and marvellous. Or, if they are a different type, peevish and small-minded, they may be permanently resentful of the circumstances of their birth.

Either way, the Act itself is (oh so gently) immoral.

We are speculating how The Manipulated will feel when he or she has grown up, but we can never know this beforehand.

We know what a good cause this is, and in practice surely most people so manipulated will find it pretty easy to forgive, after all it is forgive or do not exist.

It is immoral - but only just.

It is technically immoral.

They do something technically Wrong to get a good result, to save a life. They make a decision based on Utilitarianism, *which we'll come to again shortly.*

Thus we bring a little clarity I hope, but no simple complete solution I'm afraid, chiefly because the problem is so refined and so far removed from the wild grassy plain of Morality's true origin, where *Homo sapiens* first left the trees.

DESIGNER BABIES

What if the test tube design of the baby is done so as to produce a child that is athletic, good looking and intelligent, an all round supreme human being. The parents in this case want a child that will be a joy to itself AND THEMSELVES.

The Moral question is: has this new human being, born fresh upon this earth, already at the moment of its birth been in some way bullied - by

manipulation?
Because if it has, then this is an immoral act.
Has this child been bullied?
It seems to me that it has.

Decisions were taken to give it certain characteristics, traits perhaps that the parents admire or wish they had. While other traits that they do not like in themselves are weeded out. They mean well, but who is to say that they have made good decisions, who's to say that this creature they create will be as happy as they think?

Notice that there is no need to invoke the ridiculous phrase playing-God, a morally meaningless term based upon emotive claptrap. We can now be far more precise than this; it is sufficient to say morally wrong because it 'bullies a living human by genetic manipulation prior to the birth of that human'.

DESIGNER BABIES AND SAVIOUR SIBLINGS

Any procedure to produce a fertilised egg with certain characteristics and without others is a manipulation.

The resulting human being has been manipulated, and its manipulators are there, readily to hand to be held accountable - two in particular, the chief manipulators, its loving parents.

But when the one manipulated is a Saviour Sibling, the natural argument is that he/she has been instrumental in saving a human life, their sibling. Therefore the Utilitarian question is, does the saving of a very ill child's life outweigh the immoral manipulation?

On the other hand if the attested purpose of the manipulated birth is to "balance my family" (one male child and one female child - God help us what a concept), I suspect most of us neutrals would vote that this is NOT a sufficient reason to weigh against an immoral act.

Thus the concept Designer Baby is immoral. But even though Saviour Siblings are strictly speaking also immoral, it would seem that for most of us the rightness of the cause (itself a Moral issue - to help a dying child) outweighs the Moral Wrong. This is therefore one of those times when we must call upon the Utilitarian principle: the greatest good of the greatest number, in our endeavour to do the right thing.

Behold the subtle opposite to cruel merciless torture. *I can't think of any bullying more gentle than manipulation before you are even born. There is an irony here in the comparison with abortion.*

ABORTION

If Morality is wholly and solely Bully/Anti-bully we must decide the abortion issue based upon whether or not a foetus can be bullied. It seems to me that abortion is not immoral, because there is never an independent human life that can be bullied. You cannot bully a sperm, or an egg, or the embryo that forms in the weeks before it is ever capable of independent human life, for up to that time there is only a woman with tissue for a potential human life inside her.

There is at this time only one person, one member of this social group of humans, one human being with the full Moral Right of membership of the group, not two. And that tissue inside her, that part of her body has no rights at all separate from hers.

How could it? It has no existence. The only Rights that can possibly exist are the Rights of this woman to choose what she does with the inside of her own body. To talk of the rights of the 'unborn' is illogical. *Tom calls this the-time-of-giving-opinions, but I don't see it as an opinion, neither Steven's nor anyone else's.*

Some people consider this to be too harsh a cut off point. But that is all there is to discuss, it is the Moral issue here, the only one - where, or rather when, at what length of time after the sperm reaches the womb should we draw the cut off line for Bullying. At that very moment or sometime after - can you bully a sperm as it fertilises an egg, how old is the embryo before it can be bullied?

How can a being as yet unborn have Rights?
Sadly for the foetus, you have no rights, no existence until you are born. Only members of the Group have rights, tissue as yet unborn cannot be a member of the team. The team that first uttered the words: that's not fair, you have been wronged, you have been wronged … my fellow team member.
As soon as you are an independent being, hey presto, you have rights, the one Right-not-to-be-bullied.

Thus the irony, that the baby who is manipulated and used as a saviour sibling comes eventually to have existence, and thus the moment of its birth, is the moment at which it attains all its rights. At that very moment it immediately also has a claim for bullying and manipulation against its own parents.

Whereas the aborted foetus, sadly, never has any claim because it never has any Rights, because it never has independent existence. It is 'got at' before it is awarded its official 'certificate of humanness', and of course that is painful and mind boggling, especially now that we can photograph a foetus. But since there never exists a separate individual human being that is or has been bullied, there can never be a valid Moral claim either.

Only humans that have independent existence can have rights which vary from the rights of the mother. To juxtapose the concept of the embryo's possible future rights and place it at odds with the mother's existing Right-not-to-be-bullied, as a fully functional Team Member, is to put the cart before the horse.

Next thing you know we'll be like those Jains who wear a breathing mask when they go out, in case they breathe in and kill a gnat. Of course they do that because the gnat might contain the soul of their dead grandfather … oops! That idea - the transmigration of human souls, is of course a Belief: a Metaphysical-Religious Belief, a Mystical Belief, a Cultural Belief, an Ancient Belief, a Mumbo Jumbo Belief, whatever you prefer, but always a Belief, never Morality.

Morality is Bully/Anti-bully, and Metaphysical Beliefs just don't come into it.

And the rights of the unborn?
I honestly can't say that phrase, it's so stupid it sticks in my throat too much - the unborn have no rights.

Are the unborn standing with us on that grassy plain of long ago?
The place where we go, for clarity, to figure out any moral question, no matter how modern, that comes up? No, only living human members of the team have rights, possible future members just don't come into it.

Some find the arbitrary nature of this cut off point difficult to come to terms with, yet we choose an age for voting, 18 years old, the age of 2 years would seem absurd. We choose an age for criminal responsibility in our courts, below which a child is held to be not fully responsible.

We choose an age for sexual consent, 16 years old, giving a 6 year old girl the 'right' to consent to sex would be sick. A child is not old enough for the right to be applicable, thus also a foetus incapable of independent life ... but we hesitate, of course we do, because the stakes are so high, a life itself.

STEM CELLS

Once we ban the Metaphysical-Religious term 'playing God' from our moral language, it clarifies that there can be nothing immoral about undertaking stem cell research - how can you bully a stem cell? A blob so small you can barely see it with the naked eye, a blob that is never going to be a fully-fledged human being with the Right-not-to-be-Bullied.

Don't use either of those phrases around me please, don't insult me, the 'unborn' have no rights. And there is no question of 'playing God', the only question is - have you Bullied another sentient being or not?

1.3 Traditional Morality

Running through the numerous religions and philosophies that human beings have developed, there are when it comes down to it just three over-arching Moral systems, and in terms of western philosophy these can be summed up as:

1. Natural Law (or Biblical Law)
2. Utilitarianism
3. Kant's Categorical Imperative.

How I've wrestled with those.

When I was young, 14 maybe 15, something strange happened to me, no nothing like that, it happened inside my head. A question began to nag at me, and it nagged me from then until I was in my forties, when finally I answered it, with Steven's help. At the start I didn't even know what the questions was, but it turned out to be the oldest question in all philosophy, "what is the Good Life?" as the Greeks had it, or perhaps better put as "how should we live?"

Seems a small enough question, but the trouble is it leads to other questions and yet others, all requiring answers before you can answer it, it's a slippery little devil. The second question is; "What is justice, what is doing right?" And somehow, under Steven's influence, it gradually took over or at least became 'equal first'.

> *"Myself when young did eagerly frequent*
> *Doctor and Saint, and heard great Argument*
> *About it and about: but evermore*
> *Came out by the same Door as in I went."*

How many times did I read that poem, The Rubaiyat of Omar Khayyam, the Edward Fitzgerald translation that's not fashionable anymore. But who cares about fashion, not me I can assure you, that's some poem and always will be.

"With them the Seed of Wisdom did I sow,
And with my own hand labour'd it to grow:"

You don't have to share his sentiments or be concerned that it is a totally inaccurate 'translation', or that the reason you came across it was as a left over from your father's old fashioned self-education, over and over again and again and again I read it countless times. Until at one time, without having tried to do so, just because of the repetitions, I knew it off by heart, and it's a very long poem.

"And many Knots unravel'd by the Road;
But not the Knot of Human Death and Fate."

"What is justice, what is doing right?"
I persisted at that question, longer than anyone totally sane would do. Actually I've always thought that if I'd been any good at anything else, anything at all: singing, dancing, sport, there's a long list of things I've tried to be good at, my chosen career, even perhaps if I'd been more successful with women or at being a father, I would have given up my quest long ago.
But I wasn't, so I didn't.
You've heard that saying about evil that Steven says summed up the murdered Marc Walosh. It's from Thoreau, Henry David Thoreau, the American of the mid 1800s who came up with the concept of Civil Disobedience that Gandhi put to such good use. Mr. Thoreau has it that: "There are a thousand hacking at the branches of evil, to one who is striking at the root,"
Marc Walosh was like that apparently, but Steven wouldn't talk about him much. Much? Hardly at all. I understand why, Tom and I were his close friends once, but from another time, another life, we hadn't gained our spurs, nor ever would deserve them, in the world he later entered. I found out what evil was, and good, and doing right, and I found out because I have been lucky enough to meet one in my life who hacked at the root.
Steven was always much more concerned with a Theory of Justice than either Tom or myself, I was more interested in finding a Religion, secure and unassailable by anyone and anything. Whereas Tom was like Karl

Marx, he wanted philosophy to change things, everything, the whole world, even so we've made Steven's dance with Peter Barrow central...
    Sorry - miles off track already.

Let's get back to Natural (Aristotelian-Religious) Law, Utilitarianism and Kant's Categorical Imperative.

1. "Natural Law", has become more familiar to us as the Sacredness-of-human-life principle. This states that the gift of life from God (or from Nature), is not to be transgressed or taken by a mere human being, therefore in this system the taking of a human life in any form, in any circumstances is murder. Often expressed as 'Interfering with God's purposes' (as derived by early Christians from Aristotle), life is given from on high, and each life has a purpose ordained by God (or Nature), a gift that none should take back, except the Giver.

    I mustn't keep interrupting myself, but to be frank (and since I'm not an academic philosopher I can intrude with my opinion), to be frank I've always thought Natural Law was utter crap, even when I was a kid. Don't get me wrong I think Aristotle was a hell of a guy, the golden mean, and all that encyclopaedic writing on every subject under the sun.

    But, as Darwin and others have convincingly shown, he was wrong about 'since the purpose of a knife is cutting, therefore everything upon this earth has a purpose' - the concept 'purpose' is a facility of the human mind, the Universe doesn't have purposes, nor does the process we call evolution.

    From this 'everything has a purpose' idea, Christianity derived the concept of God's moral purposes, and now even though since 1859 CE (at the latest) the Aristotelian idea of all things having purposes has been totally discredited, indeed seen to be laughable, Christianity clings onto it. This is typical of the kind of claptrap some Religions saddle themselves with, and can't let go of. And which then before you know it brings the reputation and the good things about that Religion crashing down in flames, worst still in flames of derision.

    And then look - see! There goes the baby out with the bath water.
    I must stop these interruptions.

Many strict Mass Religionists achieve pretty much the same result by taking certain sentences in the Koran (or Bible) as moral instructions from God, so we don't need to sweat over Aristotle too much. I must just say, isn't this whole approach fundamentally flawed? Can we even call it moral philosophy? It is more like theology, in which certain sentences in the Good Book, whichever one it is, are interpreted and then proffered for our attention (rather than other sentences in the Good Book that say the opposite).

Either way, whichever way you take your Religious moral instructions, the gist of it is do what the Good Book says. And when it is a little fuzzy and unclear, do what those who are in the business of interpreting the Good Book for others say it says. *We won't be spending much time on it, you either believe that this approach has validity, or you don't.*

2. Utilitarianism as propounded by J. S. Mill *et al* is commonly known as the GREATEST GOOD OF THE GREATEST NUMBER. This states that those decisions are Morally correct which lead to the greatest happiness (or least pain) of the greatest number, happiness being defined as pleasure, compared and preferred over pain.

Where Steven does mention Utilitarianism, when he discusses Social Skilfulness, Book 1 Chapter 20, or just now in Designer Babies, he deems it to be a secondary Moral system - any decision based upon the greatest happiness, or least pain, of the greatest number is a simple Pleasure/Pain calculation.

Because...

The 'greatest pleasure' part is derived from the Pleasure/Pain Mechanism, which has nothing directly to do with Morality, while only the 'greatest number' part is taken from B/A-b Morality, when it tacks onto the greatest pleasure part, the codicil - of Others. The consideration of the Pleasure/Pain 'of Others' makes Utilitarianism into a partly moral calculation.

3. The CATEGORICAL IMPERATIVE, which states that God (or Nature) has laid down laws as part of our humanness, expressed by Jesus as: do unto others as you would be done to. And by Immanuel Kant as: do not will an act that you cannot will being UNIVERSALLY ALLOWED TO EVERYONE. For example, do not steal unless you are willing to agree that everyone should be allowed to steal.

Note here that although Kant is Seriously Religious, he does not simply 'do what the Good Book says' because it doesn't say anything coherent enough to satisfy him. We can see he is Seriously Religious because he insists that God watches us in order to dispense Final Justice, since clearly no one else can see into the hearts of others, no one else can see our Intentions. No one can see whether a particular series of our actions were Intended to Bully or not.

Oh I hope God does watch us, firstly because intentions and results are one of our biggest moral problems and there is no other solution, a lie detector test just doesn't measure up, it can't compare to God's eyes upon us. But mainly because if It does watch (God's never been a 'he' in my vocabulary), then my two young friends and I will be re-united and walk into heaven with just a nod from the guy on the gate.

But his famous dictum leads to a problem.

His emphasis on detailed crimes led Immanuel Kant to conclude that if a knife wielding maniac came to you demanding you tell him where his wife was hiding, you had to tell him, unless you were willing to accept that everyone was allowed to lie.

He was in error; clearly we can see now that in such a situation the Moral Categorical Imperative states, 'Don't Bully and don't aid Bullying, ever, no matter what'.

We can clearly lie to the knife wielder because to tell the Truth would be to assist in his Bullying-her-to-death. This lie is a white lie, a Right Lie, it is in a good cause, it stops rather than assists Bullying, and so is Anti-bully, Anti-bully, Anti-bully.

As he said, there is a single categorical imperative **to be obeyed in all circumstances**. Only it is not, as Kant supposed, in the detail of thou shalt not steal (like Robin Hood), or blackmail (like Gandhi did to the British Empire), or lie (like Schindler did to the Nazi SS), for these are all details. Too detailed to be the basis of a great philosophical issue like Morality, note instead that these thefts, blackmail and lies were all Anti-bully, all in a good cause.

The categorical imperative for which he searched is **thou shalt not bully**. *Or as he would say - DO NOT BULLY UNLESS BULLYING IS TO BE UNIVERSALLY ALLOWED TO EVERYONE.*

Immanuel Kant's Categorical Imperative lies hidden in the universality of thou shalt not bully, no matter what, in any and all circumstances. It is this, and this ALONE that is the foundation of the Human Moral Law.

We can see that of the three concepts that have been centre stage in western civilisation's search for the core of Morality, it was Immanuel Kant who was closest to the truth all along.

1.4 For Example...

In a village in some country on any continent you choose, in any century you prefer, five people are lined up against a wall: a woman, an old man and three children, the army is in town. Let's assume it's a current scene these are soldiers with rifles, and their commander repeats again his question to another man, the village head man, father of the children, husband of the woman, son of the old man.

"Either you tell me where the five criminals are hiding, or these five people die. Now, for the last time, where are they?"

I heard Steven many times on this subject, there would be a quiet moment, a lull in conversation and he'd start off. Picture a village, in some country, in any continent you choose, in any century you prefer, but I especially remember the first time, a few weeks after I'd met him in school. We were on top of some old colliery slag heaps, with a fine view down below us of the backs of the terraced houses where I lived. He lived over on the posh side of town, but in the south where I lived these heaps of waste were littered everywhere, close to each disused coal mine.

They're all gone now, flattened or moved I don't know which, it seemed to happen without me noticing. Funny how much time I spent up there, as a small child carried on my father's shoulders, then later squirming into the tops of old capped off shafts. Then later still, thinking, talking, planning, lighting fires, playing bung-off (hide and seek as you probably call it) and yet they somehow disappeared without me realising.

Anyway, we were up there that first time. As we got older it would become conversations in pubs and bars, but we always talked philosophy and we didn't need drink to do it, though we didn't perhaps quite know that that's what it was, or did we? I can't remember, I can remember very little of my childhood, and not much more of my adolescence really, and I find it hard to believe the biographies by people who claim otherwise.

Let's assume for the moment that the head man tells the soldiers where to find the rebels, and they drag them down into the village square, where the head man waits, his wife and children still against the wall, his father sitting in the shade. The commander is angry with the village, they've hidden enemies of the state, but he'll let them off, in fact he'll do more than that, he will spare four rebels as well, as long as the head man shoots the fifth, the leader, here now. He passes him a pistol, with one round in the chamber.

"You're a head man, shoot him in the head, and save four rebels and your family too."

What should he do?

At sixteen years of age how we loved to get stuck into that one, how we argued and argued. Little did we know we were going to carry on wrestling with it for the rest of our lives. And oh how wonderful that's been, life doesn't get any better than having a dream and being lucky enough to live it. For it to become you, for it to inspire you on every single day of your life, "that thou art" as the Hindus have it. Or "thou art that", I can never remember which way round that is, or whether it matters.

Anyway, 'shoot him in the head' - no contest for a Utilitarian (kill one - save nine), not so easy for the Christian village leader who believes in the sacredness-of-human-life. For thou shalt not kill is the law, thou shalt not interfere with God's purposes, thou shalt not take human life, no matter what the provocation, no matter what the duress, no matter what the temptation.

If we were to make the rebels ten or twenty in number, then a Utilitarian would find the decision even easier. But if the renegades numbered only two or three, then instead the Utilitarian would sacrifice them all and save the family of five - or perhaps a close family member counts as worth two others, or maybe more? Whatever, if he is a Utilitarian, and therefore believes that all Morality is based upon doing that which brings the greatest happiness (or least pain) to the greatest number, then he will shoot the lower number to save the many.

Or if he is like Kant, he will believe in his duty to obey the Categorical Imperative. Which in this case states that it is always wrong to kill a fellow human without at the same time agreeing that all should be also allowed to kill too. He will therefore not pull the trigger. *We argued and and disputed over who was right, the Utilitarian or the other two famous Moral positions.*

Sometimes Steven turned it around in different ways:

- A. What happens if there are three innocent villagers and three rebels? Then Utilitarianism is stuck in an embarrassing impasse. Can Morality really be based on the luck of numbers?

- B. What happens if you have to tell a lie, let's say all five are really rebels and you lie by saying that only one is, thus saving four others? Well Kant would say don't, if you don't want to condone universal lying by all and sundry, you must not lie, no matter how good the apparent cause. And yet, we think to ourselves can it really be immoral to save four from these fiends with guns?

Perhaps if we can get all three systems to agree, surely that will clarify things?

- C. Five virile young men of the village are lined up against the wall this time. In order to save four of them the headman must tell the soldiers which one of them is the renegade. He can now save four innocents by stating which one is the revolutionary. What's the problem? Point your finger, tell the truth.

None for the Utilitarian, none for the God's-sacred-purpose-of-life, and none for Kant who advises we should never tell a lie. In this version the three great rival sources of traditional Morality all agree ... and yet... Why does it not feel right - to betray even one to the soldiers?

When the people lined up against the wall are your father, wife, daughter and two sons, I think most of us would betray the rebels to the soldiers. And feel guilty. The guilt of being weak, of not having enough strength to take the other option, the ... but what is it? How can this be weakness? How can there be "another option", when in Alternative C, all three longstanding Moral positions are in agreement?

Let's go back to the first scenario, and assume that the headman betrays the rebels to save his family, as we think we would do. As a result the soldiers haul out the so-called revolutionaries, torture them, then shoot them, and leave.
These men were not from our village, the headman doesn't know them or the soldiers, they are nothing to him, his wife, family and his village are everything.

Yet he still feels bad, he feels he had no choice, but he still feels bad. Why? How can this be a Moral dilemma, when he has saved his family, from death, at the hands of someone he doesn't know over someone else's fight that is no business of his? Why are we open mouthed with a kind of horrified admiration over the person who won't give up the rebels, no matter what the price?
What is the 'other option'?

It is to refuse to co-operate with the soldiers, whatever form they ask their 'question' in, whatever pressure they bring to bear. It is the 'I WILL NOT BE BULLIED' option.

The hidden Moral issue is always between the bullying soldiers and those they are putting under duress, the Moral choice is always very simple but very hard. Whatever they do, or threaten to do, am I going to be strong enough to resist being bullied by them? The threats to wife and family, and whether or not one or two or four rebels will die, or who shoots them, are all side issues, a smoke screen hiding the real Moral issue.

In all these situations there is only one Moral question. Will you resist the Bully? Resist him no matter how high the price, no matter how great the suffering, no matter how long the pain lasts?

All the rest is illusion, camouflage, a smokescreen.

All these are not really different Moral choices at all, but merely different kinds and levels of pressure on the same Moral choice. For every time, the question hidden by all these surface conundrums is the same, is between the single citizen and the soldiers, will he give in to the different levels of pressure, what's his breaking point, will he be bullied, when will he be bullied? When will he break, will it take torture? Will it take the torture in front of him of his children, or will merely threatening to kill them be enough?

Will it be even easier - will bribery work?

Which is why bribery, the taking of money to betray a trust is yet another form of bullying, another form of the same immorality. Betraying a trust is a particularly subtle form of bullying, as in the Serpico syndrome, bullying by omission. When Serpico, the unpopular honest cop forces his way through a drug dealer's door, and meets resistance, his comrades simply hang back, they betray a trust, and let the criminals inside do their dirty work for them.

There is only one Moral answer to the riddle, to life's riddle, an answer which takes tremendous courage: the answer "let the soldiers do their own dirty work". I won't be bullied by them, even into supposedly saving five lives, I won't be bullied by them, no matter how high the price.

Bring it on, whatever it is you've got for me, bring it on, bring it on soldier boy, because frankly, I don't give a damn. No matter what it is, I'm willing to pay, willing to pay no matter how high the price - I WILL NOT BE BULLIED. *This is what takes our breath away.*

It is no coincidence that we admire those who will not be bullied, no coincidence that though we might make other choices we tend to wish that we had the courage to make the choice that resists the bully. No coincidence that we are invariably impressed by the person who refuses to succumb to blackmail, no matter what it costs them. Because the blackmailer is a particularly insidious form of the bully, and we admire the victim who resists, no matter what past bad behaviour is now made public.

1. As for Natural Law and the Sacredness-of-human-life?
A metaphysical principle created when the Chief Priest stole the Moral high ground from the Council.
Each one of us is born with the absolute certainty of our own death it is in fact the only such certainty in the whole of our lives. When you stop and think about it, the concept of inverting this certainty into an avoidance-of-the-certainty and using it as a basis for Morality is a strange idea.

If that really is the basis of Morality, then 'the Devil' always wins - but of course it's not. What we actually object to is an untimely death, and in particular an untimely death brought about by an oppressor, a torturer, a murderer, an arrogant negligent surgeon, there are many ways to die at the hands of the bullies.
All lives must face death, but all do not have to face torture, repression or an agonising death, and so the basis of Morality is the fight against BULLYING in all its many varied forms, not the maintenance of human life at any price.

2. Or the greatest-good-of-the-greatest-number?
Yes, if having made the decision not to resist the soldiers there is still a way of saving two or three people rather than only one, then this is a Utilitarian decision, but it is not the basis of Morality, it is an offshoot of Morality. Firstly the soldiers might lie to us, and kill them all anyway, Utilitarianism always involves a guess - about what might or might not happen in the future.

Secondly and more philosophically, every creature on earth is attracted towards pleasure and is repelled by pain, there is nothing Moral about it, it is a basic survival mechanism. The basic survival mechanism behind ALL LIFE, move away from pain, move towards pleasure.

Every living creature, even every plant, clinging to this earth carries with it an automatic pleasure versus pain mechanism - a calculating machine called a nervous system, but every creature is not moral. Plants are lovely but they are not moral, like every living creature before or after them they 'prefer' what makes them 'happy', they flourish when the environment they find themselves in is 'pleasant', is conducive to their growth, they die or fail to flourish when their environment is unpleasant or noxious to their growth.

3. Whereas the Categorical Imperative?

Immanuel Kant was right, his universal duty is so close as to almost be the Bully/Anti-bully principle, almost. Except he erroneously based his system on reason, whereas now we know that Morality is based upon our emotions, and also of course he got hung up on specifics: lying, stealing, killing, and said they were wrong in all circumstances.

The universality of THOU SHALT NOT BULLY is the foundation of the Moral law. Not never to tell a lie in the good cause of resisting a bully, but never to tell a lie that bullies others.

Mr. Kant, the second greatest philosopher that ever lived, considered Morality to be the most important philosophical quest facing humanity. As far as I can see it still is. How wonderful to find a consistency behind all the confusion, and even more wonderful for me, is to chat to Immanuel like that.

What you think he's dead? No, you know better than that, the dead still have a part to play. Keeping the dead alive so we can carry on talking to them is one of the good things Religion does.

I must confess that in telling Steven's story I've made him more religious than he used to be, but people change, especially when under constant pressure, and besides he was always very sympathetic to my position.

He and Tom started out as atheists, or sometimes agnostics depending on their mood and what they'd been drinking, but neither of them were quite so certain in that regard when they hung around with me, I have that effect on people I'm afraid.

And as I'm sure you've already guessed - it's not really something I'm ashamed of.

1.5 Not 'a matter of opinion'

Once upon a time there was a World in which POWER was the one and only undisputed King. And then one day, the concept Bully comes into existence, and thus, from this time on, the concept 'Doing Right' sits in opposition to it.

In the summer of 1968, the summer I was 16, I would run my hands along the shelves of books, in that small town Library, as I introduced this new exotic arrival to the delights of our little town. No not the pubs and bordellos such as they were, that summer I was still a little young for such pleasures, and so, despite his big talk, was my new friend Steven Morris. All that summer, student riots in Paris, tanks in Prague, what excitement, we stayed there all that summer, you had to pass through town to get home from school, so why not?

The sunlight, the wooden floor, I can see the motes in the air, it's so easy to conjure it up again, the smell of old Library books, History, Philosophy, Psychology, Sociology, Theology, far flung Religions from faraway places. And no one ever read them, no recent date stamps, they'd not been booked out in years.

Complication 1: Who is bullying whom?

As we have established we frequently DISAGREE OVER WHO we think IS BULLYING WHOM.

Sit down, settle yourself, feel the influence of the first moral complication over all of your relationships with others. Over how we get on, or don't, with our parents, children, in-laws and spouse. Are some of them trying to manipulate us?

How we get on better with some colleagues and acquaintances more than others. Are some of them trying to bully us?

What were they these strange exciting subjects, what might one learn, how much stronger and better might one be if one could only soak up everything that was there, what excitement. How might one change the world with this knowledge, if you only knew how, there had to be 'an answer' to the ills of the world, what excitement. If not to be found here in knowledge then where?

I was no longer a child, not because I'd just passed through puberty, but because I could think, for the first time ever in my life, I could think like an adult, could tackle questions that only adults could tackle.

Then Steven arrived, making our twosome a threesome.

"The whole history of ideas, generation after generation flows through here my friends, passed on, passed on, as we attempt to grasp the nub of things. Let's join them, let's join them and never look back."

Steven had an absolute certainty that he would do great things in the world. He would join, in an as yet unspecified form, those people, the intelligentsia let's call them, who wrote and discussed and discovered and revealed on those shelves, in the Library of that little town where I was born, and elsewhere and everywhere, wrote and revealed those things that humans had a right to know and to benefit from.

What excitement...

Complication 2: The Council

When LAWS are formulated Morality is REDEFINED, and its origins are hidden from view. It now becomes a SET OF RULES, which must have come from somewhere, somewhere outside, somewhere beyond.

If we look back to the First Council as they form the first Laws, Morality does not thereby become 'a matter of opinion'. We must watch out for those (commonly the Religious with vested interests), and in particular the Mass Religionists, who say at this point: but you have downgraded Morality into being 'a matter of opinion'. You will hear them say this, they say it even though nobody has said any such thing.

The aggregate of our Anti-bully feelings is used to formulate The Law.

Morality is not an aggregate-of-our-opinions, still less is it 'a matter of opinion'. Morality is the Anti-bully fire shared by every last one of us, the 'I hate to be bullied', that burns inside each human heart and brain. It is the human ability to speedily sniff out, recognise and condemn bullies of all shapes, sizes and guises.

Feel its presence as we did, feel the presence of Steven's big idea.

Ironically this is exactly where my own writing started, and never got anywhere. With the question, 'why is there a difference between the spirit and the letter of the law'. I never took it far enough, but at least it meant I was ready, ready to join him, because one day, one day in the Public Library of that town I read something. Back there in that town, in that hick town where I was young and that I loved so much, I read something.

> *"... we recognise our own rejected thoughts; they come back to us with a certain alienated majesty.*
>
> *Great works of art ... teach us to abide by our spontaneous impression with good-humoured inflexibility then most when the whole cry of voices is on the other side.*
>
> *...else tomorrow a stranger will say with masterly good sense precisely what we have thought and felt all the time...*
>
> *and then,*
>
> *... we shall be forced to take with shame our own opinion from another.*
>
> *Trust thyself: every heart vibrates to that iron string."*

That has always scared me - to have maybe had something, and to have not followed it up. What a fate I have always thought. That truly is a fate worse than death ... anything but not that. "FORCED TO TAKE WITH

SHAME OUR OWN OPINION FROM ANOTHER". Another who had the courage, the confidence and the strength of character to persist, to persist long enough to produce something new and worthwhile, and didn't care a damn if he looked a fool while he was doing it. As Mr. Emerson says...

> *"To believe your own thought, to believe that what is true for you in your private heart is true for all...that is the Secret.*
> *Speak your latent conviction ... set at naught books and traditions, and ... speak not what men think, but what YOU THINK.*
> *A man should learn to detect and watch that gleam of light which flashes across his mind from within.... Yet he dismisses without notice his thought, because it is his.*
> *Speak your latent conviction ... our first thought is rendered back to us by the trumpets of the Last Judgement."*

From that moment I wanted to be one of those who, I wanted to join those who ... set at naught books and traditions, and spoke not what "men thought". Instead I would speak what I thought.

I saw, that in THEM, in their words ... "we recognise our own rejected thoughts; they come back to us with a certain alienated majesty."

I saw that ... tomorrow a stranger might say with masterly good sense precisely what I have thought and felt all the time, and then I would be forced to take with shame my own opinion from another.

Well at least it was no stranger that did it to me; it was a friend I knew was a friend for life at the age of sixteen. It was Steven who forced me to take without shame my own opinion from another.

> *"We too had the experiences they had, but we did not suck those experiences dry of their secret and subtle meanings: we were not sensitive to the overtones of the reality that hummed about us."*

2. What it is not

2.1 Death and Injustice

We are Incommunicado until our brains grow large enough in size. And what is likely to prey upon this big brain most?

We are the first creatures to realise and contemplate IN ADVANCE the inevitability of our own DEATH, and not just our own death but also the death of those around us, those we know and love, those we rely on for mutual support. Of all the 'firsts' of *Homo sapiens* this one, this one surely, maybe even this one alone drives forward the human phenomenon known as Metaphysics-Religion.

Imagine when 100,000 years ago our enlarging brains start to remember for longer and longer, and to miss more and more, to long for, to mourn for, those close to us now dead and gone.
Gone where?
Surely it must have been death, but only partly the thought of the inevitability of our own deaths, mainly THE PAIN OF LOSS, that made us stop, made us think, made us take a new path.
A path no living creature up to then had ever trodden before, the path of thinking-about-whatever-lies-beyond or beneath the normal daily round, the surface phenomena presented to us and taken at face value - up to now.

No creature ever felt like this before, no other creatures keep the memory of their dead alive, via stories to the next generation, of their grandparents and great grandparents. And via graves, via sacred places where do dwell the spirits of the dead, via worship of the Spirit Gods, even worship of the dead themselves. They are still with us, surely they must be still with us, or if not, their spirits at least, their souls still somehow present in the sacred places.

We shall meet them again in the next world, we shall see them as they were in life. We will be together soon and slap them on the back in happy times, and say to them all the things we've thought since last we were together. Tell them all the things we've done and times we've missed them, times we've wished them present at some victory, wished they could see us at some special moment. Ask them all the questions we've stored up of half forgotten things they said about themselves, when we were paying scant attention because we thought they'd always be there, to ask and ask again.

Oh the pain, we cry out 'I miss you', the empty space soon to be healed, for what a meeting we will have, what a catching up there will be, what talks we shall have once we are together again, what good times await us down the road in paradise.

We humans are the first to mourn.
We mourn, mourn in pain, and ask why, why have they gone?
And this directs for the first time, the force of human curiosity beyond the surface of events, towards what lies beneath, beyond, above, below. The uncertainties of daily life prey upon the big brained *Homo sapiens*, and as consolation to handle this comes Metaphysics-Religion.

We talk of them, tell our children the exploits of their forefathers, the great sayings, the great acts of the group's great chiefs, now dead. Or surely perhaps just gone elsewhere. For how can ones as great as these be dead and gone forever?
And our children in their turn remember, remember those now dead, and yet also curiously still kept alive by memory, by the stories we retell, the songs, the dances. Still with us in spirit via our memories, via our minds, via our brains, still with us EVEN NOW, as inspiration. *Grave goods and the bereavement they indicate are not just the first SIGNS of Religion they actually are THE FIRST RELIGION.*

Now life is not confined to mere surface events and impressions, now we feel our history around us, referred to, and discussed. We FEEL PART OF something larger than ourselves, we are joined to our history, and we are stronger for it. We talk and listen to the dead, they give us meaning, they give us HOPE, we have become, we are becoming, Metaphysicians.

Along with Death and the pain of mourning another possible reason for first calling out to God is the pain of INJUSTICE.

Surely as much as when we are in pain and in mourning, we call out too when we are hurt and angry?

Do we not call out when the human justice of whatever form of society we live in has failed us? Do we not call upon God to judge when all human efforts have failed?

For the parents of a murdered child, whose killer is never caught, is there any other way to ease one's pain than to call down God's final judgement upon those who have eluded every other judgement?

Thus…

Complication 3: Religion comes to think of itself as the source of all Morality.

It was a bad day the day I realised that Complication 3 was an error on our part, on the part of the Religious. I say day, but in fact it was a lot longer than a day, I was clinically depressed for quite a while thereafter, the only time I've had to rely on drugs in the whole of my depression prone life. It was funny what finally brought me out of it, a silly thing that bugged me as a kid, and that I must have been 'still carrying', as the Buddhists say.

I can see myself with Tom and Steven, trying to deny the truth of a (to me) important statement - just an Oscar Wilde wisecrack really -- but it seemed to get under my youthful skin. In some play or other he says something to the effect that since it is unreasonable people who rage against the way things are, then it is unreasonable people who make all the progress in human affairs. I took exception to that, I hated it. Hated it because I considered myself to be reasonable, after all I was very, almost too, understanding of others, always willing to listen and to see other points of view.

And then one day, after over a year on anti-depressants, I realised with delight, I'm not a reasonable person at all. It's obvious, reasonable people don't spend all their lives in one crummy little town trying to solve a philosophical problem others don't seem interested in. Reasonable people don't, while they're at it, invent a personal Religion-of-one just for themselves, on the contrary that's what mad people do.

Oh how wonderful, I'm not 'reasonable' at all. So I let Oscar go, and with him sloughed off 18 months of at times suicidal depression. It acted as some kind of catalyst that kick started my recovery, I don't know how or why, there was a jolt and the world around me slowed down. From then on nothing was ever as intense again, as it had been before.

I could keep my Religion intact, better than intact, inviolable, isolated and separated from all Moral disputes, it meant I could Believe without the theologians (how I hate even writing that word) stealing it from me.

I'm free to believe in my own personal way, free of the God-stealers, I can have the strength of Religion, without having to believe a pack of lies as part of the so-called bargain - what a lousy bargain. I can have my

Religion, without having to believe in anyone's version of Totality other than my own - I'm free, free from the dominance of others.

Free to be religious in my own way, free to venerate my ancestors, free to remember wet windy nights, when the rain would drive under the front door and seep into the long crumbling tiled hall of that big old terraced house in which I grew up. To remember my father, a working class father who took no crap from teenage boys, remember him stuffing rags behind that front door to stem the flow, cursing the front door weather board, whatever the hell that was, I didn't really know. He would sally forth from the back room and the kitchen behind, with his anti-flood equipment, and incredibly, especially the first time it happened, would not yell at me to come out of the front room nearby and help.

All because you were there Steven Morris, no one else made such a difference, only you, only if I was ensconced there doing homework or philosophising with you, only you, not Tom, not anyone else who came hanging around. Not my younger brother, nor any of his mates, only you could work such magic. I can hear the radio echoing in that damp dreary hall, or the wireless as we used to call it then, and him there wringing out old cloths into a bucket, and cursing, half laughing and yelling for that brother of mine, but leaving us alone. Even when I would stick my head out, "no you carry on as you are, dopey Joe's on his way any minute", then yelling "Bert" again, though it wasn't my brother's name, "Bert where the hell are you?"

Silence, no sign of brother Alan.

"Bert, say something for God's sake - if it's only goodbye".

My father was a philosopher of a kind of course, much more so than those other adults I saw around him. He was a loner, like me, and despite all the arguments in my teens, I get it all from him. And that's why, though I remember his faults, I love him still, twenty years after his death, love him like I have loved no other. That mighty five foot eight pocket battleship (I'm six foot) must have recognised a soul mate too, even he with his scant regard for teenage boys, could see you were something different. Not a master though, I can't give you that much credit, that man knew no master.

And I feel his blood in me.

I am he; half my genes are his - sitting here now, closer to me than my fingertips, closer to me than anything else on earth. He's dead, dead twenty years, but he's closer to me than anything alive upon this planet now.

2.2 Slander and Blasphemy

S ay someone criticises our opinions and an argument ensues, during which evidence is brought forth by both sides and points are made and disputed. We may become angry with the sheer stupidity of the other person, but each of us has the RIGHT to express our opinion - this is Free Speech.

LIBEL AND SLANDER ARE IMMORAL
If the disagreement degenerates into personal insults and accusations that are false and that are unsubstantiated by facts, we are in the land of Libel and Slander. And these are legitimate and important limits on Freedom of Speech.

Slander (spoken) and Libel (written) occur when a group member some-how publicly slurs the character of a fellow group member, and is unable to produce evidence to prove that the something said is true.

We know and understand what Slander and Libel are, we see enough cases ending up in court and then being covered in the newspapers. It's clear enough that telling Public Lies about someone has to be a limit on Freedom of Speech. Such lies result in a slur on our reputation amongst our group, they are therefore the Bullying-manipulation of other group members into unjustifiably viewing us in a bad light.

As with the rest of Morality, the concept has long since passed over from within-groups to apply also between-groups, but not to the dead. You can't slander the dead, even though it must often be very painful for their close relatives to listen to dubious claims written or spoken about the recently dead, as 'revisionist historians' have the habit of doing.

It is an interesting question to ask why, if such historians are not able to justify their criticisms with facts, should certain categories of close relative, children, parents, siblings and spouses of the deceased not have the right to sue?
Is this still not Libel and Slander?
Lies which cause suffering to other Group members?

Maybe just parents and spouse would be best, and leave it at that? We don't want people's kids, who weren't around at the time of whatever it is their parent is now accused of, defending the family honour out of blind loyalty and dragging the thing on for another generation.

One can see of course that death is a neat legal full stop. But forgetting legal conveniences for the moment and speaking philosophically?

Hold onto that for a moment while we take a look at an allied issue.

BLASPHEMY
Blasphemy is defined as being disrespectful towards God or towards holy and sacred things.

Therefore Blasphemy cannot be immoral.
Blasphemy as it is defined above in law is not immoral because it is not an act of Bullying.

Yet one wonders can it be Right to allow Jesus, Mohammed, Confucius or the Buddha to be gratuitously insulted? Even though they are dead? Note please JC, Buddha or Mohammed, not God, and not holy and sacred things.

Can it be Right that pygmies not fit to wash their feet are allowed to get away with insulting without evidence these special people, these Saints who founded great world Religions?

After all even though they are now dead, in a sense they are always with us. I ask myself can it be Right to Libel-a-Prophet or Slander-a-Saint? And is it not this that has an element of immorality about it, and yes isn't this why we sometimes feel sympathy for the protests of fervent Mass Religionists, even when we don't share their fervour?

Don't we all despise Slander?

Isn't it the SLANDER-OF-A-SAINT rather than the strange outmoded concept of Blasphemy that disgusts us?

To the secular Open Society the concept of blasphemy is ridiculous, utterly ludicrous because blasphemy is a command driven 'wrong', it is based upon blind obedience - and the Open Society doesn't do blind obedience.

In fact that's what it is set up specifically to combat - the blind obedience demanded by all sorts, shapes and sizes of SPECIAL CASES, special rulers, kings, queens, emperors and empresses, tin pot dictators, semi-gods and demi-gods. The Open Society has developed to combat and question all those who claim Obedience, claim blind obedience because they 'know best'.

It doesn't do BLIND OBEDIENCE because not doing it is precisely how

a balance of power is maintained in society, that is how tyrants are controlled. Not doing blind obedience is Democracy, not doing blind obedience is Freedom, not doing blind obedience is Morality.
Is Morality standing upright on its own two legs.
Morality shouting out, loud and proud, for its Rights.
Shouting for the Right not to be Bullied by the Alpha Male, even when he comes hidden in clerical garb.

In the secular Open Society all accusations of blasphemy are always going to be met with laughter. Not insulting laughter, but genuinely bemused uncomprehending laughter, because those who shout "blasphemy" have missed the whole point.
Blasphemy is about insulting Authority, but the primary definition of the Open Society is that it doesn't accept 'authority'.

Just as thousands upon thousands of years ago the first human groups declined to accept the up to then unquestioned authority of the single Alpha Male.
I don't accept 'Authority', do you?
It is the policeman, politician, priest, lawyer or lowly army corporal given too much POWER. And in their hands and in the hands of oh so many like them 'Authority' becomes the Bully of all Bullies.

Not me, no thanks.
I'm free of that and I'm staying that way.
I'm free because my ancestors (and yours) fought for our freedom, and I won't be giving it up. I won't be insulting my own dead by pissing away that which they sacrificed themselves for, that which some of them died for, no not me, not today, not any day.

The concept of Blasphemy has become meaningless ever since Society became secular (based upon B/A-b Morality), and also became composed of many Religions rather than One. But we can see how there is still a case to answer - the case of the Slander-of-a-Saint.

THE SLANDER-OF-A-SAINT
Certain books, films or plays ridicule and poke fun at Religion, but in doing so make a valid point of criticism, and that's fine keep it up. Others are just a series of gratuitous insults, Jesus in a huge demeaning nappy for no apparent reason other than shock value - not so fine.

Jesus portrayed as a homosexual based upon no offered evidence, or said to have fathered an illegitimate child with Mary Magdalene, in the latter case with evidence that would be laughed out of either a court or a science lab - even less fine.

If someone walks down the street with a banner proclaiming that Mohammed was a toy boy. Or that Jesus had a bastard child with Mary Magdalene, or Moses and the Buddha were paedophiles, Guru Nanak a pederast, and Confucius a thief and a liar, they have insulted a human being once living but now dead. And the close adherents of that Saint accuse them of Blasphemy, which is utterly meaningless to most of us, but what if instead they were to be accused of Slander or Libel?

We have to be careful, we are trying to balance Freedom of Speech against the use of gratuitous insults used controversially to boost the circulation or sales of some crappy production by a second rate artist or impresario.

It is a well known fact that the dead don't sue.
A fact dear to those selfish small minded little minnows whose only aim is to create a furore, a brief sensation in order to get bums on seats, or gain the kudos of a little public notoriety. Even though I understand the legal difficulties and dangers, should we not protect the names of those special few who founded the world's major religions and have millions of adherents still today, who in a way are always with us?

It's tricky, I admit, but I'm pretty sure we should. The law should be revised and they should stand accused of the SLANDER-OF-A-SAINT. At least this would be legally clear and meaningful.

Certain of the Great Dead only: Moses, the Buddha, Jesus, Mohammed, Guru Nanak, and Confucius for example. Those special cases who founded world religions, not the founder of every tin pot sect and schism, and not those Religions whose origins are so clouded in mystery that they have no unique Founder. These have to be real people, not vague Hindu half gods avatars or mystical figures like Lao-Tzu the founder of Taoism.

To be philosophically consistent and to be Moral, we ought to introduce such a law, and kick the now meaningless concept of blasphemy into touch. *Is this realistic, or is Steven being too idealistic?*

I remember reading in one of Bertrand Russell's books him questioning the whole principle of inheritance, and that we should do away with it. No more passing on of land, no passing on big chunks of money and property to your kids. I was astounded, I was in my early twenties by then, but still thought of myself as a bit of a rebel, surely Bertie was completely off the wall it seemed. Now, thirty years later I'm far more inclined to agree with him, the old radical was spot on, hunter-gatherers don't have inheritances.

The principle of inheritance is immoral, the saying 'all property is theft' is true. The tightly bound human teams amongst whose ranks B/A-b Morality developed had no great discrepancies of wealth. Sure the Big Man and the Council members had a few more tools, weapons or clothes than Mr. Average, but that's all.

To recreate the Society in which Morality first appeared amongst us Death Duties should be doubled, trebled, quadrupled, until no one earns or owns more than about five or ten times what Mrs. Average gets.

That would be more beneficial than giving Religious bigots a helping hand to dismantle free speech - this is Tom talking by the way, this is his time-of-giving-opinions.

Oh I know if we say God, Allah or Yahweh is "a pathetic figment of an over excitable imagination" and as a result we are accused of the Slander-of-a-Saint clearly there is no case to answer. We cannot give any help to the Mass Religionists on this one, because God is a Metaphysical not a Moral term.

And I know we are therefore still at liberty to criticise Islam on Women's Rights, or the Pope on why he is against the condom when it could help control the spread of AIDS. Or to criticise the Hindus on the Untouchable issue, or Buddhists on the way they treat the Sick (as if they earned it in another life). Because clearly we are questioning the Morality of these various religion-based practises, and there is and never should be any question of giving ground to Religious 'sensibilities' where these result in a clash with Morality.

I know also that there can't be a successful prosecution for the SLANDER-OF-A-SAINT where credible evidence is put forth in support of criticism. Thus in every case Religion must argue its case in court, fair and square. But equally those who have not brought forth evidence-based criticism have told a lie and telling lies is immoral.

Dare we change the law to one that means something in real Moral terms, and take the protests off the streets and into the Courts?

Is it realistic?

No I think not, Tom's correct not Steven.

Religious bigots of every flavour would have a field day with a law like that. It would be worse than the situation now, where small-minded nothings are allowed to write tripe about Jesus Christ, one of the greatest human beings that ever lived.

It emphasises once again that we can no more attain perfect democracy, wherein everyone gets a fair crack of the whip (and no more), than we can attain perfect morality. These are not PURE concepts lying out there somewhere waiting to be discovered, like the speed of light or radioactivity, they are limitations placed upon Bullying. Limitations we cobble together as best we can, trying to limit one aspect of Bullying, while at the same time not redressing the balance so much that this then gives the other party too much opportunity to be a Bully.

Wealth creates Bullies, or if not creates them, gives them increased opportunities for domination of others. To hell with Steven, let's leave the libel laws alone and outlaw the concept 'inheritance' instead, that would be far more JUST. Bertie, that old formula on legs, was right, that would help create a far more FAIR Society.

Fat chance eh?

2.3 What Obscenity is

There are three legitimate constraints upon Freedom of Speech.

Three only, all other constraints are lies – lies told by Bullies, and would-be-Bullies.

All other constraints upon Free Speech are restraints by POWER upon our Rights of free expression.

Constraints wherein the Bully, the Alpha Male, imposes himself, as he follows his ancient desire … to dominate. Or Alpha female, in every early human Group there will always have been a head of the sisterhood too, the top female. Let's not kid ourselves, females in general are only a little less driven by ego than are males, and in many individual cases not less at all.

The second constraint to appear in our history we have just discussed, it is slander and libel. The limit on Free Speech that says thou shalt not Bully-manipulate by telling lies about others.

The third historically we will meet later, it is racial discrimination, faced when B/A-b Morality passes from operating only inside, to operate ALSO **between Groups**.

The first historically is OBSCENITY, and it is up for discussion next.

What do we mean when we say that something is OBSCENE?
It is often used in connection with sexual matters, but is also confused with Artistic Taste and sometimes even with the outmoded concept of Blasphemy.

To look inside this word, we need to familiarise ourselves with a certain type of genetic pre-disposition regarding the way we have SEX, compared to the way other creatures do.

Humans have sex in private.
Most animals have sex in front of others, but humans greatly prefer privacy. In fact most of us do not just 'greatly prefer' it's more of a 'must have' privacy.

Humans have no 'in heat' season.
Unlike most animals, which mate only at certain times of the year, instead human females are sexually receptive all year round.

Humans have sex long after the female is capable of conceiving.
No other animal, as far as I understand matters, continues to have sex when they are no longer fertile.

These are just facts of human sexual behaviour, uncontested biological FACTS that are independent of any Religion, Racial Group or sub-Group, Creed or Culture. COMMON HUMAN BEHAVIOURS that we all share.

This mechanism is from a different source than Morality.
It is from the third of the Big Six: SEX.
It is within the human version of SEX that the concept OBSCENITY lies hidden, not in any of the other five.

No one cares much either way if, in the privacy of their own home a couple have sex, for the PLEASURE of it, at any time of the year, day or night, nor if they continue to do so long after she is fertile. But how would their fellow shoppers react if this same couple were to have sex along the High Street in front of the local Marks and Spencer on a Saturday morning in early May?

They would take exception to it they would protect the eyes of their beloved children, and they would label it OBSCENE.

They take exception, not because they have been physically hurt in any way, but because this couple have offended against a SPECIAL CODE - the unanimous predilection humans have for privacy in sexual matters. If we were any other animal: chimp, elephant, deer, dog, cat, or horse, sheep or cattle there would be no issue - because they have sex in front of each other all the time.

SEXUAL PRIVACY

Thus those who indulge in sexual acts in a public place are offending the common human sex code, the instinct for privacy, the genetic aversion against public displays of sexual intercourse. If asked the man in the street would say that such behaviour IN PUBLIC is indecent or OBSCENE, the woman in the street would comment that anyone doing such a thing is offending our sense of what is proper in public, and that's just the way we are, we humans.

There are various evolutionary theories as to why this has occurred, but let's press on, observing though from whence the concept OBSCENITY arises, from our predisposition for SEX IN PRIVATE, rather than in full view of the rest of the herd, pack or group. Thus is derived the concept OBSCENITY, not from B/A-b Morality nor from anything written in the Anelects, Bible, Koran, Talmud, Bhagavad Gita or Dhammapada.

There is no Right to Freedom of Sex in Public as there is to Freedom of Public Speech, because no bully has taken away our right to public sex, virtually 100% of us just have no desire that way. Just imagine for a moment, if you are of the male gender, trying to get, let alone maintain, an erection in public on the High Street in front of M&S.

We don't want to do it, and 'they' don't want to see it.

And those deviant few who do enjoy sex in public places? Tough - either control yourself or be prepared for the consequences.

Although please note there is a world of difference between 'in public places' and 'in full public view', the former one might do when drunk or for a dare when no one much is around, the latter is rarer than hen's teeth. And especially because to get the comparison correct we must add the stipulation that, like many animals, our parents or our children must be stood outside M&S watching us.

In this case it is not 'agreed upon' in the same way that Moral Rules are, by a VOTE of the first Council. It is in-built at our birth, via the genes of all the humans born upon this planet, it is the way we are MADE.

The first Council doesn't need to organise a pow-wow and a vote on it. There is NO VOTE, because this predilection is locked in our genes from birth.

There is no vote because everyone just automatically turns up their noses at anyone they see having sex in a public place, in full view of others -

we're just not made that way. No one ever thinks that there may be extenuating circumstances in which it is Right to have sex in public, as they do regarding theft, when Robin Hood steals from the rich.

'No-in-heat-season' and 'sex-continuing-after-fertility' are just FACTS of our genetic make-up, interesting peculiarities of human sex, compared to the sex lives of other creatures. Thus we all agree that a couple (homo or hetero) having sex in their front garden is not allowed, it is Obscene because they should do it in private, and so this too is an undisputed issue, a BIOLOGICAL FACT of human life.

It is certain aspects of Public Sexual Display, rather than full intercourse that are not so clearly undisputed, and thus soon become a breeding ground for dispute. Displays that stop just short of full public sexual intercourse.

Before this though we must clear up a confusing side issue - Aesthetic Taste.

2.4 What Aesthetics is

When an artist exhibits as a serious work her unmade semen stained bed, many people find this to be 'in poor taste', and splutter with rage over it. If questioned more closely they may say something like it offends against public decency or some such phrase.

And in doing so they have just mixed up Aesthetic or Artistic Taste with Obscenity.

They have mixed up two things.
One is their opinion that the exhibition of an unmade bed of any kind is poor art, lazy art, aesthetically unprepossessing and therefore worthless Art. Two is their repugnance at the MILD OBSCENITY of the PUBLIC DISPLAY of the aftermath of another couples sex life.

They mean it is Obscene, but since obscene seems too strong a word for a case such as an empty bed, they downgrade it into 'in poor taste', and in so doing confuse things further. It would be far more accurate to accuse the exhibition of Tracy's bed of being lazy and aesthetically poor Art, and to label the semen stains alone as being mildly obscene.

AESTHETICS - the study of beauty or rather the study of the concept of beauty, taste and all things well proportioned and pleasing to the eye is a strange philosophical subject. It covers also that which is pleasing to the nose and the other senses such as touching, tasting, listening and it has a long and venerable history.

A history reaching back to Plato and beyond, a 2500 year old history, longer than quite a few Religions.

It is a rather ephemeral subject compared to Morality.

Yet it has a part to play in clarifying the limit called Obscenity that Society places on Free Speech, because one often hears the criticism: "that should not be permitted, it is in POOR TASTE" - it is a problem of terminology.

Now that we know what Obscenity is.

What is beauty? What is bad and good artistic taste?

Plato and his cohorts started this, like so much else, and like so much else they have a lot to answer for. Plato started it around 400 BCE and Darwin and his followers (also like so much else) finished it in 1871 CE - but traditional philosophers at first missed the endpoint.

Philosophers of all kinds were long in the habit of praising and raising the Beautiful up on high, as being synonymous with what they called THE GOOD, or even GOD. The good to look at, the good to eat, the good feeling when you have achieved or built something, the good feeling before, during and after sex, but especially a beautiful painting, building or sculpture.

Confusing 'the Good' born of the concept PLEASURE, with 'the Right', born of the concept MORALITY.

A beautiful painting, sculpture, dress or building is pleasing, an Aesthetic Good, a Pleasure to the eye of the beholder. It is closer to the world of fashion than it is to the world of Morality. And though it seems incredible to us that any great philosopher could mix these up, they did so for hundreds of years, in their pursuit of an ideal they called 'The Good'.

Little wonder then that us lesser mortals also get mixed up.

In his book, published in 1871 CE *The Descent of Man and Selection in Relation to Sex* (*The Origin of Species* was published in 1859), Darwin states:

"Let us suppose the members of a tribe in which some form of marriage is practised, to spread over an unoccupied continent; they would soon split up into distinct hordes, which would be separated from each other by

various barriers, (mountain ranges, rivers, deserts, etc) ... and still more effectually by ... war.

The hordes would be subject to slightly different conditions and habits of life, and would sooner or later come to differ in some small degree. As soon as this occurred each isolated tribe would form for itself a slightly different standard of beauty; and then unconscious selection would come into action through the more powerful and leading savages preferring certain women to others."

In the battle to attract sexual partners, many creatures select upon the basis of the brightest colour, the biggest chest, longer neck, wider wing, tail, eyes, lips, buttocks, in short any feature considered amongst that species as attractive (just a little more exaggerated than others around it). These attractions also include particular sounds, as well as smells and tastes, we lick, we listen, we smell, we look for that which attracts us, that which pleases us, that which is a PLEASURE, and therefore 'accords with our TASTE'.

In the majority of species it is the males who strike the pose to show how healthy and strong they are, and the females who do the choosing - by acceptance of the suitor. A young buck jumps high in the air every so often as he runs from the lion. "See how fast and glorious I am, so fast so fine that I do not even need to run in total panic. I can actually waste time jumping as I run, choose me I'm beautiful, choose me, choose me I'm strong, choose me I'm healthy choose me."

Our eyes, our ears, and in some cases our noses become utilised, not just as instruments for survival and searching for food, but also as a means of choosing between the perceived beauty of one mate compared to another, between slightly different versions of the same thing. Our eyes become able to discern the concept beauty, as an adjunct to choosing the best - by which is meant the healthiest, the strongest, the finest, the fittest.

In this process evolution has done what it always does, it has used something already available to us for an additional purpose. Our eyes are already able to tell us which things in our world look good/healthy, clean water, a fresh kill, a field of trees with tasty nuts. And which look bad/unhealthy, dirty stagnant water, putrefied fly blown flesh, barren scaly plants of low nutritional value or brightly coloured and poisonous berries.

Now it is refined further, by being used to choose the best, most robust and healthy, partners on the grounds of physical beauty, and those who choose correctly producing more healthy and surviving offspring, who in turn choose again in their turn on the same basis. Again, again and again over thousands of generations.

And so AESTHETICS or TASTE - the preference for that which we consider beautiful, that which we find appealing to one or other of our senses.

Thus millions of years later, humans with their much greater brain power develop a very wide and refined range of preferences, which their philosophers come to call Aesthetics, and they ponder it for hundreds of years. Well we can cease to ponder now, the subject of AESTHETICS developed from the choices, the sexual choices those before us made over millions of years of evolutionary time.

Hence in art, we exaggerate for effect and by so doing we attract, or sometimes repel. If the particular feature is not so well considered, we incur the judgement in others, 'that is poor or bad taste'.
Artistic taste - nothing to do with the issue of Obscenity.

Clearly humans have a far greater range of tastes than canaries mating in the wild, but in fact your classical music buff, food, wine or art snob, is saying nothing much more than: 'I find that SEXY'.
Despite all the words and all the blathering nonsense, our refined human Aesthetics owes its existence to SEX and SEXUAL ATTRACTIVITY. Pretty funny really, it is a measure of how attractive we find something - and that is all.

Thus all our supposed refinement and so-called sophistication, all the pretension, all the artistic talk, is rationalisation. All a smokescreen as we show off our plumage whilst admiring the plumage of others. As we show off our personal attractiveness or show off via our artistic works - like a Bower Bird - we parade the beauty of our pretty petty productions.

For someone whose father was an Architect Steven sounds scathing about aesthetic beauty doesn't he? Actually he was pretty scathing about his father as well. Tom and I quite liked him, at times he was an arrogant old sod I could see that though.

Steven was never fooled into believing that Aesthetic Beauty and Truth were somehow linked. He always, from the start dismissed it, dismissed music, art, food and wine, fashion, clothes "all ephemeral, all nothing, meaningless" he would say. He wouldn't even concede to call it crap, it was less than crap, a zero, pointless and useless.

Aesthetics produces many lovely things which enhance the PLEASURE of our lives, but there is no longer a great mystery about what it is, and whence it is derived, as there was in Plato's day.

It is the part of evolution called sexual selection, the part that chooses attractiveness, chooses beauty in a mate, and thereby chooses more so in the next generation, it is an EVOLUTIONARY MECHANISM not, as Plato thought, our 'imperfect imitation of a perfect harmony wherein the Gods do dwell'.

2.5 Aesthetics and Obscenity

So when we say, that picture is ugly I don't like it, we are utilising our aesthetic judgement.
That unmade bed is ugly, is neither here nor there, it is a matter of ARTISTIC TASTE. One calls the other an empty-headed philistine and on we both go to the next exhibit or the next gallery.

Those semen stains are indecent, because they are on public exhibition, that display is MILDLY OBSCENE, is something else, is a different topic altogether. We are saying then that those stains are indecent because they exhibit (a part of) someone's private sex life IN PUBLIC.
We are saying that it contravenes the human sex-is-private, genetic pre-disposition.

Most of us wince at the stagnant evidence of another couples sex life, we find it yucky, it is private and we don't want to know, we are conditioned by genetics, by our evolutionary past into not wanting to have such information thrust in our face. We think it is in Bad Taste for anyone to do so, and the moment we say that we are confusing it with bad taste in Art, the ugly, the ill proportioned that gives us NO PLEASURE when we look upon it.
When we really mean that it is OBSCENE.

This obscenity is only a mild one, far less OBSCENE than seeing Tracy and her friend on the bed having sex IN PUBLIC, in the middle of an Art Gallery. But we must pause a moment here because the self-righteous amongst the liberal wing can get very hot under the collar about this.

We are not saying that anything Tracy and her lover do on that bed is Obscene, what they do is a wonderful normal human act, blah, blah, blah, etc, etc, blah blah blah. (She's great isn't she, a crazy natural unaffected marvellous piece of womanhood. What man amongst us wouldn't trade places with him?)

What we say when we call the displayed bed MILDLY Obscene is - Obscene because it DISPLAYS A PRIVATE ACT IN PUBLIC. The doing of it is the most natural thing in the world, but the displaying of it is not. It contravenes a Common Genetic Pre-disposition.

Although in the case in question, I don't suppose the majority of us would be so offended as to vote to make the public display of Tracy's semen stained bed illegal by dint of Obscenity. Therefore we must be teetering on a boundary, and philosophically speaking, boundaries are interesting places on which to teeter.

It throws some light for example on that statement that people make from time to time, sometimes by 'liberals' and sometimes by pornographers. You know the one. It goes like this… How come Society allows violence to be portrayed on television and in the cinema but becomes all coy and uptight about the natural and beautiful act of sex?

Well here's the answer, public displays of an explicit sexual nature are OBSCENE, **because they are PUBLIC** (however privately delightful), they contravene the Genetic Instruction imprinted by our biology "do not have sex in public".

The WRONG is the Public Display, not the Act itself.
And this has nothing whatsoever to do with violence in films, because such violence is ALWAYS A B/A-b MORAL QUESTION. Hence why scriptwriters twist the plot around so that our movie heroes can use the excuse of vengeance when they behave violently. The 'he deserved it' syndrome, the bad guy got what was coming to him.

Phrases which always mean, 'this person is a Bully' he has always been a 'wrong un' and is now receiving nothing other than an eye for an eye, or even a tooth for a mouthful of teeth, because that which our hero is now dishing out is actually less than whatever the bad (wrong) guy has done to others.

He is receiving his JUST DESERTS, this vengeance is not Bullying, it is JUSTICE.

Yes, when I see a couple on the street, or maybe at a railway station saying goodbye, and involved in a long passionate lingering kiss, I've often wondered why I look at them and then quickly look away again - as if it's Wrong.

Wrong to look and somehow Wrong for them to be too intimate in public - no matter how much in love they may be?

This explains it. We feel trapped, we accuse ourselves of being voyeurs and prudes at the same time. Am I a prude to turn and look away? Or am I a voyeur to look? It's confusing - up to now.

WHAT OBSCENITY IS NOT

One hears people say for example, it is Obscene how minor potentates flaunt their wealth while their fellow citizens starve and die in poverty all around them. Or in times of war, it is Obscene for reporters to criticise our soldiers while they are out there dying for us.

These are incorrect uses of the word OBSCENE, it should be reserved purely for unacceptable public sexual displays, is it any wonder we get ourselves confused.

The word Obscene (a Biological categorisation) is used, over used and misused, because the speaker wishes to express utter disgust with the actions being criticised. Is used - to give emphasis. Obscene is, unfortunately for accuracy, a wonderful word for adding punch, adding vigour, giving emphasis to our disgust.

It should though never be used in any other context than that of either, **an act of sex undertaken in public or a public sexual display sufficiently explicit such that it borders on the sex act itself.** Since OBSCENITY is a central BIOLOGICAL issue to all human societies it is too important a word to mess around with.

Displaying wealth when surrounded by starvation and poverty is a Moral Wrong, the rich are still, despite their wealth, members of a social team, and they have taken more than their FAIR SHARE. Their greed is IMMORAL and DISGUSTING, but provided they don't also have sex in public, their behaviour is NOT OBSCENE.

In the second example, the reporter may well be telling an honest story about atrocities committed by our soldiers, if he is then good for him and the person who is trying to shut him up is a liar. If the reporter himself is lying, then he is guilty of libel, again a Moral issue and nothing to do with OBSCENITY - publicly displayed sex between two humans. *(Or, if you want to include bestiality - between a human and an animal - same thing, Obscene.)*

But we'll never change people's misuse of the word OBSCENE.

So henceforth we should use the term BIOLOGICAL WRONG, it's more accurate and also less emotive.
A BIOLOGICAL WRONG IS AN ACT OF SEX UNDERTAKEN IN PUBLIC IN FRONT OF OTHER HUMANS, or A PUBLIC SEXUAL DISPLAY SUFFICIENTLY EXPLICIT SUCH THAT IT BORDERS ON THE SEX ACT ITSELF.
A Biological Wrong is not a Moral Wrong, bit it is still a Wrong.

Complication 4:
These are two different types of Wrong we have mixed up, a mistake of history, but they are both Wrongs. A Biological Wrong is an issue of SEX MISUSED by public exhibition, whereas a Moral Wrong is always an issue of POWER MISUSED.

2.6   Two Types of Wrong

Part One of **Complication 4** is when an actual act in public or portrayed in public is not quite full on sexual intercourse - is it still not admissible? Where should we 'draw the line' is what we are often actually arguing over. Some of us are more prudish than others, some of us are so even in the privacy of our own bedrooms, nothing wrong with that, we vary from each other.
Part Two is that originally, out on the open grassland, there is no question of portrayal - that comes much later with drawings, paintings, books, sculpture, photographs, films, radio, records, television, the internet.

Where does this lead us?
To censorship of course, that *bete noire* of left wing liberalism - because they think it is dictatorial, against free speech, and prudish (against the sweet beautiful PLEASURE of SEX). We easily mix up political-censorship, which certainly is Bullying-by-Dictatorships and therefore a Moral Issue, with Censorship-for-Explicit-Sexual-Content, which is a Biological Issue.
We should be more careful to differentiate between these two.

In a world in which humans have a unique genetic sexual predisposition for sexual privacy, we should not be as afraid of sex-censorship as we tend to be. Provided that we establish it upon the rock solid basis of Biology, and not upon some Mass-Religionist, or any other opinionated twaddle. To be afraid of the principle of sex-censorship is to mix up this BIOLOGICAL issue with the MORAL issue of freedom of speech and the political-censorship that tries to control such freedom.

SEX-CENSORSHIP
Sex-censorship is actually an appropriate response to a Biological Wrong. Whereas political-censorship is itself a Moral Wrong, because it is an attempt to BULLY the rest of us into silent acquiescence in the face of someone else's OPINION, the opinion of those who assume POWER, those who assume AUTHORITY over us.

The problem is that one person's **Obscenity** is another person's prudish overreaction, hence these are issues over which we debate and argue, trying to draw a line between being overly restrictive or being too *laissez-faire*. Censorship-for-sexual-content is NOT as dirty a concept as we have come to believe, not that is, as long as we free the Censor from both the clap-trap of the religious right and the self righteousness of the liberal left.

Most societies, despite the protests of the *avant-garde*, need some form of sex-censorship. We don't trust politicians to run the country without being subject to a series of checks and balances, we don't trust the police to be always scrupulously well behaved without other checks and balances, we don't trust greedy speculators not to bend the financial laws of the Stock Exchange if they're not overseen. Why would we trust film directors, playwrights, authors, and artists to behave responsibly without some checks and balances pertinent to them?

Those who claim there should be no sex-censorship seem to believe that politicians, local government officers, directors of companies ... actually the list is endless, can't be trusted without a means of redress, but artists can. It's as if they assume that there is no pressure for critical and financial success, by hook or by crook, on a Director, Producer, Author, Artist or Theatre Owner.

Sex-censorship is a vexed and difficult, even dangerous issue, we are wary of any undue Power over our Freedom of Expression. But do we want the airwaves and bookshelves flooded with hard core pornography?
Of course not and rules are made against such activities.
Rules derived not from Religion, but from our human predilection for PRIVATE rather than Public Sex.
Many of us enjoy a bit of titillation, and perhaps we feel that a little salacious stimulation of our personal sex lives is a harmless pleasure?

And seen from this angle it is - a private matter - hence the liberal left's preference for relaxed laws.

However harking back to the animal equivalent, unless one is willing to be watched oneself during the act of sex (one's closest family, Mother, Father, children), then one should not be watching others. So all those wanting to buy pornography should first have to supply a video of themselves having sex. The video should clearly encompass the fact that their parents or children are watching, as occurs in many animal species.

Fair's fair.

That might control this Biological Wrong better than any Censor?

THE VEIL

On this analysis one can see the logic of Mohammed's original idea. Reducing the frequency of women accidentally and accidentally on purpose wafting their pretty little tails in the faces of the group's males, will also reduce the arguments, internal feuds and sexual tensions within the group. Surely this is no worse an idea than our own society awash with soft and not so soft porn, images used to sell everything from toilet cleaner to next week's TV programmes?

Mohammed's requirement, as far as an infidel like myself understands it, included a shawl covering the hair but **leaving the face uncovered and visible.** The full faced veil, where only an eye slit is left or with gauze covering even the eye slit, was not part of his original stipulation.

This is a Biological Issue because it concerns SEX, but interestingly it later crosses over into being a Moral Issue AS WELL.

Firstly there is the proposition by western liberals that men forcing women to dress in a certain way is men MISUSING their social POWER over women and that this is Bullying and so is Morally Wrong - which it is. This is weakened though when some women say it is their decision to dress with a veil hiding the face.

However I want to concentrate on something else - the philosophical core of the full hiding of the face that usually doesn't get a mention.

To hide your face from other people is generally considered IMPOLITE in all human societies, for a very good Moral reason.

Sometimes people do it by leaving their sunglasses on while they speak to you, others hide behind beards, but that's not as bad, because it doesn't hide them as much. It is even done when people hide behind the tinted glass of a car.

When you drive a car you are in charge of a potentially lethal weapon, with which you interface with others. You can tint the glass in every room in your house if you wish, it is your private space.

We like to, no we feel we must, see who we are dealing with, all attempts to disguise this, like youngsters hiding inside hooded coats, leads to a lack of trust, and it is upon trust that human Morality and indeed all human relationships are built.

We see in order to feel comfortable - in order to trust. Our instinct is that those who hide themselves have something to hide, and thus we cannot trust them.

It has been this way since the formation of the first human groups, we must see our fellows, because if we don't we do not trust them. Trust is about openness, we must see so that we can trust, or at least have a basis for trust, after which we get to know people further.

We continue to assess and re-assess, but based upon a revision and re-revision of our first impressions.

Hence those who hide, in whatever way, induce in us some nervousness, a withdrawal, a withholding of trust until we know them better - and if we never know them better then we never trust them. *Impoliteness is a low level form of Bullying, the spurning of another, and it is so slight that we never legislate against it, we frown upon it, and try to discourage it in those around us and in our children - well we used to anyway.*

Therefore in any country that is not 100% Moslem, those who hide their face beneath a veil are being impolite. The rest of the human race find it strange, we cannot help ourselves, because it is in direct contravention of our usual emphasis on openness and transparency equalling trust. All humans have developed this way for the last half million years, we trust those we can see, those we see are open with us - it's just that Moslems have got used to this masking amongst themselves, as a special Religious exception.

This is an aspect of Islam that works badly in non-Moslem countries. It is counter-productive in a multiracial society, because it engenders a lack of trust, when the whole effort of multiculturalism is to build trust between different ethnic and religious groups.

PROSTITUTION
It is neither a Moral nor a Biological Wrong when a prostitute of either sex accepts money for sexual services rendered - as long as both of the parties to this contract enter into it freely. Humans sometimes marry for money, and thus provide sexual services to an older wealthy spouse, but even when we don't, sex is a part of every marriage contract, so much so that church marriages are annulled, a step beyond divorce, for non-consummation.

The mini-contract of prostitution may be distasteful to some, but it is of the same stuff as every human marriage contract - as long as it is freely entered into.
When pimps enslave, traffic and force women into such 'contracts' it is Bullying and thus a Moral Wrong. When societies are so skewed that wealthy men can in effect coerce women from the underclass into 'contracts' they would not otherwise sign up to, it is a misuse of Power and thus a Moral Wrong.

There is no B/A-b Moral objection to legalising prostitution because it is neither a Moral Wrong, nor a Biological Wrong. Legalised prostitution would reduce the Moral abuses endemic in the current situation, and would offer a safer environment for the women involved.

INCEST
Incest between close blood relatives is a Biological Wrong.
We can see this in our observations of the sex lives of many animals beside ourselves, we now know that in evolutionary terms this is because the resulting genetic defects in the offspring frequently lead to their early death. They die and so do not pass on their tendency towards sex-with-blood-relatives, and thus we have an aversion to it.
It is uncommon amongst us and this is just another BIOLOGICAL FACT.

But...
SEX is so strong an urge that it sometimes overrides our Biological aversion. Occasionally a brother and sister do love each other genuinely and also sexually, and provided this arrangement is entered into freely by both parties then it is not a Moral Wrong, but it is still a Biological Wrong, if they have children together.

However most cases of incest are Moral Wrongs IN ADDITION to being Biological Wrongs because there is usually a dominant older partner who coerces, and thus bullies the younger into having sex. All too often this is a trusted father who misuses his special position of trust, MISUSES his POWER.

When the younger 'partner' is a child under the legal age of consent, then the manipulative elder is a paedophile as well as an older bully, a second Moral Wrong, a second layer of Bullying laid onto the first.

We have come to the end of the subjects that overlap with Morality along the northern and eastern shores of Steven's Inland Sea.

In Section 3 we look next at the historical trials and tribulations of the journey Morality has had to make amongst us. In preparation for our return, in Section 4, to the southern shore called the Moral Response, where we will go back, back to - what is Justice? What is doing Right?

3. Where it has been

3.1 Democracy appears

Who is it who first shouts stop bully stop? Who is it that says HOLD IT RIGHT THERE, not so fast, I think this person's protest is legitimate? Who is it in the whole history of the human and pre-human race that first claims the RIGHT not to be bullied?

Who knows for sure?
We can only guess - in an educated way.
It must happen many times of course, many many times. Over and over again until it becomes established as a specifically pre-human trait.

We do know though who the biggest Bully must have been, and still is potentially, because we see him operating all around us.
He is the Group Leader, the Alpha Male. The head of the herd, the leader of the pack, just as we see amongst our primate cousins and in many other animal groups around us to this day. Ha, what am I saying, just as we see in numerous human groups to this day, being the biggest bully is how the position is gained in the first place, and then kept, against all comers.

There must have been squabbles in all the pre-human Hominid groups, just as there are now in chimp and monkey groups, but the biggest and most serious squabbles are challenges for leadership. Often these are nothing other than one bully pitting himself against another bully.
But amongst primates…
Leaders of chimp and monkey groups don't rely totally on throwing their own weight about, they also FORM ALLIANCES.
They form alliances with certain other leading males.

Would-be challengers must themselves have backers, must have allies, or at least potential allies, males at least willing to change sides if they see the way the wind is blowing. No one rules alone, not even bullying chimps.
In Primate Groups no one rules alone - the Alpha Males have their favourites, their inner circle their lieutenants.

We will never see that first stop bully stop, but against this background who might we reasonably suspect of being the first to build on and extend

the edifice of this beginning? Who claims, and claims most vociferously, in return for Duties performed, the Right not to be bullied?
Who, in effect, first claims the RIGHT of FREE SPEECH?

It has to be someone who is not cowed, someone not dominated, or at least not fully dominated. Someone strong enough to have a voice, and yet not quite strong enough to be the dominant and all-powerful Alpha Male. To be strong enough back then he must be male.
He is a male almost-leader, one of the henchmen of the Leader, the Alpha Male. And he is watching, watching, waiting, waiting - for his chance.

What is The Council?
A band of the toughest males, next strongest after the leader - a band of henchmen. They are the heads of pre-human 'households' consisting of younger males, women and children, gathered together in family groups to form a larger group. The Council members are the Leader's loyal lieutenants, his storm troopers in times of disputes with neighbouring groups, his right hand men - his (almost) equals.
And in times of peace…

Amongst human hunter-gatherers extant today there is no Alpha Male, there is no all powerful Chief, instead there is what anthropologists call a Big Man, first amongst (almost) equals. The position of Alpha Male, common in other pack animals, has become instead a temporary appointment, abolished as soon as the crisis of a looming war with a neighbouring group is over, or a time of famine ceases. Signalled as being over by the simple expedient of any (or all) of the senior males IGNORING ORDERS AND COMMANDS given by the Leader.

Ignoring also even statements that sound as though they could be interpreted, or misinterpreted by either party, as being construed as an order, rather than a request. In hunter-gatherer societies every senior male does his own thing and will not be subordinated by or to any other male, except in times of war, or on a hunt, or some other temporary and specific mission.

This is not an imaginary society, not one of Jean-Jacques Rousseau's wet dreams. This is a description of the vast majority of hunter-gatherer societies that have been studied in the last 100 years. It therefore seems highly likely that **it is the Alpha Male's loyal lieutenants who first claim the RIGHT not to be bullied**. Who in effect thereby **claim the RIGHT of FREE SPEECH,** and while doing so **ALTER FOREVER THE STATUS OF THEIR LEADER** - change him from Alpha Male into Big Man.

This surely is one of the great moments in the history of humanity - maybe the greatest moment of all - and all unseen and unrecorded.

This first happens in a simple hunter-gatherer Society (half a million years ago, maybe more, maybe less) and it is this, NOT THE GREEKS, that formed the first Democratic Society. And in its time, this limited first hunter-gatherer 'democracy', ruled EVERY HUMAN ON THIS EARTH.

This temporary-and-limited leader compromise is not achieved by some 'idealised harmony' or 'time of sweet simple innocence' as that clown Rousseau once claimed existed, but instead by a BALANCE OF POWER. Which, as we know with our own modern version, is the only reliable and believable restriction on UNBRIDLED POWER.

When the, accepted on sufferance due to practical necessity for the present Big Man, steps arrogantly one half pace beyond his jurisdiction, he is slapped down so quickly it makes the later invention (by KNOWLEDGE) of supersonic flight seem slower than a crawling snail.
He is simply ignored, humiliated, and most crushing of all, laughed at, by any and every high ranking male whose fierce independence he attempts to usurp in this high handed manner.
By having the temerity, the stupidity, to issue an order beyond his remit.

LAUGHED AT - this is the start of FREEDOM of SPEECH - the first limit upon those who were once unquestioned dictators. LAUGHED AT, how simple, how immediate, and how effective. The first limit on the unbridled Power of the former Alpha Male is the scorn and derision of his almost-equals. Hence perhaps why we are so expert at recognising the slightest nuance of arrogant behaviour in others.

This then truly is the Moral Age, when B/A-b Morality takes its hold on governance. Thus comes the first uniquely Human Society, a time, the first time that a Leader's POWER is limited.

No longer the brutal sexually domineering Alpha Male of earlier primate groups (and of other pack animals too), there are now social limitations placed upon him. It is the first time others dare to speak freely in his presence, more than this, claim the RIGHT to SPEAK FREELY any time they wish - without fear.
The Alpha Male has been demoted, demoted to the Big Man, and we can see him still alive and well, in the few hunter-gatherer societies left in

existence today.

On a hunt if he makes a good kill, his senior males belittle it - the prouder he proclaims his worth, the greater is the tumult of piss taking. Nothing more subtle is used than mercilessly taking the mickey out of any male arrogant enough, big headed enough, to put himself forward as any kind of permanent superior to the other leading males.

It's maybe how and why making fun of someone first originated, a non-violent way of taking someone down a peg or two, and it is how it is done to this day amongst the nomads of the Kalahari desert. It is how it is done to this day in every organised human enterprise, group, club, business or bureaucracy - isn't it?

It is the self-same entity that we credit the Greeks with inventing around 500BC and ourselves in Western Europe with re-inventing over 2000 years later.
It is THE FIRST DEMOCRACY.

Well it turns out that the Greeks were re-inventing it actually, and that it had been in existence for as long as 500,000 years before them. The Greeks were re-inventing democracy for use in an AGRAGARIAN SOCIETY, while we, with modern democracy, have re-re-invented it for INDUSTRIAL SOCIETY.

Thus do we have Democracy - the form of government decreed by Morality. Nay DEMOCRACY is the form of government that is Morality in its governmental form, the only form of government that follows from the premise of its creation. THOU SHALT NOT BULLY - even if, especially if, thou art THE STRONGEST OF THE GROUP. *Even if thou art the richest merchant, the sharpest trader, the most successful farmer, best hunter, toughest warrior, highest ranking priest, smartest lawyer, whoever you are you are also a MEMBER OF THE GROUP.*

For THOU SHALT NOT BULLY, is the whole of the law.

THE GUARDIANS
Those who in the packs of the primates, were the able lieutenants of the dominating leader, helping him maintain control and thereby earning for themselves a share of the feeding and sexual spoils (while also awaiting their chance to one day become top dog themselves), these now have become something else. Have become the first Guardians of the first DEMOCRACIES, democracies without written constitutions, with

nothing more than the Anti-bully instincts of the leading males to rein in the former Alpha Male.

This Demand is the first limitation placed on Dictatorship. The LAWS the Council make include, in fact primarily include, restrictions on their former Alpha Male. These men, for they are always men, men watching, jealous of another's power. Men with clubs, no bows and arrows yet, we're too far back for that, men with stone clubs, these men are the FIRST to claim FREE SPEECH.
Thus they are also the FIRST GUARDIANS of DEMOCRACY.

Of course! Of course they are - jealous men with stone clubs are the first foothold of Democracy.
While in times of war or other crises they will still act as the Big Man's lieutenants and are willing to die for or with him, in normal times they act also as his JAILER.
They hold him in check, limit and proscribe his dominance, make him constantly aware - there is a line - DON'T CROSS IT.

In all the books you will find the Greeks given credit for the founding of Democracy. That is an error, when we look back we see that Democracy originated within simple hunter-gatherer societies.
EUREKA - of course it did! Of course it did, this form of Society is not just the result of Morality, it feeds back into Morality to enhance its progress, to enhance its establishment and permanence amongst us even further.

These watchful jealous men are the first Judiciary, the first Parliament, they are the first foothold of the new phenomenon MORALITY-in-Governmental-form. No, this is to insult them, Parliament, *habeas corpus* and modern legal systems are but pale imitations of these men, are but shadows of their brilliant INSTANTANEOUS EFFECTIVENESS.

A laugh of contempt, and a walking-away-to-sit-down-and-ignore.
A laugh in the face of he who would issue an order beyond his remit.

Would that it were that easy these days.
The humiliation, the utter humiliation, and all done in front of other 'Council-men', who are watching, watching, waiting, waiting.

The Greeks or Western Europe the inventors?
Don't make me laugh, no way - what hubris.

3.2 Democracy assailed

Wait though. If this is true, why do we have to keep re-inventing Democracy? Why do many countries, even modern societies, reject Democracy? Surely if the new Bully/Anti-bully Society actually forms, or helps to form Morality, we should not have to struggle so much to achieve a Moral Society?

THE SECOND COMING OF KNOWLEDGE
About 30,000 years ago KNOWLEDGE achieved a truly great triumph, it learned to take the seeds of certain grasses, plant them, harvest them, and subsequently improve them from harvest to harvest. Also around the same time, in many of the same fertile river valleys of China, the Euphrates, the Tigris and maybe the Nile, KNOWLEDGE figured out how to domesticate animals.

As a result the human world changed, and changed forever. From being wandering nomads it became possible for us to stay in one place, static, for the whole of our lives, bringing the food to us rather than us following it. And this tolled the death knell of the once totally dominant hunter-gatherer form of society, the final throes of whose demise continues to this very day on the edges of the driest deserts, frozen tundra and inside the deepest jungles.

By about 10,000 years ago, largely unseen, reminiscent in this respect of the all consuming challenge of Metaphysics-Religion 60 to 90,000 years earlier, comes a new challenge to MORALITY - this time from POWER. POWER RE-SURGENT and enjoying its own second coming, though it never really went away, on the back of this great upsurge in Knowledge.

Being stationary allows the build up of food stocks, the hoarding of grain reserves and animal products. Next comes ownership of a larger spread of farmland than your neighbour, by dint of either hard work, better farming abilities, or both plus a streak of ruthlessness. And thus is WEALTH built up, wealth, a concept unknown in hunter-gatherer society.

Wealth makes Big Men into separated Leaders again, they become Tribal Chieftains who OWN more, then most, and eventually ALL, of the land within their domain.
The Alpha Male returns, after maybe as long as half a million years in remission he's back, this time as a King, and now with POWER beyond his wildest dreams.

TRIBAL CHIEFS

From a hunter-gatherer society that has no concept of land OWNERSHIP, there develop Chiefs and Kings who tax their neighbours, neighbours who have now become their subjects. Tax them to offset the expense of their households, the expense of administering their leadership duties you understand. Their many responsibilities, their retinues, their standing armies, required to protect THEIR PEOPLE, and to protect THEIR LAND.

In the new AGRAGARIAN SOCIETY, brought into being by inventions due to KNOWLEDGE, the Alpha Male reasserts himself in a flash, as those who are both successful farmers and also successful TRADERS build up stores of goods, stores of WEALTH. And Wealth is POWER. And so the new Alpha's neighbours become his subjects, his underlings, peasants, farmers, and herdsmen. While the Chief, and the lieutenants who swear loyally to support him, become a special warrior class, a caste soon to become The Army, who vaunt themselves above those others, their former neighbours, those without - 'aristocratic blood'.
THE ALPHA MALE IS BACK.

And not just back, but back with a vengeance, back with knobs on, back *fortissimo* - oh boy he's back, he's back all right, back like he's never been away, back like he's never been seen before.

Back with weapons, wealth, land and property, new forms of POWER, he even has subordinates now. Subordinates to do his dirty work for him - the torturing for example. There's always some torturing required - it has to be done, to keep things organised and controlled, to keeps people 'on side' a regrettable practical necessity, *pour encourager les autres*.
   Of course the dictators never really went away. You can see its seed ... in every school playground, in every family, where brutal father, nagging mother or spoilt brat rules the roost. In bosses bullying their employees, in the committee bullying the individual, in bullying businesses not paying their debts, while those they owe the money to go bankrupt. In every bribed public official, in every policeman who misuses the trust he holds, in every secret policeman, in every torturer, every rapist, murderer and thief. In cruel dictators starving, terrorising and imprisoning those they are supposed to be protecting.

Until to following generations, the origins of Democracy are lost, lost along with the origins of Morality. And now the double insult, the irony of all ironies, these people who steal the Moral concept Democracy from the rest of us, convince both us and themselves that kingship, monarchy, aristocracy, dictatorship, call it what you will, is the right and ONLY WAY to administer human society. They steal our birthright from us and convince us, and themselves - which is why they're so convincing, that we never had it in the first place!

More yet, worse yet, they even steal our Metaphysics from us too, they use Religion to bolster their claim of the Divine Right of Kings. They steal our Religion from us, steal our crutch and comforter, our inspiration when all we have is it and nothing else, they steal it from us and feed it back to us as A STATE SPONSORED **MASS RELIGION** - to bolster their claim to POWER, to bolster their POWER over us.

And thus ever since we have been engaged upon wrestling back our Right (not to be bullied) from POWER - from the Alpha Male with all his modern trappings. And this is where we find ourselves, having now established even bigger and more complex Industrial as well as Agrarian Societies. Some of us still struggle to establish working democracies in the face of naked Power, and even those of us who have managed this now grapple with the shear size and stratification of modern society.

Complication 5:
The huge societies we have created confuse and hide the core of these issues more than ever.
They result in a further Moral Complication, the LOSS OF IMMEDIACY - wherein persons from a higher stratum of society judge those from a lower. Are the people who live in this country really a single society of 60 million, or are they actually many fragmented sub-societies? Can we really expect a moral system that evolved amongst groups of 60 or so individuals to be equally successful when applied to 60 million?

Such Societies can never match the direct simplicity of the inventors of Democracy - the Council armed with stone clubs, who laughed in the face of the Dictator. Nothing we have come up with, separating the Executive from the Legislature, separating both from the Judiciary and the Police, every single modern democratic artifice just doesn't measure up, each is a clumsy ad hoc makeshift device for controlling POWER, a device for laughing in the face of the Dictator.

He-who-laughs-in-the-face-of-the-Dictator is the first democrat, the first Guardian of the New Order that soon we humans call Morality. He has the courage to laugh directly in the face of Power AND DEFY IT because he knows that when he correctly smells a whiff of arrogant presumption, and challenges it, his fellow 'Councillors' will back him, with their stone clubs.

Notice he doesn't defy Power as previous challengers to the Alpha Male have done, so that he can then be Boss himself instead. He defies it ON BEHALF OF OTHERS, on behalf of the whole Group.

He does it out of arrogance, out of pride, this male egoist who-will-not-be-dominated even does it to some extent out of jealousy.

But this is neither here nor there, because nonetheless he is Anti-bully glaring back - glaring long and hard at the Bully.

These democracies we are so proud of are but poor substitutes for the Council-men, with their scornful laughter and their opportunistic piss taking, and their antennae always turning, always primed to spot arrogance, primed to spot those who are trying it on. Primed to spot any bid for POWER, any bid for POWER-beyond-a-limited-remit, and primed to slap it down in an instant.

The time of the stone clubs was the golden age of Democracy.

All lost 10,000 years ago, when more and more of us became farmers instead of hunter-gatherers, and the Alpha Male came back, disguised as the Tribal Chieftain, the King, the Emperor, the father, of HIS PEOPLE.

3.3 Golden Age

The time of the stone clubs was the golden age of Democracy. Well, let's say a Golden Age. Certain aspects were not so golden, but in some respects this truly was its Golden Age.

Yet even here, and it is important to remind ourselves of this again, even here in the age of its conception, it was NEVER PERFECT - which tells us a lot.

The golden age of instant MORAL retribution and response was not so golden for the women and children of the troop. Because, judging also by our studies of extant hunter-gatherer groups, Democracy stopped at the front door of each individual household. Here the Balance of Power worked out between competing males stops, and within each household a dictator rules, the same dictator who outside, will not be subordinate to any other, the human male rules - his wife, or wives, and children. *Which confirms for us, if confirmation were needed, that it is A BALANCE OF POWER that keeps these males in check, not some lost innocence.*

As we see in humans alive around us today, no doubt some of these household dictators were more benevolent than others - but HE RULES,

rules because it is his ancient primate inclination. And that which holds him in check elsewhere, the force of other males with similar inclinations, is not present in his family group.

To some extent his own finer feelings, by which we mean his more Moral behaviour, developed in order to be able to get along with others, holds him in check. As does a strong wife, but as we also know to this day, there's nothing quite like a bit of external pressure, just to be sure.

And the realisation that even here, in the hunter-gatherer societies that for half a million years bred and nurtured Morality, the GOLDEN AGE WAS NOT 'PURE', opens our eyes a little further.

We can see exactly what Morality is…
It is and has always been a RELATIVE SCALE of values, and NEVER AN ABSOLOUTE SCALE.
All our judgements in any situation are about who is bullying whom, who is the bully, who is the unjustified bully, who is the worst bully, who is being a bully but was picked on themselves by another bully, but always firstly - is there any bullying going on here at all?

MORALITY IS RELATIVE.
People who twitter on and use the term Moral Relativity as a sarcastic putdown, as a criticism of whatever they're arguing against, are talking rubbish - they're incorrect. Moral Relativity is the only Morality there is. There is no Absolute Morality.

And so the search, be it by atheists, agnostics or religious metaphysicians, for an Absolute is as illusory as the search for the philosopher's stone. Fool's gold - an ILLUSION.

Morality is not some golden ideal handed down from 'on high', handed down from God knows where by God knows who. It is a sliding scale for the identification, condemnation and control of the many-headed-beast-of-Power-Misused.

It is simply a constant battle against selfishness, our own selfishness, locked inside every last one of us - our 'selfish' evolutionary biological survival mechanism in fact. Our 'selfish' tendency to look as though we are fully committed to the principle of "all for one and one for all", while really being a little more concerned with "all for one" - ME.
Personally I find that recognising Morality's lack of perfection explains a lot of what I see around me, and removes the frustration, the pressure

that we are "getting it all wrong", when things are less than perfect in our Society. Recognising what Morality is allows us to do our utmost to make the best of a bad job, rather than give way to those with 'perfect' solutions, that if only we follow them will bring utopia.

Dear me, that sounds awfully preachy, it must be Tom talking. Yes let's blame Tom, he was the hippie - peace and love will change the world man. Personally speaking the world can go hang, let it save itself, let the young save it, they've got the energy.

How could it be ABSOLUTE?
How could it possibly ever be an ABSOLUTE?
We see before us at this time Morality born and fully formed, yet it has not even begun to grapple with the problems caused by trying to apply it between Groups...

3.4 Racial Prejudice

As soon as Groups start to exchange artefacts and keep in contact with those who marry outside the Group, comes the problem 'my new trading partner, or my new brother-in-law has been injured by my brother. Who should I support?'
My brother, even when he's clearly in the wrong? Or this outsider?"

In other words, do I support my fellow-group-members because they are racially the same as me, against the wogs next door, even when my racial group is behaving badly, by bullying those in the neighbouring group. Or should I do the RIGHT thing, the MORAL thing, and support the one who is being bullied, whether he's of my (racial) Group or not?
Shall I cast my VOTE against the BULLY because he's in the WRONG?
Against the Bully, no matter whether he's of my group or not?

Complication 6:

This is the 'moment' that **Morality jumped, from being within Group to applying between Groups as well**. We're still struggling with it now.

Actions against, or inflammatory speeches inciting hatred towards, or violence based upon, racial differences are a legitimate limitation on Free Speech because to be PREJUDICED is, according to the dictionary, to be biased and unjust.

Biased against what, prejudiced and unjust according to what standard?
We have seen the standard, it is the one and only commonly shared Moral code:

Thou shalt judge thy fellows by Bully/Anti-bully, BY THE FAIRNESS
OF THEIR ACTIONS, NOT BY THE COLOUR OF THEIR SKIN.

The phrase defines itself.
Once these funny foreigners were OUTSIDE our GROUP, were potential
enemies in the constant uneasy tension between neighbouring groups, but
now the Group has been extended - to ALL HUMANITY.

RACIAL PREJUDICE IS THE 'LEFT OVER' BARRIER THAT ONCE
DIVIDED THE **ISOLATED GROUPS** WITHIN WHICH MORALITY
FIRST DEVELOPED. The first crossing of this boundary was massive,
was probably the second biggest step in the whole history of Morality.

At one time the boundary between neighbouring Groups was a place
where Morality ended - there was no compunction, NO DUTY, to treat
those outside your Group FAIRLY.
They were BEYOND.
At this time the whole purpose of The Group...
The purpose of Our Group, was for protection against fast fierce wild
animals, and also against **other humans in other Groups**, trying to steal
OUR food, OUR hunting ground, OUR territory in which we hunt and
collect the fruits, seeds, nuts and berries we need - to SURVIVE.

Morality is for helping OUR GROUP to SURVIVE, those outside are just
that, OUTSIDE, beyond the call of Morality.

We are in fact still at that boundary, some of us hanker after the old days,
crave a return to the other side of that boundary. In some ways they were
simpler days I suppose, but things are actually going the other way - the
world is smaller than it has ever been. And so Morality stands against
those who make statements based upon, "my racial or religious group first
- right or wrong".

COMRADES-IN-ARMS
Where do we find today, in our huge societies, that feeling of 'The Group'
and the special strength and pleasure we have in the feeling of belonging,
of unquestioning loyalty to the Group above all else. Teenage gang
culture obviously, young men adrift, not finding a fit or even perhaps any
employment in the huge society around them drift into Gangs, into
primate Groups, and find there a fit, a niche and a special ancient pleasure
not found or felt elsewhere.

They even create what we might call fake wars, with nearby rival gangs, so that they can re-visit the way of life long gone in which loyalty to the Group was everything. Treat all inside the Group fairly and with full respect, but for those outside, the same within-Group rules need not apply.

Is it any wonder soldiers can never recapture the intense camaraderie of human beings together under fire when they leave the army, and that many search for something to replace it all their lives, without success? This camaraderie is the stuff of our birth as humans, a call back to that first grassy plain and the Group that stood upon it. Thou shalt trust thy comrade with thy life. This is the revolutionary law of the later primates, the law that blew away millions upon millions of years of evolution based upon self, self, self, any left self again, this is the stuff that made us what we are.

Made us human, part selfish animal, part selfless friend.

Men who have fought together in wartime often remark on the special bond formed between them and their comrades in arms, such friendships formed during the Second World War are still alive thirty, forty, fifty and sixty years on. That bond is formed by what people went through together, formed by each one not wanting to let his fellows down, not wanting to lose the respect of his comrades under fire. Not wanting to be anything other than a fully paid up member of the team, and feeling Good (Right) about it, feeling Good about being respected. Feeling Good about being Human.

Not feeling good about the horrible hell of war, of times spent in terror under fire, surely the feeling Good can only come from the special form of comradeship, loyalty-to-the-Group. Feeling Good about being willing to give up everything including life itself for the man next to you, and knowing that he feels the same way towards you.

This situation truly is a special time, a pure, almost experimental case; to the front is the enemy, to the rear are the generals some of whom these men respect many of whom they don't. To the rear also are the second stringers, engineers, logistical troops, headquarters staff, artillery and backup, some of whom they respect, but many they don't. And even further to the rear are their families, the homes, towns, relatives, children and lovers they have left behind, some of whom they love and some of whom they don't.

Their whole lives are concentrated for the months or years of the war, into this special pack - their front line comrades. For a short time there are no divided loyalties, no claims from wives against the tyranny of mother-in-laws, no squabbling children crying about who's picking on them, no boss to work so hard to please while colleagues please themselves and seem to get away with it.

For now there is a pack of comrades, comrades who will give their lives for you and you for them and nothing ever feels so Good again. Because this is the same all male troop that leaves its village in the dark before the dawn half a million years ago - to hunt. To face huge fast animals with crude weapons, improved verbal communications, increased cunning from their special brains, and … TRUST in each other.

They go to drive part of a herd over a cliff, to trap and kill, to spear the slowest, to stand together by the kill and drive off other predators, carrion feeders, vultures, thieves of every kind, including other Groups of hominids, by sticking close together. By knowledge, by planning yes of course, but these are of only theoretical use if you cannot TRUST those next to you.

Trust them not to let you down.

Trust that they, like you, desire the mutual respect of others more than they desire life itself. Trust that they will give their life for yours.

Behold the birth place of Morality in modern garb - no wonder that they never find the like again, in oh so complicated Civvy Street. Civilian life, that messy intermeshing clash of conflicting overlapping loyalties that is the modern world.

Notice the difference between the Soldier and the Policeman.

THE POLICEMAN'S DILEMMA

A policeman is surrounded by colleagues who he knows and sympathises with, and who know and understand him and his life. Like the soldier he hopes and believes he can count on them in a crisis, count on them when his life is on the line.

Then one day he is asked to 'shop' one of them and he can't bring himself to do it.

"I don't care what you say he's done, there was a time, a day, a situation where he saved my life, he stuck, he didn't run. He was with me that day and so I'm with him now - until we both lie rotting in the grave."

But the police are not like soldiers.

They live on Civvy Street, surrounded 24/7 by Moral dilemmas. Thus they can't be afforded the luxury of 'my comrade right or wrong' no matter how much, as humans gathered together in a GROUP, they gravitate that way. The policeman and woman's job is to protect members of society from being bullied, including bullied by one of their own colleagues. Yet the bureaucracy of the law is often faceless, modern societies are almost theoretical concepts compared to those Groups of our beginnings. Whereas one's colleague has a face, a face one hopes one can rely on, a face one hopes one can trust.

There is a similarity here with bribery…
   Like racial prejudice, it is designed to circumvent the basis of Morality we call being FAIR, or judging on merit. We are racially prejudiced when we judge people by the colour of their skin instead of on whether or not they are honest and trustworthy in their dealings with us. Similarly with a bribe, an illicit payment is made to skew our judgement unfairly, against someone who is trustworthy, and in favour of the bribe giver.
   Hence why bribery is immoral – because it is manipulation of another.

3.5 Complication upon Complication

Complication upon complication, and more to come. See how the complications mount up, is it any wonder that international relations between countries have become so complicated? All from the same basis, whether it's me arguing with the bloke next door or disputes and agreements between countries and continents.

We start by struggling to decide who is bullying whom, then the Council re-define Morality as communal rules. Next Metaphysics-Religion, in its effort to improve human conduct, claim Gods not humans have produced these rules.
Now we have seen the hidden complication of Biological Wrongs and the problem of racial prejudice between groups.

We can see that the size of The Group increases dramatically when we change from being nomadic hunter-gatherers to large scale static farming and later industrial size societies. Wherein soon there come to be Tribal Chiefs and their henchmen who rule and dictate, often re-writing the laws to suit themselves, including even the 'laws' of Mass Religion.
Thus there come to be groups within groups: a landowner class or caste, an army class, a merchant class, a tradesmen class, a peasant class, a slave labour class and thus gang versus gang, group after group and group

within group. To which somehow we must apply feelings of what's right and wrong that first coalesced inside us when we still lived in hundred strong groups with no sub-groups half a million years or so ago.

To keep this clear in our heads we can turn the list of the Six Threads into a timetable that includes these Complications. *They are numbered in the order Steven has written about them, which is not the order they have occurred in our history. In particular, numbers 4 and 6 come before Metaphysics-Religion.*

1. The PLEASURE/PAIN Mechanism: 2,000 to 3,000 million years ago.
2. POWER: complex cell forms start to 'eat' other single cell forms.
3. SEX: a new way of procreation by mixing genetic material from two individuals.
A gap in time…

4. KNOWLEDGE: when creatures first begin to learn and pass on what they've learned to others within their Group.
Another gap…

Complication 4 - Obscenity is a Biological Wrong, later mistaken by us all, but particularly by Metaphysics-Religion for a Moral Wrong.

5. MORALITY: 0.5 million years ago.
Complication 1 - Who is bullying whom?
Complication 2 - The Council re-define Morality by publicly stating certain dos and don'ts.
Complication 6 - Racial Prejudice between members of distinct (and often rival) Groups.

6. METAPHYSICS-RELIGION: 0.1 million (100,000) years ago.
Complication 3 - The Medicine Man takes the Council's redefinition and explains where it 'really' comes from.

The Second Coming of KNOWLEDGE to humans: farming 30,000 years ago.

Thus as a result of remaining static, the Second Coming of POWER: Tribal Chiefs and Kings: 10,000 years ago.

Complication 5 - The Group becomes dominated by a ruling caste, and is now so large that loyalty to it is stretched to breaking point, as it splits into sub-groups within the whole. As a result those on the political left see that the upper castes have no Right to judge the lower, because these upper classes are manipulating society to their advantage, while those on the political right wing attack the left who they accuse of being too soft on lower caste criminals.

Complication 5 is clearly the last historically, in fact it is increasing in complexity as we speak on an almost daily basis, as populations get larger and emigration runs rampant worldwide.

Hence the terrible complication when we see one of these tribal, religious or racial sub-groups who happen to be in power in a country scourging, raping, murdering and ethnically cleansing another sub-group. We wring our hands and try to do something because as neutrals we hate to see Bullying, and at the same time are told not to interfere - inside another country is another country's business - claim some. When really it is often the two Groups, who are the real separate 'countries' that just happen to live inside the same bureaucratic boundary lines drawn by someone somewhere years ago upon a map.

Thus does one tribal group inside one of these giant countries with many sub-groups visit genocide upon another sub-group. Then afterwards, after the horse has bolted we try to shut the stable door, by having a long drawn out trial in the International Criminal Court for one or two of hundreds involved in genocide. Which though it doesn't bring the dead back, is an improvement on the world before such trials - when murder went unchallenged - because 'inside another country is another country's business'.

Complication 7 - Nature-Bully or Nurture-Bully?
We're coming to this now, in a way it's part of **Complication 1**, but it's time to re-visit it in the light of the history above and the decision still to come. Is the Death Penalty ever Justice, even for Peter Barrow, one who tortures-unto-death?

The Second Coming of METAPHYSICS-RELIGION: the world Mass Religions - from about 3,000 years ago.
The Second coming of Democracy: the 'Ancient' Greeks - 2,500 years ago.
The Third Coming of KNOWLEDGE: the Scientific and the Industrial Revolutions - from 300 years ago.
The Third Coming of Democracy: the Open Society and the struggle to establish it over the last three hundred years, in the wake of the Industrial and Technological Revolutions.

It's happened without us noticing, **Complication 5** has I mean, the effect upon Morality of the incredible size of modern society. It's a big factor, a big Complication on top of all the others, one of the many gathered as Morality has wended its way amongst us. Until nowadays our loyalties stretch out in all directions, like ripples on a pond ... getting less and less as they are located further and further away from the centre. Modern Civvy Street is so confusing, so confusing for us all, if only we could get back to our comrades in that Group.

The Group that leaves its jungle home and living now upon the open grassland ... takes a turn down a different evolutionary road.

4. Is it Justice? Is it Doing Right

4.1 Limited Forgiveness

S *teven gave away his copyright to prolong Tom's life, but for all we know he has this written out somewhere, waiting to correct us wherever we've gone wrong. I hope so, because that means I'll be hearing from him again. We are back now to his question: is it Justice to kill Peter Barrow?*

Clearly this has implications for the issue of the Death Penalty, so we'll address this here briefly as well, even though that isn't the main thrust of his story. The Death Penalty is a thing people argue about, and if moral philosophy doesn't directly address things people argue about, then what in God's name is its purpose.

If you accept the principle of assisting someone who is terminally ill to put themselves out of their misery, then you also accept that there are fates for humans that are worse than death. We can now come back to those four categories of moral-response: overkill, an eye for an eye and limited or unlimited forgiveness.

The operation of a criminal justice system hinges around whether to be tough or soft, whether to forgive or hit back. Let's have a look at this, because it throws light on the origins and boundaries of Morality and how its dilemmas grew in us, really they are Moral-response dilemmas.

Over the course of the last fifty years, some computer people have come up with a simulation of human behaviour that shows how co-operation developed in those funny, awkward, slow, weak creatures with small teeth - our ancestors. In its original form it is called The Prisoner's Dilemma, a part of Game Theory, but it could just as well be called The Moral Dilemma, and this is how selflessness, or rather occasional-acts-of-selflessness, derived itself via the evolutionary process, from its ancient ancestor - SELFISHNESS.

FORGIVENESS/CO-OPERATION
Let's call the choices we have out in the wild as either to bully or co-operate (rather than forgive).
We see it in the wolf pack gathered around the carcass once the hunt has succeeded - should I observe the pecking order, or fight for a higher place within it?

Let's set up a seemingly simple computer game in which each player has that choice in each round of the game, to bully or to co-operate with every other player they interface with, amongst the various players in the game.

Surely to always bully is a winning strategy?
Well one time it was, half a million years ago, and maybe earlier, before the primates came to play.

If you bully and your opponent gives way (co-operates), then you take all you want, to eat, to have sex with, and your opponent, especially when times are hard, gets nothing, you get five points and your opponent gets zero, hooray, you've won!

Not so fast, this game is different to any other game you've ever played - it never ends.

It is the ENDLESS GAME, it goes on forever, the game that doesn't end even after you're dead, via your genes, passed on to others like yourself it continues, continues, continues on and on and on and on.

In the next round of the game, in the wild at the next hunt a few days later, your opponent last time is still on the team, he's hungry and he knows your face, he's a primate and he has a good memory for faces.
This time he doesn't co-operate.
Just as you attempt to bully him he bullies-you-back.

In fact you fight each other almost to exhaustion. Now neither of you eat much, catch much, because of your injuries, because of your mutual opposition.
Let's give you one point each, you ate a little more than he who lost last time, but at the price of injury, exhaustion, pain, wasted time while others of the pack ate well, or worse, neighbouring packs ate well.

Next time, at the next round of the game, you both decide to go for co-operation, partly because you've now tried out each other's strength and realise you're almost equal, and partly because you're still too hungry from the last round to waste time fighting again. Your co-operation is successful, it is a good hunt, you both eat well, you have meat for the kids, and for the females, everybody has a good time.

You didn't get as much as when you bullied, and got away with it, but you're still well ahead of the game. Well ahead of the time you fought yourselves to a standstill, you both get three points, which while not as good as five, is a damn sight better that one or zero.

Of course quite often your opponent, or should we say playing partner, looks a bit weaker than you, a bit less sure of himself. So you push him a bit, bully him a bit, try to get four or five points, by hustling him, by crowding him, putting him in his place.

Sometimes you get away with it, and sometimes you don't, but the scary thing is that sometimes it's seven, eight, nine, or even more rounds later before you find out you haven't got away with it.

These creatures have long memories, these creatures wait and wait, and then suddenly, they bully-from-behind, just when you thought you'd got them where you wanted them. They stab you in the back, or simply hang back at the vital moment on the next hunt, when they're positioned next to you. *They do a Serpico on you.*

Back in Computer World, more impressive than even this, is that when you play this game by computer simulation, with real people partnered together, devising permutations of strategies, between the two extremes of always co-operate and always bully; in the same way that the game has been played through the thousands of years of our evolution, and the results fed back into our genes, as those who play best survive longer and procreate more, the thing is, that RECIPROCITY ALWAYS WINS MOST POINTS overall.

RECIPROCITY - DO AS YOU WOULD BE DONE TO.

That is, a friendly strategy of co-operation on the first round, followed by doing on the next round whatever one's partner/opponent did on the last, always stacks up more points than any other behaviour pattern.

Except, when the game gets really subtle, when by feeding back this information to all the players and running the whole thing again for another hundred rounds, a strategy of one more forgiveness / co-operation stacks up even more points.

That is instead of tit for tat, tit for two tats.

One extra round of forgiveness before you strike back.

Behold the mechanism that creates the mechanism ... that creates ... MORALITY.

LIMITED FORGIVENESS is the building block, is the dawn of the concept 'too harsh', of the idea 'over reaction', of the human feeling 'that is Bullying'. Thus it is the **means by which the B/A-b response was built,** which in turn is the means by which MORALITY was BUILT. The means by which co-operation was built from harsh competitiveness - wolves never forgive *(not quite true)*.

Witness the gene that says - first be friendly, if hit forgive, if hit again, hit back or sometimes forgive just one more time.

Witness how it appears and is nurtured by the evolutionary process. As it works its way amongst this species learning to co-operate like no other individual mammal ever has, in a way new upon this earth half a million to a million years ago.

Over generations bullying amasses fewer survival points than it did in former times, and the human Moral Gene, the gene for ACTS-OF-SELFLESSNESS takes pride of place. Or should we say carves itself a niche, for make no mistake, that other selfish dog is yapping at its heels - the dog that is the selfish-bully won't just fade away.

For wolves and many others, the pecking order - wherein the strongest rules - is sacrosanct, inviolable, the rule of rules. The rule which shapes their social world, the rule which is their whole social order, the rule which governs every single one of their relationships. Not so with us…

'Here take this food, take this water, come closer to the fire. Sit here by me, let me protect you, it is my PLEASURE so to do.'
And now we come FULL CIRCLE.

For it is LIMITED-FORGIVENESS, that first DECISION to hold back a moment, (and he or she who responds by taking it, not as weakness, but as a sign of magnanimity, a sign of friendship, co-operation, TRUST), that builds a different SOCIAL ORDER.

That holding back, by both parties, takes us down a road that leads further and further away from the wolf pack mentality, a road that soon…
Produces NEUTRALS, who DECIDE, this is Right, that is Wrong, who decide when asked: yes, you have been treated badly, too roughly, unfairly, UNJUSTLY. You have been BULLIED, when there was no need for such a HARSH RESPONSE, no need to … OVER REACT, no need to … BULLY.

Behold the last piece in our puzzle is the first piece also.

4.2 The Biology of Forgiveness

I *know - that was my first reaction too, Morality isn't a game. The first time I came across Game Theory it seemed ridiculous to me that it could throw light on the subject of human Morality. So I understand how one's first reaction is to be doubtful, but this computer simulation does model, and therefore represent, generations of human behaviour using real humans.*

To forgive a specific low number of times is a limit of Morality, is one of its boundaries, not necessarily its only boundary, but a definite demarcation line it seems. So many of us, including Steven and myself, but not Tom, find it difficult to forgive when people hurt us, yet others, often under the influence of their Religion find it in them to forgive many times. Like Steven I too am interested in finding which of these different classes of people and their responses are 'correct' and which are 'incorrect' in different situations.

Tit for two tats may seem to you rather a sudden end stop to Morality, but when you look around do people really forgive each other more than that? Isn't giving people another chance (just one) about as far as our forbearance usually goes? Maybe, or maybe not, either way we can reasonably stretch the concept of Limited-forgiveness to three or four tats - at least.

Another reason Steven was looking for a limit to forgiveness is his awareness of an argument in the world of Evolutionary Biology, it revolves around whether we can ever be altruistic. No it revolves around how biologists say we cannot ever be altruistic if evolution is correct. Yet we appear to be so - sometimes.

Appear is the important word.

There's a mix up here that biologists have got us into, and that Mr. Morris wants to get us out of, let's take a look.

All actions within the context of Evolution are undertaken via the mechanism of Pleasure. Hunger is unpleasant and it is therefore a pleasure to eat. Sex is a pleasure and so we survive to procreate. If we do not eat first others will eat and we will starve to death, if we do not have sex first others will take our potential partner and we will not propagate our lineage.

Therefore all creatures are selfish, because all of us pursue our own pleasure, and the whole of Evolution is based on this. Fair enough, but Biologists use the term 'altruism' to mean acts whereby a sacrifice is made that **benefits another's capability and opportunity to breed,** while reducing our own. But human altruism is much subtler than that.

We humans have evolved via hunting and gathering Groups such that we take great pleasure (sometimes) in helping others, and it is this feeling of pleasure that we seek. Mostly our pleasures are selfish, but look what happens when a creature also SOMETIMES is able to gain pleasure from helping others.

'Here, come sit by me, lay down your burden and let me bind that wound. Listen, there's a storm coming, a herd of wild beasts coming, let me help you with that.'

By this act I think of myself as generous and unselfish, AND OTHERS SEE ME AS THIS TOO, and they love and TRUST me for it. But in order for me to believe this even myself (and thereby claim this special Pleasure), let alone convince others, I must perform acts that are genuinely at a cost to me - and ideally they must be public acts that others notice or (more subtly) hear about. The fact that I gain the secret, and in some cases almost unconscious, PLEASURE of thinking of myself as a genuinely unselfish person, and am therefore 'really' a hidden egoist, not an altruist, is neither here nor there as regards the way others are treated by me.

Thus whether our helping hand is given from 'biologically altruistic motives', or because being altruistic gives us selfish pleasure (the warm feeling of 'I'm being a Generous and Right person'), the act is still done at some cost to ourselves, and is a benefit (though not necessarily a reproductive benefit) to the recipient. Because if it costs us nothing in the world external to ourselves, no money, no effort, no time, then we cannot even convince ourselves, let alone anyone else.
We cannot feel the wonderful internal special human pleasure that says to us inside our own heads 'you are a generous, giving, unselfish person'. You are GOOD (though as ever we really mean you are RIGHT).

In Kant's terms - you are doing your Duty, you are behaving Morally because you make a sacrifice on behalf of others, and others in the Group see you make it. They see you can be 'counted on' in a crisis, they see you give to others freely, and so, they RECIPROCATE. You get something back in addition to the pleasure of feeling good about yourself, you receive help from others when you need it - because they see you are unselfish, and therefore worthy of their friendship and their trust.

Out in the real world as long as it is a genuine sacrifice on our part, which confers a benefit on the recipient, then it matters not to that recipient that

ALSO there is a secret pleasure in it for us. I-help-others-free-of-charge and thus I am fully human, even maybe a great human, is like so many of our pleasures, a private pleasure.

And this is all there is to the great biological confusion over altruism, as with so many philosophical problems, it is due to the misuse of a word. The Biologists use altruism ONLY AND SOLEY IN THE CONTEXT OF REPRODUCTIVE SUCCESS, whereas the rest of us use it far more widely, meaning any time we give freely to others.

Our generosity gives us a certain kind of private inner Pleasure, and so, for all it matters, we probably are, Biologically speaking, 'really' always acting Selfishly. This then complies with evolutionary expectations: creatures are always seeking after their own Pleasure, which nine times out of ten equals their own survival (as this generous act of ours may do, when in the future others in the Group reciprocate).

'One day you'll guard my back without me even knowing it...'
If they think of me as a 'genuine altruist', they will come to no harm by it, because, no matter my secret pleasures I am the genuine article in my acts towards others.

Whereas were they to mistakenly think some selfish bastard (who gets far more pleasure from his own gratification than he does from acts of generosity) was an altruist, and place reliance on him, that could be a mistake from which they would suffer hurt, even death - when they are let down at some critical time. They will not be let down by me, despite, no wait, they will not be let down by me, because of, my secret Pleasure.

They will not be let down by me because to act selfishly would negate the view of myself that I have, would negate the core of my ego, my view of self.

And we all have egos, even the Buddha. Don't be fooled by that Buddhist stuff about peeling off the layers of self via meditative practice, the only people without egos are the glorious dead. For sure we should be engaged all our lives upon controlling our egos more and more, via Buddhism or whatever, but not destroying our egos very existence.

Let's get these terms correct, to be without any ego is to be dead, or dead inside - the concept of being 'ego-less' is just a convenient term that is neater than the term ego-under-control, and so we fall into the trap of using it. An ego-under-control is our true goal, never no-ego, not ego-

less, I've tried it, and it's my favourite Religion, but that doesn't mean that there's no such thing as Buddhist claptrap.

For scientific research into Evolution this split between evolutionary-altruism and everyday-altruism is important, and I suggest that the use of these two separate terms is long overdue, instead of the present situation where biologists use the same word 'altruism' for both. Meanwhile for you and I, our judgement of which amongst our acquaintances tend to be selfless (everyday-altruists) and which are selfish egoists is enough.

Is everything.

Of course egoists often try to masquerade as altruists, but the sniffing out of such people is a different day to day matter from the question of whether or not there is in the final analysis such a thing as 'genuine altruism', by which is meant evolutionary-altruism. Game Theory is much more than a game, the game is an experiment, an attempt to see how real human beings react to the series of mini moral dilemmas they are presented with as they interface with those around them.

How they really react mark you, not how they talk, not how they say they will react, talk is cheap. This is how they do react. Tit for two tats, tit for three tats at a stretch, and when the behaviour of others starts to push us beyond this we begin to suspect ... here is an egoist - one of the selfish - taking the piss. Taking advantage of my easy-going nature.

You're still a bit doubtful - how about a little example illustrating that Biologists can often miss out the bit that's important to the rest of us, in their concentration on testing Evolutionary Theory?

You will have heard wildlife commentators say something along the lines of: "the new male lion kills the existing cubs so that the female will come into heat again, and the cubs that then result from their union will propagate his line not her former mates". No doubt this statement is biologically correct, but there's a mistake hidden in it. A step they miss out, unintentionally gloss over, call it what you will, but it's an important step, when dealing with everyday matters, and it's an omission repeated for many creatures.

The male lion does not kill the cubs so that he can propagate his lineage, he kills the cubs so that he can have the PLEASURE of sex with his new partner.

If we were talking about humans, his new girl would have sex with him even though she had young children from a previous marriage, because human females have no in heat season. With many other creatures though she will not be sexually receptive until the young are either weaned, which takes time, or off the breast due to 'sudden infant death syndrome'. The new male lion kills the cubs for sexual gratification, for the Pleasure of having sex with her. This is his immediate, indeed is only purpose, and it just 'happens' that due to the biological construction of life upon this planet, this also procreates his lineage.

4.3 The Biology of Hypocrisy

R asputin is reputed to have once said that there is only one sin: hypocrisy. We have learned that the word sin is an inappropriate Moral term, but we ought to take seriously the proposition that there is only one immorality - hypocrisy.

We hate hypocrites because they manipulate us into behaving one way, while they do the opposite themselves - they fool us, they betray us. Many times in our disputes and moral arguments we accuse others of hypocrisy. So let's have a look at the concept of Hypocrisy, what is it and who does it.

Of course people are hypocrites, from what we have been saying they are bound to be - to an extent, and as with altruism, it is the 'to an extent' that is important. They are bound to be because we each have a personal battle to keep our hypocrisy down to the bare minimum. A few Saints manage to banish it altogether, the rest of us never really do. And the reason for this is simple - we are set upon a road to hypocrisy from the moment of our birth. Born like all life forms fighting for life, fighting for breath, for food, for water, for air, for sufficient attention and care from our parents so that our little selves will survive.
But…
Humans survive by TEAMWORK, and to work as a team you must be inclined and willing to SHARE.

All creatures must think **primarily** of themselves in order to survive - but human creatures must, AT THE SAME TIME think of OTHERS. So that the whole group, the whole team also survives - because without the team you're dead. Here, in this dichotomy lies the elusive hidden core of so many moral dilemmas. those dilemmas we set out to investigate so long ago are partly hidden by our need to sometimes be selfish, in order to survive.
First yourself, but ALMOST equally THE TEAM.

This ALMOST is the seedbed of HYPOCRISY, the seedbed of those dilemmas where we are not impartial but involved, a protagonist. We tend to talk more morally than we behave, and tend to spot this habit more in others than in ourselves, and then we get angry and call them hypocrites. Sometimes with justification, when those we call hypocrites, are incapable of doing anything more than pay the vaguest lip service to the team.

Those we call hypocrites are the ones who talk, loudly and a lot, as though they put the team equal first, but really they always put themselves and their needs and desires way way out front. When we see through them, we despise them for it, and we call them hypocrites.
They say one thing, but do another.
They say SHARE, but do SELF.

The important thing to realise is that we all do this to some extent. Biology has made us that way, all creatures look to themselves first, in order to survive. Our ever present Moral Dilemma on becoming team players is to keep this 'to some extent' down to a minimum.

We are all hypocrites, to some extent...
We all behave less Morally (more selfishly) than we should, WHILE AT THE SAME TIME ESPOUSING THE IMPORTANCE OF MORALITY. But some do this far more than others, some are ALWAYS, always secretly looking after themselves while trying to kid the rest of us they are making personal sacrifices for the team. They are liars, they are the special kind of liar who live a lie about their own motives, and they are the ones we specifically brand Hypocrites.

SAINTS
Those we call Saints, don't just share, and don't ever share grudgingly. They give what little they have WITH PLEASURE TO OTHERS of the group. They give beyond the call of duty, the call of 'think of other team members ALMOST as much as you think of yourself'. They think of others at least equally and often - oh no wonder they receive our incredulous admiration, even our adoration, of course they do, often they think of others MORE THAN THEY THINK OF THEMSELVES.

They fly in the face of the whole of the Natural World, the whole world of 'look after yourself at all costs', survive, survive, survive come what may, survive.
THEY TURN NATURE ON ITS HEAD.

They are MORALITY at its STRONGEST, no they are beyond Morality. These are the ones who contemplate, believe in and are actually capable of GRANTING UNLIMITED-FORGIVENESS.

And note please that they are not necessarily Religious, though they often are, and certainly not of one Religion only.

On one level they are fools. Idiots to be taken advantage of. Call them what you will, they do not care. Call them what you like, they don't give a damn - they are SAINTS. They care only to give, give, give, more and more - they take our breath away.
Names?
What do they care what names we puny nothings call them?

They are those who live in poverty, and give their lives up working for the poor - and enjoy it. They are those who stay behind to help when others flee, and go first to the places where only human misery survives.

They are the opposite of the leach, the bully, the hypocrite who thinks only of self, self, self, the freeloader who thinks it's clever to 'get one over' on others. They are Saints, they are those who spirit Jews away from Nazis, no matter what the personal risk. They spirit Jews away from Nazis while the rest of us look the other way.

They are the Unselfish, and not just occasionally unselfish like the rest of us aspire to be, but the TOTALLY UNSELFISH, THE SELFLESS, they are the opposite of Evil, the opposite of the ultra-selfish.
And they are very few in number.
   The idea that we are all hypocrites can be a bit hard to swallow, but I see it now as Steven says…

You will understand as well as I do that these Saints come in different shapes and sizes, from different cultures and from many different countries. It will be as clear to you as it is to me that they are pink, white, yellow, black and brown, every colour and from every religion under the sun.
And as a result…
You will see as well as I do, that Morality cannot be a question of which Religion you are, but instead must be about how you practise the one you happen to be.
Are you Bully, or are you Anti-bully?
EVIL or GOOD?
EVIL or RIGHT? as we should, more correctly ask.

You will see as well as I do, that Morality cannot be a question of which Holy Book you happen to take your Metaphysical-Religious inspiration from, but instead must be about HOW YOU BEHAVE TOWARDS OTHERS.

Selfish or Unselfish?

It will stand out to you now like the nose on Mohammed's face, or like the Buddha's fat belly.

Morality is inherent in our ANTI-BULLY STANCE.

And is utterly independent of any one Religion.

Take for example when two sets of Religious adherents clash or dispute over something or other, a little country for example, each claiming their religious literature confirms they are in the Moral Right. In such a situation right and wrong, justice and injustice can only be judged by the one impartial Moral standard we all share - by Bully/Anti-bully, not by what it says or doesn't say in the traditional Holy Book belonging to one side or the other.

If you think the Israelis are the bullies you side with the Palestinians, and if you think it's the other way round you take Israel's side. We neutrals don't judge by Holy Books, we judge by Bully/Anti-bully - every time, every single time, without exception.

Many of the protagonists involved in this particular issue seem to want it to be a Religious war. But Right and Wrong in the international sphere is decided in exactly the same way as in every other situation - who is the bully here and who the victim?

Then I'll cast my vote.

If this weren't the case would each side really spend as much effort as they do to convince the world's media of the atrocities (gross bullying) committed by the other side?

Morality is independent of any one Religion, and so can be, and already is, used as a meeting place and common ground for discussion and mutual understanding.

The best way to rescue MORALITY from the extremists and lunatics on either side (on every side) is to call it what it is, not to cling to a Belief that one Religion and one alone can define Morality.

Call it instead what it has been from its birth.

A DETESTATION OF BULLYING.

ANGER at those we see Bullying others of the troop, a troop that's now got so much bigger. ANGER at those we see DOING WRONG.

There is only one moral absolute - to BULLY is WRONG.

And the absolute certainty that sits alongside it is that we are all capable of it, we are all potential hypocrites.

4.4 Nature and Nurture

*W*hen I was young, a teenager growing up I mean, I believed a saying from that old film 'Boy's Town', that there is no such thing as a bad boy. Tom believed it too, though I'm not so sure that Steven ever did, I still believe it now, but ... back then I also believed, as logically I should, that Nurture was more influential in bringing up a child than was that child's original Nature-at-birth.

I believed that environment and my own efforts could mould and change what the mix of genes had presented me with at birth. Oh there were many things I planned to do, many aspects of myself I planned to tackle. Many many things I was far from satisfied with about myself that I would change, and change forever.

Some people tell us every wrong is a response to a previous wrong e.g. a delinquent son has previously been bullied by his father, or Capitalist Society has bullied him by turning him into a member of the underclass. In other words every bully has been bullied, every perpetrator of a crime has also been a victim of some kind, and therefore it is society who is to blame, not individuals.

If they go too far in that direction others call them the loony left, but as we've seen they have a point, regarding upper castes condemning lower castes having first made sure of and sure of maintaining their position of privilege - hypocrisy or what? To avoid mix-ups let's be a little more precise, right wing or better still rough-justice-right will mean inclined towards an eye for an eye.

Left wing will mean inclined to forgive many times, even though I've known quite a few Communists who were far from forgiving types. So we should call this response the forgiving-left, to distinguish it from those old fashioned left wingers, such as my mining forebears who were, like Ruth, strictly Old Testament, not inclined to forgive transgressors at all.

There maybe a lot of truth in the position that 'every bully has been bullied', but is it the whole story? The opposing rough-justice-right wing view would say the proposition that 'every bully has been bullied' is beloved of do-gooders, and is idealistic nonsense. That on the contrary there are some amongst us who would always have been prone to bully others, no matter what.

NATURE or NURTURE?
This every-bully-is-a-bullied hypothesis would only be true if Nurture (the way we're brought up) was totally responsible for our attitudes and

actions in the world, without any contribution whatsoever from our Nature (the mix of our genes at birth). And though the Nature versus Nurture issue is by no means settled, it seems clear that neither one is solely and wholly responsible for the development of our personalities.

Evolutionary Biologists say that at bottom we are all selfish, and our trawl through the struggle Morality has had and still has with Power-Misused suggests they're correct. Therefore Morality has arisen as a response to the Misuse of Power, and thus Bullying must be inherent to some extent in our genes.

As we look around at our fellows, are not some more selfish than others? Are not some more inclined to be assertive and aggressive with others? Are not some, by dint of their Nature from a young age, more inclined to BULLY than others? And so to gain perspective, Nature: this having an instinctive inclination to bully at birth, or at least a tendency to be aggressive, should be set alongside Nurture: people bullying because they themselves have been bullied, every-bully-is-a-bullied.

Surely those of us born of aggressive parents (Nature) are more inclined to be aggressive, more inclined to bully? If we are also born into a tough neighbourhood, in tough economic times, (Nurture) we may become even more of a bully to survive, a double dose, Nature-bully plus Nurture-bully.

Historically and still today: the **element born in us** is that which we designate **IMMORAL** (Nature-bully).
Let's clarify this, all humans consciously or unconsciously designate Nature-bully IMMORAL, and Nurture-bully as being, with extenuating circumstances, maybe understandable.

What we humans call IMMORAL BEHAVIOUR IS THE AMOUNT OF BLAME we apportion to others for THEIR TENDENCY TOWARDS UNPROVOKED BULLYING.
And therefore in particular THE BULLYING THEY-WERE-BORN-WITH VIA THEIR INHERITED GENES, since clearly this is ALWAYS UNPROVOKED, because it is THE WAY THEY WERE MADE.

When courts ask for 'reports' before sentencing, they are trying to assess the circumstances (Nurture) which have contributed to the defendant doing whatever it was he did. All of us in fact ask constantly for reports on those around us (gossip), so as to be FAIR in our assessment of their actions towards us. 'To be FAIR', is to judge how much circumstances have contributed to an act, and how much is due to unprovoked bullying. We blame them much less or sometimes not at all for their tendency to Bully caused-by-their-environment, but far more for their innate, inborn tendency to bully.

And like it or not, this is how we make our MORAL JUDGEMENTS upon others.

If the judge asks for psychological or psychiatric reports as well, then in addition there is a query over sanity, and in particular whether or not this person understands the difference between Right and Wrong. Provided the accused does know Right from Wrong, the next consideration is how much his circumstances (acts of bullying committed against him) should be taken into account in deciding sentence, in deciding how Bad/Wrong he is.

By an accident of birth some of our number are born with an inclination to be aggressive in order to survive in this world, and this aggression, when directed WITHOUT PROVOCATION towards one's fellow group members, we call Bullying. These we designate anti-social, or when taken to further extremes IMMORAL, WRONG, EVIL.

We tend to avoid social contact with such people as we know that sooner or later they will hurt us, because they are selfish-plus-aggressive and cannot be trusted to be fair towards others. They will unhesitatingly push us down as they pull themselves up in what they consider to be the rough and tumble of life.

Incidentally these are not by any means always 'street bullies', there are wealthy and respectable 'Capitalists' whom it suits to believe that life is a jungle, conveniently forgetting that the whole purpose of us humans banding together in the first place was to combat that jungle. What they do now is to import that jungle back inside the human group, back into the very place created by early humans to offer some protection from its pain and rigour. And think when they say life is "the survival of the fittest" that they are telling us a great truth! They tell us this having received support and a leg up from the Group they now so roundly condemn as weak. Now that's hypocrisy.

A young boy of 15 comes out from the big city slums one night with a couple of older men, to break into a house out beyond the edge of town. A wealthy country house, where he gets himself shot and killed by the householder.

Is he Nature-bully or Nurture-bully?

Some of us side with the owner against the boy, who wouldn't have been shot if he hadn't gone stealing. And some of us side with the 15 year old lad who never got a chance in life, a Nurture-Bully shot by a Nature-Bully, shot by a privileged fat cat. Shot by a member of the upper caste, with his big house, his cars, his wealth, his dogs and his guns.

The forgiving-left side with the boy and the rough-justice-right with the homeowner, but all of us, left wing right wing and those in between, make our decision based upon whom we see as the bully and whom we see as the bullied. And it makes it easier for us if we can believe that those we designate as the bully are nature-bullies, otherwise the water gets very muddy, the decisions get very tough.
It is then that the left and right call those of us in the middle indecisive. They call us pusillanimous vacillating cream puffs, and we return the compliment by calling them bigots.

We judge less harshly when they treat us roughly those we consider have been badly bullied themselves. We are more inclined to forgive those we think have 'never had a chance in life' due to their social circumstances.

It is the ones born with an inclination to bully, by which we mean to use their in-born aggressive streak unfairly against members of the Group, those who give free rein to aggression without control, that we condemn. It is these we dislike, these we reserve our anger for, these we are pleased to see get what they deserve in books, plays and films, as well as in real life.

Sometimes it is argued that "they cannot help it" or "it is their nature", and this is true, but it doesn't take us very far. The fact is that it is these traits, the in-born tendency to Bully, that humans judge and have always judged to be immoral, to be WRONG. Whether it is the hard fisted, hard drinking husband, the murderer, the thief, the lying adulterer, the cruel torturer or the merciless dictator, all are condemned.

All are judged immoral, irrespective of whether they can 'help it' or not.

That some of us are born inclined to be aggressive is just a fact of evolution. And remember that these are looking out mainly, usually only, for themselves, themselves, themselves … themselves alone. The rest of us, having formed co-operative groups, have to try and protect ourselves against freeloaders.

We must protect ourselves against the ravages of individuals born so selfish that they treat others of the Group as though there is no group. No Group which offers a protective umbrella.

These Bullies-from-birth are the violators, and whether they can 'help it' or not is immaterial, it is still this behaviour which we designate IMMORAL.

In fact it is because they can't help it that they stand condemned.

WE DON'T CARE if they can't help it.

If you happen to be born an aggressive bully and claim therefore you can't help it, SOCIETY DOESN'T CARE - it never has.

It's in your genes?
It's in your genes - and so you say that you can't help it.
Again, Society STILL DOESN'T CARE.
We don't care, NOR SHOULD WE - you have been born with a tendency to look-after-yourself-at-the-expense-of-others.

The first Societies were created to share the burdens of life and thereby all would have a better life. The rest of us have to keep an eye on you, because you have a tendency to take more than your FAIR SHARE (you were born that way and can change it only a little), you have an in-born tendency TO BULLY.
We have to accept the way you are, and make allowance in our dealings with you.

Is it really such tough luck to be born a Bully?
Generally most of them seem to get by pretty well, the Nature-Bullies the BULLIES-FROM-BIRTH, get by in this world pretty well I think.

But with Societies now so large, some say that in practise there is no longer a Group that offers a protective umbrella. Society now looks after its higher castes and does little or nothing for its under employed and unemployed lower castes. Except condemn them when they 'step out of line', they're quick enough and hypocritical enough to do that. And on this basis the forgiving-left forgives them.

Another difficulty in our huge modern societies is that of telling which of the many people we don't know intimately are Bullies-due-to-circumstances and which are Bullies-from-birth. The bigger the Society the greater the difficulty of having to decide: "has another bully made this one who's bullying me the way she is?" or, "has he been like this from birth, born with an aggressive gene". And with neither credible 'reports' nor village gossip available the forgiving-left tends to give them the benefit of the doubt - and forgives these cases also.

Either way what we humans call immoral behaviour is the amount of blame we apportion to others for their tendency towards **unprovoked bullying**, and in particular therefore the bullying they-were-born-with via their inherited genes.

Most bullies-from-birth get by pretty well in life…
They do so very often at the expense of the rest of us.
Let's not be too soft on them - let's not get too misty eyed.

4.5 Unlimited Forgiveness

Now we can see that: we are all guilty of hypocrisy, except a few Saints, and we must be aware of this when we accuse others. We see: Nature and Nurture, wherever you stand on it 50/50, 75/25 or 90/10 whichever way round, is a live issue - because it is how we judge, it is part of why we instinctively condemn or forgive, the actions of others. And we see Limited Forgiveness is the basic building block of Morality, it is the fundamental response we used and still use in all our relationships with others.

LIMITED FORGIVENESS is the SEED behind the gradual flowering of the ANTI-BULLY SOCIETY.

Via it we can see that every social relationship is like a mini-democracy, it is a balance of power. There is a tendency for one to dominate, be it as slight as impoliteness, or the public snubbing of another, thereby forcing the other party to formulate A RESPONSE, albeit a fairly gentle one in many cases.
We can see how that which starts with those who make petty spiteful comments in our social group, ends at the opposite extreme, with those who take us into a dark dungeon in the dead of night, and at the behest of a powerful dictator apply electrodes to our genitalia. It is a question of degree regarding the same phenomenon, and thus we can also see a little more clearly which of those around us are manipulating us, as opposed to those we can trust.

Forgiveness between individuals in the pack is the mechanism by which we come to be able to pass JUDGEMENTS in the first place.

The members of the troop learn forgiveness, and as those who master this art best (knowing when to forgive and when to slap down) flourish more than others, they breed progeny more than others. Breed offspring inclined also to forgive a time or two before they strike, and thus the PERFORM-ACTS-OF-SELFLESSNESS gene is fixed amongst those creatures we now know as *Homo sapiens*.

They learn to stand in judgement. This troop member, he's OK, he's tough, but fair, he never shirks his DUTIES, or hangs back when danger threatens - he can be TRUSTED. But this other one hurts those who're weaker than the rest, eats all he can, is lazy and hangs back in times of trouble - he is forgiven less.

Because if you forgive him he'll only take advantage rather than repay you like for like. I DO NOT TRUST HIM. He's quick, oh so quick to claim his Rights, but slow so very slow to undertake his DUTIES. The contribution to the Group that earns for him his Right-not-to-be-bullied.

And as they learn to judge during the squabbles round the carcass, they form the early bonds of loyalty, to those less selfish members of the group. The selfish are now marginalised, they become less successful in keeping mates and procreating. Strength alone is not enough - it has begun - the laws of evolution do the rest.

But …
Not once in all this time do humans ever think to grant UNLIMITED Forgiveness, even to fellow group members. No one until the Buddha and 'soon after him' another, Jesus Christ, ever thinks to go so far as to advocate UNLIMITED FORGIVENESS.

   Except a parent, a parent does, and a lover, but not average Group members, it is between typical members of the tribe Steven means.

   Although the fact that we do grant Unlimited Forgiveness to certain categories of our fellows shows that it is there inside us as we should expect from Evolutionary Theory, which in turn suggests to me that it is part of Morality, rather than something other than Morality.

We have seen that in strict moral parlance there is no UNLIMITED FORGIVENESS, forgive once, maybe twice, certainly not more than thrice, THIS IS MORALITY - this is how it was made, the evolutionary result of co-operation amongst partially competitive individuals. In a world in which we tend to act for biologically selfish reasons, it could not have developed other than by the gradual iterative process that Game Theory illustrates.

Unlimited Forgiveness is still in transit - whether Jesus and the Buddha present it to us, or modern psychologists speaking in terms of soaking up the insults, barbs and pain, until the one dishing it out begins to heal themselves.

But do they always heal themselves?

Does this new technique always work?

And if it does work sometimes, but not others, what are the limitations of its successful use?

There seems to have been a limit to Morality during its derivation, a boundary. After you have forgiven someone one, two or three times at most, and decide to keep on forgiving rather than lashing out, then you have gone towards extended-Morality.

You have gone beyond its derivation, beyond its roots ... and before we can come to a conclusion as to whether it is justice to kill Peter Barrow, as well as self-defence, we must acknowledge this 'place beyond'.

We are using the terms forgiving-left and rough-justice-right, and while these are crude labels, they are far more accurate than talking in terms of Muslims, Christians, Hindus, Atheists. Because there are plenty of patient forgiving-left wing Muslims, Jews and Hindus and plenty of wrathful rough-justice-right wing Christians and Atheists, and *vice versa*.

Every Religion, indeed every human institution has its left and right wings, its forgiving and retributive wings, its doves and hawks.

Why - because our Bully/Anti-bully feelings stretch across all human Religions and Institutions, because B/A-b is the institution behind all our institutions.

I don't want to knock the contribution Religious Belief can make - do we see anyone other than those with such Beliefs, or similar beliefs, being capable of Unlimited Forgiveness?

Here though is something I've pondered over.

"You have heard that it was said, An eye for an eye and a tooth for a tooth. But I say to you, Do not resist one who is evil. But if anyone strikes you on the right cheek, turn to him the other also."

I remember looking that up in Matthew 5, expecting to see the turning of the cheek, and expecting to be able to say: he turns the other cheek once, maybe twice, three, four, five, six, seven or more times, maybe 77 times ... but not forever. But it doesn't say that, it says "you have heard that it was said; Do not resist one who is evil". Full stop.

Can that be right?
Are those words really what he said?

Is that, "Do not resist one who is evil" even a correct translation?
Elsewhere, in Matthew 18, he does say; I do not say to you 7 times, but 77 times.
That's a limit, it's a lot of forgiveness, a hell of a lot, it's a mountain of perseverance and patience, but it's a limit too - and that is what makes the big difference between these two seemingly similar statements.

'Do not resist one who is evil', is endless Unlimited Forgiveness, whereas 'I do not say to you 7 times, but 77 times', is I suppose an extension of Limited Forgiveness, albeit an incredible extension.

There is a problem with unlimited compared to 7 times. If everyone knows your forgiveness is endless, then they can take it as a given, they can in effect do what they like to you, knowing you will always forgive. Whereas with 3, 4, 5, 6 or 7 times, your forgiveness has to be earned, the offender has to put in some effort to make things Right, even if it's only a promise to do better, to try harder next time.
Otherwise what?
We should grant our forgiveness, as a matter of course? As a given, give our answer before the question has been put? Before the circumstances are known? Pacifism for example can be seen as giving your answer in advance for all time; that you'll never respond with violence no matter what is done to you.
   Don't give your answer, make them guess, make them wait, make them miss the point. Don't allow them to take you for granted. Forgiveness is a sliding scale. Should we really grant it in the same degree to someone we don't really trust, as we would to a close friend or lover?
   "Master Confucius, should one forgive ones enemies?"
   "How then will one treat one's friends?" came the old one's answer.

But at its best what does Unlimited Forgiveness do?
It sends a message of Trust, it says I forgive you because I believe you are a person of worth, and your bad behaviour can be reformed, with a little help from me, but mainly … by your own efforts. Now, go and … live up to my expectations, which I'm sure you will.

Earlier I asked if Unlimited Forgiveness does work sometimes but not others, then what are its limitations?
Here is one, A MASSIVE MODERN STATE compared to a small group of HUNTER-GATHERERS. Even if Unlimited Forgiveness works well

amongst a tightly knit band of 50, 100 or even a couple of hundred people, is it as effective in huge societies where we don't know everyone so well?

When their Big Man (or Big Woman) is in close touch with the whole group he or she commands respect from Bullies along with everyone else, his/her opinion of them is important, without it they will have a reduced status within the group. When the Big Man or Woman frowns everyone reacts, even bullies take note, they want to impress, and are willing to an extent to modify their behaviour to do so.

No one wants to gain the respect of a faceless State, and so one means of coercing bullies into improved conduct is lost, or at least curtailed in effectiveness. When the Big Man slaps you down it's personal, when he forgives you more than once, or twice, or again and again, it means something - it means he believes in your potential, believes in YOU.

"I forgive you because I think you will make something of yourself, will when you grow older you young pup, be a worthwhile member of our Group. I forgive you, not because I forgive everyone as a matter of course, but because I think you are worth my time and trouble - what do you say to me, how do you respond, what do you have to say? Speak sonny boy speak, respond daughter respond."

This is lost in a large scale Society with a faceless justice system.
Is Unlimited-DEPERSONALISED-Forgiveness effective?
Is it as effective as the Unlimited-Personalised-Forgiveness of those we respect?

One would think not - the anonymity of the State helps to stop personal vendettas between rival males and their families, it has the advantage of administering justice in a neutral disinterested way. As is common though, something is also lost in return for this gain, the forbearance of the Big Man/Woman, the forgiveness and trust of those-whose-respect-is-sought. In a large faceless state Unlimited Forgiveness can be taken instead as a sign of weakness, a sign of state sponsored stupidity.

Forgiveness, and especially Unlimited Forgiveness, is tied into personal relationships. A faceless State doesn't grant Unlimited Forgiveness, often all that is granted by a faceless State is a let-off, to be laughed at and taken advantage of.

Let's admit that this is one of the disadvantages of large scale societies to set against the many advantages.

Steven always said that philosophy can't answer everything, can't solve all 'the world's problems', whereas Tom, bless him, thought the opposite - if you found the Truth it would 'fix human society' once and for all. How innocent we were, well Tom and I anyway.

4.6 Death Row

We've come a long way, through the whole of moral history, all in order to properly address the great Socratic question, "what is Justice, what is Doing Right". What can we say now?

Firstly that it is surprising that we do as well as we do, as well as some of us do anyway. We manage to just about organise massive societies of 20, 50, 60, 100, 200 million and more relying upon an instinct bred into us by the evolutionary process when we lived in small groups of 20, 50 100 or 200 souls at most.

Where else are we? Well personally, at the start of my 30 year search for the core of human Morality I believed that humans were 90% what their Nurture, their environment and upbringing, made them. Whereas now I've switched to the other way round and believe that 90% of what we are is set at birth within our genes. Oh you can completely and utterly mess a human being up by treating them badly as a child, but you can't achieve the reverse using some brilliant nurturing technique.

I wouldn't dream of boring you with the banal minutiae of my life, especially when compared to Steven's, that forced a change of mind upon me, my little trials and tribulations. That's just the way it's gone with me, you'll have your own ideas and opinions, and I'm not trying to change them, I have no cause, no axe to grind. It's Tom that has the axe not me, and he's too weak now to even read the final versions of the books we've laboured on together.

Next I want to use those poor unforgiven souls on death row to illustrate something: appropriate, inappropriate and 'not inappropriate' Responses to Bullying. Often of course we call this MORAL RESPONSE by the name punishment.

Is punishment aversion therapy for the offender? A warning to others? Or a comfort to the one offended against? Or all three - and if all three, how weighted? I think it is probably all three and the weighting and success of the policy varies with different situations, but I'm not going to digress, it's a book in itself, and one I'm not qualified to write. We are focussed instead on digging into every last corner of the phenomenon we humans call Morality.

Any punishment is 'not inappropriate' that does not break the Bully/Anti-bully rule, **tit for two tats,** and that is ALSO **not disproportionate to the offending act.**

The term 'not inappropriate' is used because we are entitled, some would say even obligated, to forgive more times than twice, at our discretion.

But provided we forgive twice, and when we do Respond we do so on the basis of Reciprocity, an eye for an eye, then our responding, or punishing, actions are 'not appropriate'.

Tit for two tats may be appropriate, but for many of us tit for three tats is more appropriate, or some may want to forgive 7 or 77 times and would consider this appropriate. So because we differ, we can only ever say 'not inappropriate' with any certainty, to say appropriate is to give no latitude for additional forgiveness.

He is going over old ground, I know, but only for the sake of clarity, and because the subject is so important.

When a thief grabs your handbag on the street it is not inappropriate for you and your friend to chase after him, catch him and dish out a little physical chastisement to encourage him to hand your bag back. This giving him a thick ear is clearly not forgiveness, but neither is it INAPPROPRIATE, if you are only as rough with him as he was at the theft.

Whereas if you and your friend were to corner him and savagely beat him to within an inch of his life in an alley, disfiguring and crippling him for life, you yourselves would have become bullies, by punishing him INAPPROPRIATELY.

It's simple stuff that we're all familiar with - the concept of sufficient or reasonable force.

The MISUSE of CAPITAL PUNISHMENT
Before we take the step of looking at whether there really are instances where Capital Punishment may be Morally 'not inappropriate' we must recognise the vile and grossly unjust ways in which the Death Penalty is TOTALLY INAPPROPRIATE. These are instances that B/A-b Morality designates as Bullying-by-the-State, and which are therefore immoral, as follows.

1. Firstly - crimes for anything other than murder.
At one time sheep stealing was a hanging offence, but that is BULLYING BY THE STATE because it is clearly nothing like an eye for an eye. In China citizens can and frequently do receive the death penalty for such things as tax evasion.

Like our own sheep stealing era, this policy is immoral and is Bullying by the State.

Some other countries also use the death penalty for crimes other than murder, and all such cases are clearly immoral. The Death Penalty can only ever be even considered for repeated murders, or for torture-unto-death, for all other lesser crimes it is clearly bullying by the State, and therefore INAPPROPRIATE.

On the principle of tit for two tats, only the second murder someone commits (after a warning prison sentence for the first), is an appropriate crime for Moral consideration of the death penalty.

2. Secondly - the social circumstances of those who commit the murder.

One could argue that the Death Penalty is always unjust in large scale stratified societies because of the privileges of the upper castes, and the lack of such of the lowest stratum, the underclass without jobs or education. Thus we often see that the person condemned, 'never had a chance in life'.

For example there is something immoral afoot if a country consists of say 10% black and 90% white people, and yet its death row consists of 90% blacks and only 10% whites. When a country, such as the USA, consists of such glaring disparities between certain sections of the population, it is clearly not sufficient to use the simple rule of "two strikes and you're out". Or rather this rule should only be used for the wealthy and privileged white sections of that society.

What it boils down to is that in small societies there are no in-built injustices, but in large ones we see vast inequalities, some of which are themselves Bullying by the State, let alone following it up with State sanctioned murder.

Those are the two categories under which there can be no moral question but that the DEATH PENALTY IS INAPPROPRIATE. And there is a strong forgiving-left argument that says this covers virtually every case in the book, so much so that it is simpler and more effective to campaign against the Death Penalty worldwide, than to split hairs over a handful of cases.

Well yes, but that's practicalities not philosophy, and it is philosophy we're here to discuss, not what may or may not be politically most effective, we are striving to grasp things as they truly are.

3. Thirdly - the issue of whether the death penalty is ever appropriate.
Is it really morally sufficient to use tit for two tats as our guide when the punishment is so final? The problem of Finality includes of course the many cases where the wrong person is convicted, with the Death Penalty there is no going back.

The rough-justice-right counter argument is that imprisoned murderers are constantly coming up for review, and they then seem to receive a lot of publicity and sympathy, things not afforded to their victims. The case is raked over again and again, and all the relatives of the victim can do is listen to never ending cringe making crap about the Rights of merciless torturing murderers.

Both sides have a point.
However that's enough about arguments regarding the Death Penalty, we are here for something else. We are here to look behind these arguments, at some befuddled thinking that lurks there.
   An offshoot of which follows here.
   It is sometimes said that the Death Penalty is the violation of a human right, the right to life, we have already seen that this is philosophically absurd.
   Every human right a society grants is 'earned' by the individual member of society concerned fulfilling a certain duty, the DUTY-NOT-TO-BULLY-OTHERS of that same society. As soon as any individual breaks this contract, by murdering, there is then no automatic 'right' that somehow absolves the murderer from the Death Penalty.
   There may well be mitigating circumstances, some as listed above, that do absolve the murderer, but the asinine repetition, as if by rote, of a clause of Human Rights legislation is to demean our intelligence and the importance of many aspects of that legislation.
   For God's sake - think before you speak.

One might think that just about covers everything, sadly it does not, let's remind ourselves of the special circumstance surrounding Peter Barrow's life, and death.

We now approach the circumstance for which the Death Penalty may be considered appropriate, or rather NOT INAPPROPRIATE, the case of TORTURE-UNTO-DEATH. We approach it not to advocate the Death Penalty, but instead to pick a hole in something people say, something that is ... a philosophical mistake.

THE 'STATE NO BETTER THAN' ARGUMENT

As philosophers we have no truck with vague phrases like "the Death Penalty is not what a civilised society does" or "the Death Penalty makes the State no better than the murderer". Our immediate response to such phrases is, what do you actually mean by that?

And if now, after our long discussion, the answer comes "because to do so is Bullying by the State", that's fine, we accept it - when it is Bullying by the State.

But, is it true that to execute those who commit endless-torture, those who torture-unto-death, makes the State no better than the offender? State inflicted murder, as some people argue?

No better than this grossest of offenders?

What - no better than he who tortures-unto-death, and particularly he who does this many times?

That can't be correct?

It's just not logical.

If the State inflicts on one of these purveyors of endless-torture a quick pain free death, isn't it difficult to argue that the State is now as bad as he is? They have let him off with a speedy end - how many of us will pray for the same before we're done?

Once you define a civilised society as one that doesn't bully its own citizens, fine, now we're getting somewhere. Where we are getting is that on this definition it is clearly nonsense to say that a society is uncivilised if it grants a quick death to a Dictator, such as Saddam Hussein, who has had thousands murdered and hundreds tortured-unto-death.

Hitler had 5 to 10 million killed, including the mechanised horror of the Holocaust, Stalin upwards of 10 million and Mao more than 20 million human beings, starved, tortured and murdered. Are we really saying that the mark of a civilised society is that it would not condemn such monsters to death - are we really saying that it would be uncivilised and unjust to execute these mass murderers?

And are we really saying that these three were, and the others like them are, all Nurture-bullies? All Bullies created 100% by they-themselves-being-Bullied? Are we saying that 'society' is entirely to blame for creating these ultra-selfish brutal maniacs?

Or are they in fact, and those like them too, actually in large part Bullies-from-birth? Alpha Males gone exponential, given an opening in a vast mega-society and gone utterly, totally, completely berserk.

Is each Alpha Male and Alpha Female, as they scramble to the position of top dog, driven by 'something society has done to them' or by something born inside them at their birth?

That is all - you can ban the Death Penalty worldwide if you wish. As long as when you do so you don't attempt to back it up by the claim that judicial killing, for those who have TORTURED-UNTO-DEATH makes one no better than the perpetrator. Ban it because it is misused so often by all kinds of murderous regimes, that the only way to stop them is to ban it too for those few cases where it is actually morally 'not inappropriate'.

It's fine by me to get rid of the Death Penalty, but I'm not going to tell a lie to do it - because philosophy is a search for Truth.

And all any of us are entitled to is JUSTICE.
Give every man his due.

4.7 Mutual Understanding

T *hat's it, he finishes there. Peter Barrow, as described to me by Steven was a monster. So fair enough, I concur, killing him was Justice. I can't really recall Steven's views on the Death Penalty back when we were in our teens, I think he was like me, a 'don't know', Tom I remember was vehemently against it.*

For many people who use 'the Death Penalty is uncivilised' argument, the issue is to halt it at all costs worldwide, and I understand that, but it's not philosophy. I see instead an argument that people use in error and, like Steven I can't stand that.

To say something is uncivilised is meaningless unless you define what you mean by civilised. Steven and I are not going to use the Death Penalty, except in the extenuating circumstance of torture-unto-death, but why not keep it there. Why give your answer before the question has been put? Before the crime has been committed, why tell them that they're safe? Why not make them wait? Don't give them absolution before we know the ferocity, the brutality, the extent of their crimes.

Personally I have another agenda that comes out of this, something more important than philosophical purity.

Isn't it obvious from the Moral difficulties of Capital Punishment, how similar we humans are one to the other? Is it really so hard for us lefties to understand the rough-justice-right wing rage at those of us they see as too forgiving to murderers. To them society seems to go to the opposite extreme, and frequently let murderers back onto our streets to murder again.

We can use B/A-b Morality to understand each other better, when we admit that there are a handful of brutal cases involving torture-unto-death that probably do deserve the Death Penalty. Isn't that healthier than carrying on in denial? Isn't that more honest than the philosophical oversimplification of 'civilised societies don't do that'?

The Death Penalty is not like Abortion, where once you agree the principle the question is answered for all time, every murder is different. Is the battered wife who turns on her tormentor the same as Adolf Hitler? Let's take a vote, the Jews can all have a hundred votes each while the rest of us get one, let's dispel this illusion of certainty.

Right wing rage should not be summarily dismissed, there is something important in it, and if we don't acknowledge it, then they are able to make a claim (however false) for the moral high ground. They are able to make this claim because the liberal principles, and indeed the liberals, who run the Open Society on secular Bully/Anti-bully lines, are failing to have the courage of their convictions.

The Open secular Society is based upon B/A-b Morality and upon it alone and we should be living up to its tenets. To fail to do so, and instead to pay woolly minded lip service to a soft floppy version of our own values, is to give 'fundamentalists' of various kinds an excuse, give them an opportunity, give them ammunition. When we ignore and belittle their genuine feelings of Right and Wrong, we help bolster the enemy camp.

We can understand right wing rage and also give it nowhere to go when we annihilate the vague sanctimonious overtones, the smokescreen of 'civilised societies don't do that'. Let's NAIL THE LIE that, in its shrill unthinking voice results in philosophical confusion.

'Civilised Societies don't do that' is meaningless nonsense.

Whereas 'Civilised Societies shouldn't Bully members of their own Society' (including those born and trapped in the underclass), is clear and meaningful. And by accepting this we throw light on Morality instead of confusion, and by accepting this we concede that sometimes it is NOT INAPPROPRIATE for civilised societies to execute those murderers who have tortured-endlessly before they killed and killed again.

It is JUSTICE.

NOT INAPPROPRIATE - even though we may choose to forgive, and not invoke it.

4.8 Whoo-Whoo, Whoo-Whoo

I see clearly the wonderful power that Unlimited Forgiveness has, when granted to us by someone we respect. It is a healing tool, a psychological tool, maybe something even greater than Justice.

It is powerful not only via the reaction it engenders in the one who it is practised on, but also in what it drags out of he or she that it is practised by - it changes the lives of the giver and the receiver.

But what does it take to have the forbearance, patience and ability to suffer humiliation, insults and pain while you are waiting, waiting, and waiting for the healing of a Nurture-Bully, (and hoping all the while that you are not wasting your time on a Nature-bully)? It takes Belief.

Belief in something...

When I first lost track of Steven I was still a young man, all agog, watching, living, learning and experimenting. At one time I would think this or that was the system for me, at other times something else was 'the way'. My beliefs altered many times, and as the years passed they would zigzag this, then that, and then another way. Until one day it hit me, it was not what I happened to believe at any one time of my life that made me happy or strong, it was that I believed at all.

It was whenever I believed that I had focus, that I had strength and purpose - compared to times without belief, times of doubt. Of course - it was BELIEF ITSELF that counted.

Of course!

It wasn't Hinduism or Buddhist Meditation, this or that, Christianity or Communism - it was my Belief in any one of those things at any one time that made the difference to my life. All Religions reward us with the special present of the strength we take from Belief.

Belief, the great gift of Religion to humanity, is nothing other than a super-duper version of the Placebo effect. We give one patient a harmless Placebo, a sugar tablet, while we give another the latest hot off the press drug. When both patients make equal progress we can be pretty sure this is due to the power of BELIEF in their Doctor, the Drug Company or the Hospital they are attending.

Never underestimate the power-of-the-Placebo.

The power of human BELIEF is nothing other than the Placebo effect.

But that doesn't mean I'm belittling it, quite the reverse.

I'm recommending it.

Don't focus on what the Religion you choose says or doesn't say about underlying reality, focus on what Belief does for you, focus on what Developing a Religious Outlook does for you.

Hardly the words of a Religious fanatic?
Therefore Religion is safe in my hands.
In the end I followed all Religions.
And therefore no single one dares rule me.

Try it and see. Pick and choose - it works!
Why not?
Especially since to join at least one of the world's great religions (the Buddhist one) you don't even have to commit yourself to believing in God. If it were not BELIEF itself that provides the key, rather than what is believed in, then one Religion alone (the correct one) would stand out ALONE as being able to generate that fantastic feeling we get when we BELIEVE.

Yet when we look at how human beings live and behave in the real world, we see that those who gain solace and strength from Religion come from every Belief system.

You don't have to take my word for it, what about Carl Jung, or what about Kierkegaard and his leap of Faith? No wait, a cautionary word about Soren. What exactly is his existentialist 'belief even in the face of overwhelming evidence to the contrary', how does that fit?

KIERKEGAARD

He says we must just close our eyes and JUMP, we must leap into the unknown, into the ABYSS, he tells us. He suggests having Faith in God, EVEN WHEN ALL THE AVAILABLE EVIDENCE SUGGESTS THE OPPOSITE is True.

On one level this is sickening, disgusting and perverse, the foundation stone of all bigotry, prejudice and a petty minded inability to reform one's views. Yet one can see the appeal, because his attitude is also a cry to free ourselves from every little bit of mental dominance by others, let alone physical dominance - it is a triumph of defiance, a triumph of the human spirit refusing to kow-tow, no matter what.

No matter what the pressure I will not acquiesce, I will not give in to you. No matter what the evidence to the contrary I will not agree to 'see things your way'.
Stuff you, up yours.

He is a triumph of our unwillingness to be dominated by others, a triumph of ANTI-BULLY even over KNOWLEDGE. The triumph of, 'I don't care that what you say is probably True, I am going to deny it. I am going to deny it because I dislike you and what you stand for and I suspect that you are trying to use Knowledge to dominate me'.

Morality stands with Soren Kierkegaard only when he is fighting against a dominating Bully, which is why his crazy argument has survived at all. Because MORALITY gives not a hoot for KNOWLEDGE when it is being used by POWER, instead it lunges straight through Knowledge to resist the machinations of Power, to fight the BULLY with every ounce of its strength. Including when Power uses and usurps Knowledge or Metaphysics-Religion to try to dominate us.

So come on with Kierkegaard, who is surely the ultimate case of I-will-believe-what-I-CHOOSE, not what you choose for me, come on.

Climb on board, join him and me on the speeding focussed Juggernaut called I-BELIEVE-IN-SOMETHING.

Let me recommend it to you.

Do what the priests tell us not to do, build your own Religion from the stuff you find lying around in the World's Religions.

As for me, I'm still C of E on Sundays and Mondays, but for the rest of the week I live by all the World's Religions, I sit, just sit and feel the closeness of my ancestors. The closest loyal friends you have, so close so close INSIDE YOU, their genes sit safely right inside you - could anything be closer?

Trust them, trust them, trust the glorious dead.

Come on climb on board, come back with me.

I feel my father, his mother, his mother's father, that miner of Lancashire coal, the Iron Man as he was known within my family. Back, now through them back, back, back, over time and distance ... we can talk to all of them, to all of those now gone.

Repeat with me the creed, repeat with me the prayer of those of us who are Religious, without being Mass Religionists.

I believe Metaphysical Belief is the most potent of human medicines.
But Metaphysics is not Scientific Knowledge.
And so Metaphysics-Religion CANNOT DEFINE Morality.
Belief is not Morality.
One single Religion is not Morality.
And thus Religious Revelation is a meaningless empty phrase.

There are no revelations or special truths, hidden from all except the Mass Religionists, except for the TRUTH that BELIEF ITSELF can be as powerful as any psychotic drug we've ever invented.

Come on, climb on board, climb on board our steam train ... hear its engines roar. Feel the throttle rumble, feel the rhythm of its wheels, hear its whistle sound across the empty plain.

The deserted deadly plain of fear, despair and loneliness - hear its screeching whistle banish every single doubt, banish every single fear you've ever had...

WHOO-WHOO, WHOO-WHOO, WHOO-WHOO
Let that throttle out ... go back ... go back to THEM.
Shout it out, shout it loud...
WHOO-WHOO, WHOO-WHOO, WHOO-WHOO
Back, back, journey back.
Sing it if you like...
WHOO-WHOO, WHOO-WHOO, WHOO-WHOO

BELIEF-in-something is a wonderful, wonderful thing, but it is not the same as TRUTH.

Belief makes us FEEL GOOD.
But that is not the same as what-we-believe being TRUE.

Clearly it's NOT TRUE that my (and your) physically dead ancestors are still alive today. But it feels like they are, when I deliberately create their presence, from my memories, from what I've heard, what I've been told - they feel so close.

I INDUCE THIS FEELING of course, as part of my Religious Outlook, as part of the Religious part of me, the need to feel AT ONE WITH TOTALITY. The need to change the vast empty nothing of the vast empty Universe into a warm close friend.

So if all else fails, and no other Religion suits, try the first and oldest Religion in the world, try the very act that shows us when Metaphysics-Religion first began in us, try ancestor veneration.

Try the oldest of them all, why not? Try talking to the dead.
And above all else you'll know it's real - it's locked already in your core. Securely locked inside you, safe from all who would 'interpret' for you, interpret the message hidden in your genes - it is already you.

And it sits there waiting.
Waiting, waiting for your call.

And if to you I seem insane, so what, my system does no harm to you. For whenever I deal with you, my fellow human, whenever I am called upon by events to judge you, to comment or respond to your actions, I do so Morally, BY THE BULLY/ANTI-BULLY PRINCIPLE.

Come on, be my guest.

Try veneration of your ancestors, veneration note not adoration, we disagree as much as we agree.

Come on what is there left to lose?

Try making contact with the spirits of the dead.
Waiting, waiting for your call, they sit there waiting...

Climb on board and travel back.
WHOO-WHOO, WHOO-WHOO, WHOO-WHOO

My Metaphysics - that which makes my heart soar, my step spring, my eye gleam with love of life, is no concern of yours, unless you want to emulate it in yourself. It cannot and it should not touch you, for whenever I touch you I always do so based upon the single principle that lies behind each human pack that ever lived or still lives now upon this earth. I JUDGE BY BULLY/ANTI-BULLY AND BY IT ALONE.

Whenever and wherever people cry out for JUSTICE, they cry out for B/A-b.
When people say: I've been Wronged, give me Justice.
They always mean: I've been Bullied, give me Anti-bully.

So bend your knee. And with me pay homage one last time ... to absent friends by shouting out:

It is the job of all Religions to bow their knees and doff their hats to Morality, not the other way round.
One of the functions of Religion is to serve Morality.
It is NEVER the function of Morality to serve Religion.
Morality is the older partner.

WHOO-WHOO, WHOO-WHOO, WHOO-WHOO

WHOO-WHOO, WHOO-WHOO, WHOO-WHOO

*

Lightning Source UK Ltd.
Milton Keynes UK
23 September 2010

160272UK00001B/22/P